# THOMAS
# HARDY

Other titles by the same author:

*Tyneham: The Lost Village of Dorset* (Tiverton, Halsgrove, 2003)

*Sir Francis Drake: Behind the Pirate's Mask* (Tiverton, Halsgrove, 2004)

*Dunshay: Reflections on a Dorset Manor House* (Tiverton, Halsgrove, 2004)

*Enid Blyton and her Enchantment with Dorset* (Tiverton, Halsgrove, 2005)

*Thomas Hardy: Christmas Carollings* (Tiverton, Halsgrove, 2005)

*Agatha Christie: The Finished Portrait* (Stroud, The History Press, 2007)

*Mugabe: Teacher, Revolutionary, Tyrant* (Stroud, The History Press, 2008)

*The Story of George Loveless and the Tolpuddle Martyrs* (Tiverton, Halsgrove, 2008)

*T.E. Lawrence: The Enigma Explained* (Stroud, The History Press, 2008)

*Agatha Christie: The Pitkin Guide* (Andover, Pitkin Publishing, 2009)

*Purbeck Personalities* (Tiverton, Halsgrove, 2009)

*Arthur Conan Doyle: The Man Behind Sherlock Holmes* (Stroud, The History Press, 2009)

*Father of the Blind: A Portrait of Sir Arthur Pearson* (Stroud, The History Press, 2009)

*Jane Austen: An Unrequited Love* (Stroud, The History Press, 2009)

*Hitler: Dictator or Puppet* (Barnsley, Pen & Sword Books, 2011)

# THOMAS HARDY

## BEHIND THE MASK

ANDREW NORMAN

*He slid apart*
*Who had thought her heart*
*His own, and not aboard*
*A bark, sea-bound …*
*That night they found*
*Between them lay a sword.*

From the poem *To a Sea Cliff* by Thomas Hardy

First published 2011

The History Press
The Mill, Brimscombe Port
Stroud, Gloucestershire, GL5 2QG
www.thehistorypress.co.uk

British Library Cataloguing in Publication Data.
A catalogue record for this book is available from the British Library.

ISBN 978 0 7524 5630 0

Typesetting and origination by The History Press
Printed in Great Britain

# Contents

# Author's Note

My interest in Thomas Hardy was aroused when I discovered a connection between my ancestors and the great Dorset novelist, poet and dramatist: that connection being the Moule family of Fordington.

Fordington, which lies on the outskirts of Dorchester – Dorset's county town – is situated only 2 miles from Thomas Hardy's family home at Higher Bockhampton. My paternal ancestors, who were yeoman farmers, lived here, and were baptised, married and buried at its parish church of St George, by the vicar, the Revd Henry Moule (1801–80). The Revd Moule's son, Horatio Mosley Moule (known as Horace), was Hardy's mentor and also his dearest friend.

# Foreword

Thomas Hardy was an immensely shy person, who surrounded his house, Max Gate, Dorchester, with a dense curtain of trees, shunned publicity and investigative reporters, and when visitors arrived unexpectedly, slipped quietly out of the back door of his house in order to avoid them. So that no one should penetrate this mask of shyness, Hardy kept a rigid control over what aspects of his life were to be divulged and what were not. His first wife, Emma, behaved in a similar way, at least as far as her and her husband's letters to one another were concerned: she burnt all that she could lay her hands upon.[1] As for Hardy, following Emma's death he burnt, page by page, a book-length manuscript of hers entitled *What I Think of My Husband*, together with most, but not all, of her diaries.[2] When Hardy's second wife, Florence, wrote a so-called 'biography' of him, he retained control by dictating to her virtually the whole of the manuscript. When Hardy himself died in 1928, Florence destroyed a great deal more of his and Emma's personal papers.[3] This begs the question, did Hardy have something to hide, a secret of some kind; and if so, is it possible, eight decades after his death, to discover what this secret was?

At first, this appears to be an impossible task, bearing in mind the vast quantity of 'evidence' which was deliberately destroyed by Hardy and his wives and others[4] during their lifetimes. Also, when Florence died in 1937, her executor, Irene Cooper Willis, destroyed 'a mass of the first Mrs Hardy's incoming correspondence that had sat undisturbed in her former attic retreat at Max Gate ever since her own death twenty-five years earlier'.[5] However, for a diligent researcher with an open mind, who is alive to the various clues to the conundrum which Hardy left behind, the task, as will shortly be seen, is not an impossible one.

For much of his adult life, Hardy laboured under a terrible burden of grief, the details of which he kept very much to himself. He required an outlet for this grief, a means of expressing his inner torment, and this outlet came through his writings. Hardy once told his friend, Edward Clodd, in respect of his novels, that 'every superstition, custom, &c., described therein may be depended on as true records of the same – & not inventions of mine'.[6] What he did not tell Clodd, and what only a very few of his contemporaries managed to discern, was the phenomenal extent to which his own personal life was reflected both in his novels and in his poems. However, even in this he was hamstrung, in that he could not afford to be explicit – at least while Emma was alive – for fear of offending her.

The purpose of this book is to pierce the veil of secrecy which Hardy deliberately drew over his life; to decipher the coded messages which his writings contain; to find out why his life was so filled with anguish, an anguish which led to the creation, by him, of some of the finest novels and poems in the English language. Only then is it possible to discover the real Hardy; the man that lies behind the mask.

The journey is a fascinating one. It leads to Hardy's former haunts, including his family home at Higher Bockhampton (he disliked it being called a cottage, preferring it to be called a house); to St Juliot in Cornwall, where he met and courted Emma, and to Dorchester County Museum, where many important artefacts associated with him – including the contents of his study – are to be found. It also leads, surprisingly, to various mental hospitals, known in those days as 'lunatic asylums', located in such places as London, Oxford and Cornwall.

# Acknowledgements

I am grateful to the following:

Dr J.H. (Ian) Alexander; Elizabeth Boardman; Vanessa Bourguignon; Jane Bradley; Patricia Burdick; Mandy Caine; Brian Carpenter; Sue Cathcart; Kim Cooper; Caroline Cox; Helen Day; Mike Dowell; Dawn Dyer; Aidan Flood; Helen Gibson; Valerie Gill; Jennifer Hancock; Rachel Hancock; Pat Heron; Dr Jonathan Holmes; Vanda Inman; Renée Jackaman; Stephanie Jenkins; Basil Jose and family; Joanne Laing; Nuala LaVertue; Mark Lawrence; Hannah Lowery; Jasmine Metcalfe; Professor Michael Millgate; Jon Murden; Mike Nixon; Susan Old; Roy Overall; Eric H. Prior; Stephen Rench; Maureen Reynolds; Michael Richardson; Chris and Sally Searle (The Old Rectory, St Juliot, Boscastle, Cornwall); Reg Sheppard; Alan Simpson; Derick Skelly; Alison Spence; Judith Stinton; Lilian Swindall; Revd Robert S. Thewsey; David Thomas; Deborah Tritton; Toni Tuckwood; Jan Turner; Deborah Watson; David Williams; John Williams; Gwen Yarker.

Bodmin Town Museum; Bristol Reference Library; Bristol University Library: Special Collections; University of Bristol; The British Library; Colby Special Collections, Miller Library, Waterville, Maine, USA; Cornish Studies Library; Cornwall County Council; Cornwall Family History Society; Cornwall Record Office; Cornwall Studies Library; Dorchester Library; Dorset County Museum; Magdalene College, Cambridge; Oxfordshire Family History Society; Oxfordshire Health Archives; Oxfordshire Photographic Archive; Oxfordshire Record Office; Oxfordshire Studies Library; Oxfordshire Studies: Heritage & Arts; Plymouth Central Library; Plymouth and West Devon Record Office; Poole Central Library; Plymouth Central Library; Queens' College, Cambridge; Redbridge Local Studies and Archives; Royal Geographical Society; Solicitors Regulation Authority; Thomas Hardy Society.

My thanks are also due to the Clarendon Press, Oxford; Cassell and Company Ltd, London; Mid–Northumberland Arts Group and Carcanet New Press; Oxford University Press; Macmillan Publishers Ltd; The Hogarth Press, London; David & Charles Ltd, London; MacGibbon & Kee, London; The Toucan Press, Guernsey; Longman Group Ltd; Colby College Press, Maine, USA.

A special mention is due to the enthusiastic and dedicated staff of the Cornwall Record Office, Devon Record Office, London Borough of Redbridge Local Studies and Archives, and Oxfordshire Health Archives.

I thank Professor Michael Millgate for his selfless generosity, and his diligence in preserving so much literature relating to Hardy which may well otherwise have been lost. I also thank my dear friend of many years, Dr Stuart C. Hannabuss, for his kindly words and valued criticism. And I am especially grateful, as always, to my beloved wife, Rachel, for her invaluable help and encouragement.

# Maps

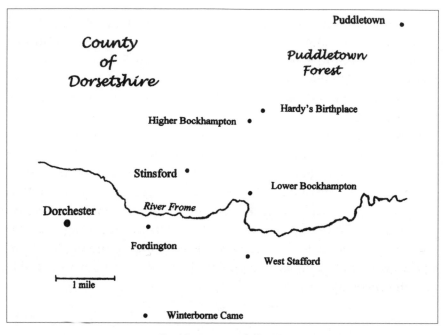

Bockhampton and district.

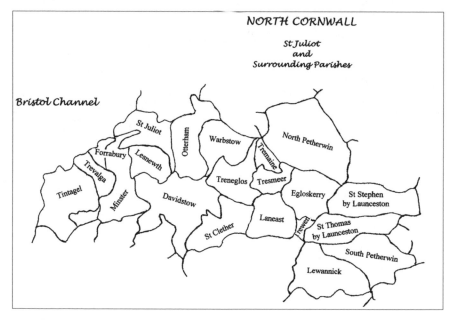

St Juliot and surrounding parishes.

North Cornwall.

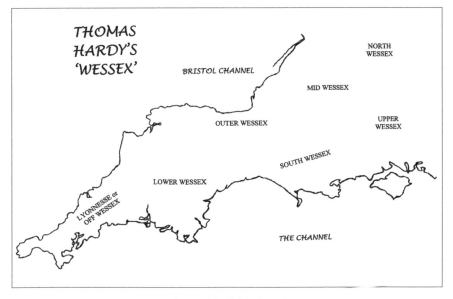

Thomas Hardy's 'Wessex'.

# Family Trees

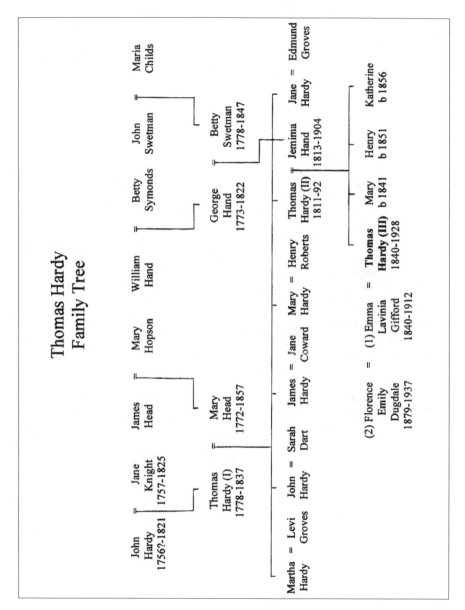

Hardy Family Tree.

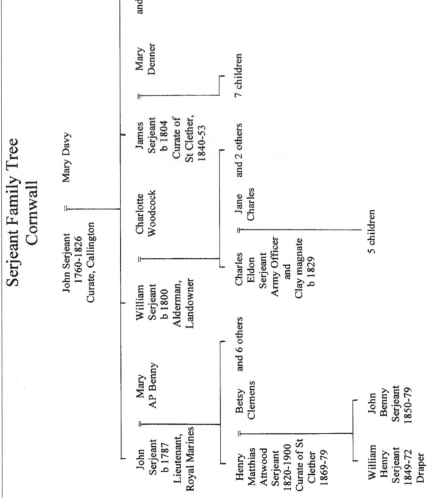

Serjeant Family Tree.

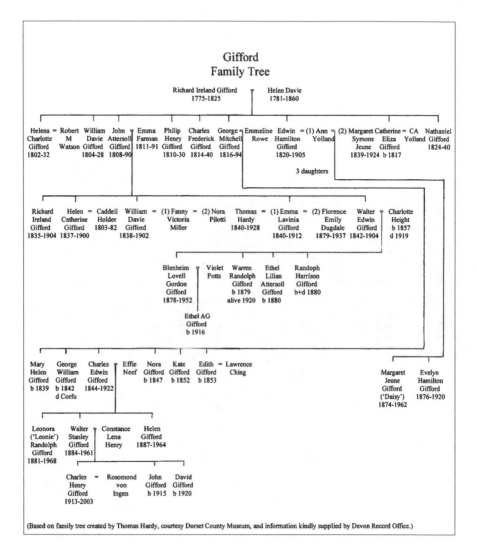

Gifford Family Tree.

# 1

# Early Life: Influences

## Birth: Forebears

Thomas Hardy – the third generation of his family to bear that name – was born in a remote house in the hamlet of Higher Bockhampton in rural Dorset, on 2 June 1840. His entry into the world was an inauspicious one, and his life almost ended even before it had properly begun, for the infant Thomas was 'thrown aside as dead'. 'Dead! Stop a minute,' cried the monthly nurse (who attended the women of the district during their confinement). 'He's alive enough, sure!' and she managed to revive the lifeless infant. Shortly afterwards, when he was sleeping in his cradle, his mother discovered 'a large snake curled up upon his breast' – which was also asleep. Because of its size, it may be deduced that this was probably a harmless grass snake rather than a poisonous adder, which is smaller.[1] Thomas III, the subject of this book, was the firstborn of his family. The following year, 1841, his sister Mary arrived on the scene, but it would be another decade before brother Henry was born; to be followed by Katharine in 1856.

The Hardys firmly believed that they were descended from the more illustrious 'le Hardy' family of Jersey in the Channel Islands: John le Hardy having settled in Weymouth in the fifteenth century. They also believed that they were distantly related to Admiral Sir Thomas Masterman Hardy, who served under Horatio Nelson as flag captain of HMS *Victory* in the Battle of Trafalgar. (As yet, no documentary evidence has been produced to substantiate these claims.)[2]

Thomas III's family, on both sides, were hardworking and creative people, but their lives were not without incident. His paternal great-grandfather, John Hardy (born 1755), came from the village of Puddletown, 2 miles north-east of Higher Bockhampton, and 5 miles north-east of Dorchester. A mason, and later a master mason and employer of labour, John married Jane Knight and the couple had two sons: Thomas I (born 1778) and John.

Thomas I carried on the family tradition by adopting the same occupation as his father. At the age of 21, he 'somewhat improvidently married' a Mary Head from Berkshire; a person who had known great hardship as a child through being orphaned.[3]

Thomas I and his wife Mary had six children, the oldest being Thomas II (born 1811). Under Thomas II the family business flourished with as many as fifteen men in its employ, including the 'tranter' who transported the materials to the building sites.

Hardy's maternal grandmother, Elizabeth Swetman of Melbury Osmond – a hamlet in north-west Dorset situated on the boundary of Lord Ilchester's estate – was descended from a family of landed yeomen. She was of a romantic disposition, had an excellent memory and could be relied upon by the parson to identify, in cases of doubt, any particular grave in the churchyard. Also, she was skilled in ministering to the sick of the locality; her authority being the English herbalist Nicholas Culpepper's (1616–54) *Herbal and Dispensary*.

When Elizabeth met and secretly married a servant, one George Hand, so great was her father John's disapproval of the match that he disinherited her. This was to have grave consequences; for soon after her father's death, Elizabeth's husband also died, whereupon she and her seven children were left destitute. One of these children, Jemima, born at No 1, Barton Close, Melbury Osmond, in 1813, was destined to become the mother of Thomas Hardy III.

Jemima was skilled at tambouring (embroidering) gloves and mantua (gown) making; she worked as a servant and cook in several Dorset houses, and also in London. In late 1836 she became cook to the Revd Edward Murray, vicar of Stinsford's parish church of St Michael (Stinsford being a hamlet situated less than a mile from Higher Bockhampton). On 22 December 1839 Jemima married Thomas Hardy II at her mother's family's church of St Osmond, at Melbury Osmond.

When she married Thomas II, Jemima was already more than three months pregnant. In those days, however, conception before marriage was considered by the Dorset farm labourers (and even by the lower middle classes) to be nothing unusual. In fact, among such folk, a marriage did not normally proceed until the pregnancy had become obvious. There was a good reason for this: it was considered essential for a woman to prove her ability to bear children, who from an early age would be required to help support the family. In nineteenth-century Dorset, children as young as 8 years of age were commonly put to work in the fields.[4]

## Hardy's Bockhampton Home

Even today it might prove difficult to negotiate one's way through the host of labyrinthine lanes to Hardy's former house, were it not for the fact that the route is adequately signposted. The house lies on the boundary of woodland and heathland, and may therefore be approached either from the woods or from the heath, or alternatively from a lane known as Cherry Alley. In Hardy's time, Cherry Alley contained seven other houses, each one occupied by a person of some standing in the community. These occupants included 'two retired military officers, one old navy lieutenant, a small farmer [presumably it was his farm which was small, rather than he himself] and tranter, a relieving officer and registrar, and an old militiaman, whose wife was the monthly nurse that assisted Thomas Hardy III into the world'.[5]

The Bockhampton house was a two-storey building with a thatched roof. It had been built in 1800–01 by Thomas III's great-grandfather, John, for his son Thomas I and his wife Mary on land leased from the Kingston Maurward Estate. (In those days, a man with sufficient means could erect a dwelling for himself, or for a relative, and be thereafter permitted to live there for his lifetime; such a person being called a 'livier'). Also included with the property were two gardens (one part orchard), a horse paddock, sand and gravel pits, and 'like buildings'.[6]

The entrance to the house was through a porch leading directly into the kitchen, which had a deeply recessed fireplace on its south wall. Adjacent to this was the parlour, and then a small office where the three generations of Hardys – who were stonemasons-cum-builders – did their accounts and kept their money. Their workmen were handed their wages through a tiny barred window which was little more than a foot square and situated at the rear. From the office, an open staircase led up to the first floor which had two bedrooms. These upstairs rooms, being built into the eaves, had sloping ceilings and it was in the main bedroom situated above the office, that Thomas III was born.

The house had a chimney at each end and was thatched with wheat straw. The walls were made of cob (a composition of clay and straw), with a brick-facing at the front. The ground floor was paved with Portland-stone flagstones; the first floor with floorboards of chestnut 7in wide. Candles were used for lighting, as was usual in those times.

At some later date a self-contained bedroom and kitchen were added, the materials used being of inferior quality to those used in the construction of the original dwelling. It is likely that this extension was built some time around 1837 in order to provide accommodation for Thomas III's grandmother, Mary Hardy (*née* Head), who in that year had been left a widow. (This would explain why Mary appears in the 1851 census as living in the parish of Stinsford, of which Higher Bockhampton was a part.) Later still, perhaps after Mary's own death in 1857, the two buildings were conjoined.

Adjacent to the Hardy house was Thorncombe Wood, where swallet holes are to be found, together with a natural water feature, Rushy Pond. The wood is bisected by the Roman road linking Dorchester (*Durnovaria*, 2 miles distant) with London (*Londinium*) via Badbury Rings and Salisbury (Old *Sarum*), and also by an iron fence dating from the Victorian era and marking the boundary between two estates. On the periphery of the wood, on the south side, lies the hazel coppice; this species of tree being specifically grown for hurdle-making. Beyond the wood, the River Frome meanders through a fertile valley, with the distant ridge of the Purbeck Hills in the background. Ten miles to the south lies the town of Weymouth. Behind the house there extends a huge area of heathland, which in Thomas III's time was dotted with isolated cottages. This was subsequently given the name 'Egdon Heath' by Hardy.

This was the landscape which Thomas III came to know in intimate detail, and also to love. It imprinted itself indelibly on his mind, and through him it would one day become familiar to people in all parts of the world, even though the vast majority of them had never seen it at first hand. During his lifetime, Hardy would live for a period outside of Dorset, but his beloved home county would never be far from his thoughts.

One of Thomas III's favourite occupations was to lie on his back in the sun, cover his face with his straw hat and think 'how useless he was'. He decided, based on his 'experiences of the world so far … [that] he did not wish to grow up … to be a man, or to possess things, but to remain as he was, in the same spot, and to know no more people than he already knew' – which was about half a dozen.[7] In other words, he was perfectly happy and content.

At other times he would 'go alone into the woods or on [to] the heath … with a telescope [and] stay peering into the distance by the half-hour …' or in hot weather, lie 'on a bank of thyme or camomile with the grasshoppers leaping over him'.[8] When one cold winter's day he discovered the body of a fieldfare in the garden, and picked it up and found it to be 'as light as a feather' and 'all skin and bone', the memory remained to haunt him. The death of this small bird revealed not only Hardy's love of animals, but also his understanding of the frailty of life itself.[9]

# Music: Books: School

Thomas Hardy III was born into a musical family and he himself developed a love of music and musicianship which remained with him all his life. His grandfather, Thomas I, in his early years at Puddletown, played the bass viol (cello) in the string choir of the village's church of St Mary. He also assisted other choirs at a time when church music was traditionally produced by musicians occupying the raised 'minstrels' gallery' at the end of the nave. Having married Mary Head, he moved into the house at Bockhampton, provided for him by his father. From that time onwards he attended the local thirteenth-century parish church of St Michael, situated a mile or so away at Stinsford, where he commenced as a chorister. He was also much in demand to perform at 'weddings, christenings, and other feasts'.[10]

Thomas I was dismayed, on attending Stinsford Church, that the music there was provided not, as was the case at Puddletown, by a group of 'minstrels', but by 'a solitary old man with an oboe'.[11] With the help of its vicar, the Revd William Floyer, he therefore set about remedying the situation by gathering some like-minded instrumentalists together to play at the church. And from the year 1801, when he was aged 23, until his death in 1837, Thomas I himself conducted the church choir and played his bass viol at two services every Sunday.

At Christmastime there were further duties for the members of Stinsford's church choir to perform, including the onerous task of making copies of those carols which had been selected to be played. On Christmas Eve it was the custom for the choir, composed of 'mainly poor men and hungry', to play at various houses in the parish, then return to the Hardys' house at Bockhampton for supper, only to set out again at midnight to play at yet more houses.[12]

After his death in 1822, the Revd Floyer was succeeded by the Revd Edward Murray, who was himself an 'ardent musician' and violin player.

Murray chose to live at Stinsford House instead of at the rectory, and here, Thomas Hardy I and his sons, Thomas II and James, together with their brother-in-law James Dart, practised their music with Murray on two or three occasions per week. Practice sessions were also held at the Hardys' house. As mentioned, in late 1836, fourteen years after the arrival of the Revd Murray at Stinsford, Jemima Hand became Murray's cook, and this is how she came to meet her husband-to-be Thomas Hardy II.

Thomas II is described as being devoted to sacred music as well as to the 'mundane', that is 'country dance, hornpipe, and … waltz'. As for his wife Jemima, she loved to sing the songs of the times, including *Isle of Beauty, Gaily the Troubadour,* and so forth.[13] However, although the family possessed a pianoforte and the children practised on it, she herself did not play.

A diagram was subsequently drawn by Thomas III, with the help of his father, of the relative positions occupied by the singers and musicians of the Stinsford church choir in its gallery in about the year 1835, five years prior to Thomas III's birth. At the rear were singers ('counter' – high alto), together with James Dart (counter violin). The middle row consisted of singers (tenor), Thomas Hardy II (tenor violin), James Hardy (treble violin) and singers (treble). In the front row were singers (bass), Thomas Hardy I (bass viol) and singers (treble). Finally, at the rear there were more singers, stationed beneath the arch of the church's tower.[14]

What of the young Thomas Hardy III? He would never have the pleasure of meeting his grandfather and namesake, Thomas I, who died in 1837 – three years before he himself was born. Nevertheless, he inherited the family gift for making music and was said to be able to tune a violin from the time that he was 'barely breeched'.[15]

When he was aged 4, Thomas III's father gave him a toy concertina inscribed with his name and the date. Thomas III was said to have an 'ecstatic temperament' and music could have a profound effect on him. For example, of the numerous dance tunes played by his father of an evening, and 'to which the boy danced a *"pas seul"* in the middle of the room', there were always 'three or four that always moved the child to tears'. They were *Enrico, The Fairy Dance, Miss Macleod of Ayr* and *My Fancy Lad*. Thomas III would later confess that 'he danced on at these times to conceal his weeping', and the fact that he was overcome by emotion in this way reveals just what an immensely sensitive and emotional person he was.[16]

As Thomas III grew older he learned, under the instruction of his father, to play the violin and soon, like his forefathers before him, was much in demand on this account. He always referred to the instrument as a 'fiddle', and to those who played it as 'fiddlers'.[17] It was the rule, laid down by his mother, that he must not accept any payment for his services. Nonetheless, he did on one occasion succumb to temptation, and with the 'hatful of pennies' collected, he purchased a volume entitled *The Boys' Own Book*, of which his mother Jemima disapproved, since it was mainly devoted to the light-hearted subject of games.

Hardy's maternal grandmother, Elizabeth Hand, was well-read and the possessor of her own library of thirty or so books (which was unusual for one who occupied a relatively low station in life). She was familiar with the writings of Joseph Addison, Sir Richard Steele, and others of the so-called '*Spectator* group' (those who contributed to the *Spectator* magazine, founded in 1828): also with John Milton, Samuel Richardson and John Bunyan. The ten volumes of Henry Fielding's works which she possessed would one day pass to her grandson, Thomas Hardy III.[18]

Elizabeth's daughter, Jemima, inherited her mother's love of books, together with a desire to read every one that she could lay her hands on. Under Jemima's influence, therefore, it seemed inevitable that her own offspring, including the young Thomas III, would follow in her footsteps. And there were others, including Thomas III's godfather, Mr King,[19] who encouraged the boy in his reading; for example, by presenting him with a volume entitled *The Rites and Worship of the Jews* by Elise Giles, even though he had not, as yet, attained the age of 8.[20] In fact, according to his sister Katharine, Thomas III had been able to read since the age of 3, and on Sundays, when the weather was considered too wet for him to attend church, it was his habit to don a tablecloth and read Morning Prayer while standing on a chair, and recite 'a patchwork of sentences normally used by the vicar'.

Thomas III was considered by his parents to be a delicate child, and for this reason he was not sent to school until he was aged 8 (instead of 5, which was the normal practice). And so it was not until the year 1848 that he arrived at school for his first day of lessons. He was early, and he subsequently recalled awaiting, 'tremulous and alone', the arrival of the schoolmaster, the schoolmistress and his fellow pupils.

The Bockhampton National School, which had been newly opened in that same year, was situated a mile or so from his house, beside the lane which led from Higher to Lower Bockhampton. The school was the brain-child of Julia Augusta Martin, who, together with her husband Francis, owned the adjoining estate of Kingston Maurward. This they had purchased from the Pitt family three years earlier, in 1845. The couple inhabited the manor house, built in the early Georgian period, not to be confused with the estate's other manor house nearby, which dated from mid-Tudor times. A benefactress of both Stinsford and Bockhampton, Julia had built and endowed the Bockhampton National School at her own expense; collabo-rating with the Revd Arthur Shirley (who in 1837 had succeeded the Revd Murray as vicar of Stinsford) on the project.

The Martins had no children of their own and Julia came to regard Thomas III as her surrogate child. In fact, she had singled him out as the object of her affection long before he had even started school. Passionately fond of 'Tommy', Julia was 'accustomed to take [him] into her lap, and kiss [him] until he was quite a big child!' Thomas III, in turn, 'was wont to make drawings of animals in water-colours for her, and to sing to her'. That he reciprocated Julia's sentiments is borne out by his statement, made some years later, that she was 'his earliest passion as a child'.[21] One of Thomas III's songs contained the words, 'I've journeyed over many lands, I've sailed on every sea',[22] which would, no doubt, have amused Julia, who must have realised that Thomas III had never ventured beyond his native Dorset. It transpired, however, that the boy was shortly to widen his horizons when he and his mother Jemima paid a visit to her sister in Hertfordshire, and on the return journey caught the train from London's Waterloo Station to Dorchester. This was Thomas III's first experience of rail travel – the railway having come to Dorchester only as recently as the previous year, 1847.

At school, Thomas III excelled at arithmetic and geography, though his handwriting was said to be 'indifferent'.[23] Meanwhile, his mother encour-aged him with the gift of John Dryden's translation of Virgil, Dr Samuel Johnson's *Rasselas* and a translation of St Pierre's *Paul and Virginia*. A friend gave the young Thomas III the *New Guide to the English Tongue* by Thomas Dilworth[24] and he also possessed *A Concise History of Birds*. Perhaps, how-ever, his greatest joy was to discover, in a closet in his house, a magazine entitled *A History of the (Napoleonic) Wars*.[25] This would one day inspire him to write two books of his own, namely *The Trumpet Major* and *The Dynasts*.

When a year later, in 1849, Thomas III's parents decided that their son should transfer to a day school in Dorchester, Julia Martin was offended, not only at the loss of her 'especial protégé little Tommy', but also because this new school was Nonconformist. This may have been a deliberate gesture of defiance by the Hardys who had developed a great antipathy towards Stinsford's vicar, the Revd Shirley. This was because, as will shortly be seen, Shirley had been instrumental in destroying not only the fabric of their cherished medieval parish church of St Michael, but also its cherished tradition of providing live music for its congregation.

And so, at the age of 9, Thomas III commenced the second stage of his formal education, walking to and from his new school in Dorchester – a distance of 6 miles in total. Here he flourished, winning at the age of 14 his first prize: a book entitled *Scenes and Adventures at Home and Abroad*.[26] The headmaster, Isaac Last, was by repute 'a good scholar and teacher of Latin', but because this subject was not part of the normal curriculum, Thomas III's father was obliged to pay extra for it. Nevertheless, his confidence in his son was amply rewarded when, in the following year, the boy was awarded Theodore Beza's *Latin Testament* for his 'progress in that tongue'.

Other authors with whom Thomas III was familiar were William Shakespeare, Walter Scott, Alexander Dumas, Harrison Ainsworth, James Grant and G.P.R. James.[27] He also commenced French lessons, and at the age of 15 began to study German at home, using a periodical called *The Popular Educator* for the purpose. He was clearly a prodigious worker, and it is difficult to imagine that any other child in the county of Dorset (or anywhere else for that matter) was better read than he.

From whence did the impetus come that led Thomas III to drive himself so hard? From his father? Probably not, for Thomas III did not deny that the Dorset Hardys had 'all the characteristics of an old family of spent social energies', and it was the case that neither his father nor his grandfather had ever 'cared to take advantage of the many worldly opportunities' afforded them.[28] Instead, the likelihood is that the drive came from his mother, the provider of books, who had insisted on him changing school in order to better himself; she, having experienced abject poverty as a child when her mother was left destitute, had no desire to see any child of hers in the same predicament.

Thomas III's move to Dorchester was not without its repercussions. So annoyed was Julia Martin at having her protégé removed from her own school, that she forthwith deprived the boy's father of all future building contracts connected with her Kingston Maurward Estate. Fortunately, Thomas II was able to obtain such contracts elsewhere, such as one for the renovation of Woodsford Castle – owned by the Earl of Ilchester and situated 5 miles to the east of Dorchester, by the River Frome.

When Thomas III subsequently met with Julia Martin, on the occasion of a harvest supper, she reproached him with having deserted her. Whereupon he assured her that he had not done so and would never do so. It would be more than a decade before the two saw one another again; by which time the Martins had sold their Kingston Maurward Estate and moved to London.

## Domicilium

When he was aged 16, Thomas III composed a poem about his home entitled *Domicilium*, which reads as follows:

It faces west and round the back and sides
High beeches, bending, hang a veil of boughs,
And sweep against the roof. Wild honeysucks
Climb on the walls, and seem to sprout a wish
(If we may fancy wish of trees and plants)
To overtop the apple trees hard by.

Red roses, lilacs, variegated box
Are there in plenty, and such hardy flowers
As flourish best untrained. Adjoining these
Are herbs and esculents, and farther still
A field; then cottages with trees, and last
The distant hills and sky.
Behind, the scene is wilder. Heath and furze
Are everything that seems to grow and thrive
Upon the uneven ground. A stunted thorn
Stands here and there, indeed; and from a pit
An oak uprises, springing from a seed
Dropped by some bird a hundred years ago.

In days bygone –
Long gone – my father's mother, who is now
Blest with the blest, would take me out to walk.
At such time I once inquired of her
How looked the spot when first she settled here.
The answer I remember. 'Fifty years

Have passed since then, my child, and change has marked
The face of all things. Yonder garden plots
And orchards were uncultivated slopes
O'ergrown with bramble bushes, furze and thorn:
That road a narrow path shut in by ferns,
Which, almost trees, obscured the passer-by.

'Our house stood quite alone, and those tall firs
And beeches were not planted. Snakes and efts[29]
Swarmed in the summer days, and nightly bats
Would fly about our bedroom. Heathcroppers
Lived on the hills, and were our only friends;
So wild it was when first we settled here.'

The poem is quoted in full, and for two reasons. Firstly, because it would be presumptuous of any person to believe that he or she was capable of describing the Hardys' house better than Thomas III himself; and secondly, because it sheds important light upon his character.

From the poem it is clear that Thomas III possessed an excellent vocabulary, and was capable of writing with both style and fluency. He is poetical and knows how to make his words chime pleasantly with each other. He senses how, with the passing of time, everything changes. He also has a vivid imagination, where he sees the honeysuckle ('honeysucks') as having a will of its own, as it reaches upwards towards the sky. On a practical level, he has an extensive knowledge of local flora and fauna.

Surely Thomas III's poem, *Domicilium*, is an indicator of the direction which his future life will take.

# 2

# Religion: Love: Crime: Punishment

Thomas Hardy I died in 1837 which, as already mentioned, was the year in which the Revd Murray was replaced by the Revd Arthur Shirley as vicar of Stinsford. Shirley was a vigorous reformer and innovator who embraced the ideas of the High Church, as advocated by the leaders of the 'Tractarian Movement' (the aim of which was to assert the authority of the Anglican Church). This, for the Hardys, was no less than a disaster, and the 'ecclesiastical changes' which were imposed by the new vicar led Thomas Hardy II to abandon (in 1841 or 1842) all connection with the Stinsford string choir, in which he had played the bass viol, voluntarily, every Sunday for thirty-five years. Nevertheless, the Hardys continued to attend church every Sunday; the 'Hardy' pew being situated in the aisle adjacent to the north wall.

Nor did the rift between Shirley and Thomas II dissuade the latter's son, Thomas III, from attending the Sunday School (established by Shirley) where, in due course, he became an instructor along with the vicar's two sons. In this way he gained an extensive knowledge of the Bible and the Book of Common Prayer, and was said to know the morning and evening services by heart, as well as the rubrics and large portions of the psalms.[1]

There was a great deal of antipathy on the part of Anglicans towards Catholics at the time. This was apparent when Thomas II took his son to Dorchester's Roman amphitheatre, Maumbury Rings, to see an effigy of the Pope, and of Cardinal Nicholas Wiseman (the first Archbishop of Westminster), being burnt during anti-Papist riots. As for Thomas III, despite the rigour and intensity of his Anglican upbringing, the age-old conundrum of religion was one which he would struggle with and agonise over throughout his life.

⌒

Quite apart from his infatuation with Julia Martin, and hers with him, Thomas III, like many people of artistic bent, was of a deeply romantic and impressionable disposition and likely to fall in love at any moment. However because of his natural shyness the objects of his desire were, as often as not, completely unaware of his lovelorn state. Such young ladies included one who passed him by on horseback in South Walk (one of Dorchester's several tree-lined streets), and unaccountably smiled at him. Another was from Windsor; a third was the pretty daughter of the local gamekeeper who possessed a beautiful head of 'bay-red' hair – and was later to be recalled in his poem *To Lisbie Brown*.[2] Finally, there was Louisa, whom he recalled in another poem, *To Louisa in the Lane*. Thomas III would also immortalise the first romantic meeting of his own parents in his poem *A Church Romance*.

Doubtless the young man was destined one day for a great but more tangible romance. When it came, however, the question was, would it live up to his expectations?

⌒

Despite the seemingly idyllic and tranquil surroundings of the Hardys' Bockhampton abode, woe betide anyone who dared to transgress the law or to flout the authorities; for if they did, harsh penalties awaited them. Thomas III's fascination with hanging may have been the result of his father telling him that in his day he had seen four men hanged for setting fire to a hayrick, one of whom, a youth of 18, had not participated in the burnings but had merely been present at the scene. As the youth was underfed and therefore frail, the prison master had ordered weights to be tied to his feet in order to be sure that his neck would be broken by the noose. 'Nothing my father ever said,' declared Thomas III, 'drove the tragedy of life so deeply into my mind' as this account of the unfortunate youth.[3] Thomas II also told his son that when he was a boy and there was a hanging at Dorchester Prison, it was always carried out at 1 p.m. in case the incoming mail-coach subsequently brought notice of a reprieve of sentence. Another piece of information that Thomas III gleaned was that the notorious hangman, Jack Ketch, used to perform public whippings by the town's water pump, using the cat-o'-nine-tails.

As a youth himself, Thomas III was to witness two executions. The first was of a woman, when he stood 'close to the gallows' at the entrance to Dorchester Gaol.[4] The night before he had deliberately gone down to

Hangman's Cottage, situated at the bottom of the hill below the prison beside the River Frome, and peered through the window, where he observed the hangman inside as he ate a hearty supper.[5] The woman to be hanged was Elizabeth Martha Brown, who paid the ultimate penalty for murdering her husband. 'I remember what a fine figure she [Brown] showed against the sky as she hung in the misty rain,' wrote Thomas III later, and 'how the tight black silk gown set off her shape as she wheeled half-round & back [on the end of the rope]' – an indication that perhaps the incident induced in him not revulsion, but a measure of sexual excitement.[6]

The second hanging occurred one summer morning two or three years later. Having heard that it was to take place, Thomas III took his telescope to a vantage point, focused the instrument on Dorchester's prison, and as the clock struck eight, witnessed the public execution of another murderer, this time a male.

Again, images of these harrowing events made a permanent impression on the sensitive mind of the young Thomas III.

# A Career: London: First Novel

Thomas III had been brought up to believe that his family was connected, albeit distantly, with other more illustrious 'Hardy' personages in the county – past and present – such as Admiral Sir Thomas Hardy, his namesake; Thomas Hardy, who had endowed Dorchester's grammar school in Elizabethan times; and several others including, of course, the Channel Island Hardys and in particular one Clement le Hardy, Baillie of Jersey. From this it may be inferred that his family was desperately anxious for the young Thomas III to succeed in the world and make something of himself; to reverse what was seen as the trend, in their case, of a family in decline. However, before he embarked upon the journey of life, his mother Jemima issued him with a warning. Said he, it was 'Mother's notion (and also mine) that a figure stands in our van [path] with arm uplifted, to knock us back from any pleasant prospect we indulge in'.[7]

While Thomas II was working on the Earl of Ilchester's Woodford Castle, it so happened that an associate of his, one John Hicks, architect and church restorer, was present there with him. Thomas II duly introduced Hicks to his son Thomas III – who also happened to be present on the day – and on the strength of this meeting Hicks invited Thomas III to assist him in a survey. Hicks liked what he saw, and the outcome was that he invited

Thomas III to be his pupil. Thomas II duly agreed to pay Hicks the sum of £40 for his son to undergo a three-year course of architectural drawing and surveying. So, in 1856, when he was aged 16, the young Thomas started work at Hicks' office in Dorchester's South Street.

By now, Thomas III had progressed from the frailness and fragility of his childhood into a vigorous manhood. He threw himself with gusto into his new apprenticeship, but at the same time, this did not prevent him from pursuing his study of the Latin language, which enabled him to read the New Testament, Horace, Ovid and Virgil in the original. Likewise, by teaching himself Greek, he was able to read Homer's epic poem *Iliad*. This necessitated him rising at 5 a.m., or 4 a.m. in the summer months, in order to fit everything into the day. Hicks, being a classical scholar himself, was well-disposed to Thomas III's efforts in this respect.

With fellow-pupil Robert Bastow and two other youths – both recent graduates of Aberdeen University, who were the sons of Frederick Perkins, Dorchester's Baptist minister – Thomas III had furious arguments as to the merits and de-merits of 'Paedo-Baptism' (the baptism of infants). This led the latter to consider whether, having himself been baptised as an infant at Stinsford's church of St Michael, he should now be re-baptised as an adult.

Adjacent to Hicks' office in South Street was the school of poet and philologist William Barnes, who would often be called upon to adjudicate in matters of dispute between Thomas III and Bastow on the subject of classical grammar. Barnes, a Latin and oriental scholar of great distinction, had compiled *A Philological Grammar* in which more than sixty languages were compared.

The year is 1859 and Thomas III (who henceforth will be called Hardy) is aged 19. His three-year apprenticeship is over and he is now given the task, by Hicks, of making surveys of churches with a view to their 'restoration'. In reality, this was a euphemism for what Hardy regarded as 'ruination', and the fact that he had become a participant (albeit unwilling) in this process would, in later years, cause him enormous regret. Its legacy remains to this day and is easily borne out by a comparison of, say, the 'restored' Stinsford church of St Michael and Puddletown's church of St Mary, which escaped restoration and in consequence has retained its exquisite and fascinating historical artefacts in their original condition and situation.

The restoration of Stinsford church had begun under the aegis of the Revd Shirley in 1843, when the main part of the west ('minstrels') gallery was removed. Shirley also removed the chancel pews and replaced the string choir with a barrel organ. For this, the Hardy family never forgave him. Hardy would one day get his revenge (although these traumatic events had occurred when he was a mere infant) in a poem, *The Choirmaster's Burial*, in which 'an unsympathetic vicar forbids [deceased choirmaster] William Dewey old-fashioned grave-side musical rites'.[8]

Hardy was now at a crossroads: the question being whether he should pursue a career in architecture or immerse himself ever more deeply in the Classics, and in particular, the Greek plays of Aeschylus and Sophocles. In this, he was to be guided by his literary friend and mentor Horace Moule, son of the Revd Henry Moule, vicar of nearby Fordington. Born in 1832 and therefore eight years his senior, Horace Moule had studied at both Oxford and Cambridge universities and had recently commenced work as an author and reviewer. It was he who introduced Hardy to the *Saturday Review* – a radical London weekly publication which attributed the major- ity of social evils to social inequality – and who also made Hardy gifts of books, including Johann Goethe's *Faust*.

Hardy now commenced writing, in the hope of being published. He was successful, and his first article, an anonymous account of the disappearance of the clock from the almshouse in Dorchester's South Street, appeared in a Dorchester newspaper. The poem *Domicilium* followed, together with articles published by the *Dorset Chronicle* about church restorations carried out by his employer Hicks. Meanwhile, Horace Moule's advice to Hardy was that if he wished to make his living in architecture, then he ought not to continue with his study of the Greek plays. This advice was accepted, albeit reluctantly.

Why did Hardy now make the decision – bold for a country youth – to leave Dorset for London? Was it because he did not find working in Dorchester for Hicks challenging enough, and hoped to better himself in the capital? Or did he have a pecuniary motive, as Desmond MacCarthy (an acquaintance of his) implies? According to MacCarthy, Hardy's thoughts turned to writing when he heard that George Meredith – poet, novelist and reader for publishers Chapman & Hall – had received the sum of £100 for writing a novel. It was, therefore, Hardy's 'desire to make a little money that first made him turn to fiction'.[9] And if he did not succeed, at least he would have the consolation, when in London, of getting a glimpse of some of the great writers and poets of the day whom he wished to emulate.

In April 1862 Hardy found temporary employment making drawings for one John Norton, architect of Old Bond Street. This introduction was made by Hicks who was a friend of Norton's. Soon, Norton in turn introduced Hardy to a Mr Arthur Blomfield, whom Norton had met at the Institute of British Architects. On 5 May Hardy began work as Blomfield's assistant architect.

One of the duties which Blomfield assigned to his 21-year-old assistant was to supervise the removal of bodies from the churchyard of Old St Pancras, through which the Midland Railway Company proposed to make a cutting. On a more cheerful note, Blomfield invited Hardy to sing in his office choir, and also in the choir of St Matthias' church, Richmond, where he himself sang bass.

In August 1862 Hardy wrote to his sister, Mary, describing how he had attended evening service at St Mary's church, Kilburn; and also how he had received a visit from his friend, Horace Moule, who had accompanied him to a Roman Catholic chapel built by the architect Augustus Pugin (1812–52). Two months later, Hardy told Mary how their father (who had evidently made the journey up from Dorset) had been to an opera at Covent Garden and had insisted on seeing the Thames Tunnel (which linked Wapping on the north bank of the river to Rotherhithe on the south bank).[10] This was the year in which Hardy made a proposal of marriage to Mary Waight, who was employed in the high-class 'mantle showroom' (retail shop selling women's cloaks) in Dorchester and who, at 29, was seven years his senior. Mary, however, rejected his offer.[11]

Early in 1863, again in a letter to his sister Mary, Hardy describes his office which overlooks the River Thames and all its bridges, and tells her how he has visited the underground railway, then in its infancy. The smog, however, which hangs over the city like 'brown paper or pea-soup' had been a problem. He tells Mary how he intends to enter a competition for a prize, offered by Sir William Tite (the architect who rebuilt the Royal Exchange and designed many of England's early railway stations). The competition is open to members of the Architectural Association, of which he is one, and his entry is to be his own design for a 'Country Mansion' – Hardy subsequently won the prize. He had also entered the Prize Architectural Essay competition of the Royal Institute of British Architects: the subject of his dissertation being 'The Application of Bricks and Terra Cotta to Modern Architecture'. For this he was awarded a silver medal.[12]

In the latter part of 1863, Hardy recommends to Mary that she read the works of William Makepeace Thackeray, whose writing he esteems as being of the 'highest kind', and a 'perfect and truthful representation of actual life'. He himself is now, in his spare time, throwing himself once more into the study of literature.

The funeral of former British Liberal Prime Minister, Lord Palmerston, took place on 27 October 1865, which Hardy was able to attend, having purchased the necessary ticket. The following day he writes again to Mary, recommending Anthony Trollope's novel *Barchester Towers* to her as the author's best work. Hardy also mentions that his father (who is apparently again staying with him at the time) has 'taken to reading newspapers'. He himself has resumed his study of French and is spending much time in the National Gallery studying, one by one, the great masters; attending a series of Shakespeare's plays, and also live readings of the works of Charles Dickens by the author himself.[13]

A formative influence on Hardy was the poet and writer Algernon Charles Swinburne, born in 1837 and educated at Eton and Oxford. Swinburne's *Poems and Ballads*, published in 1865, showed contempt for conventional morality in favour of sensuality and paganism. Although this evoked violent criticism, Hardy, who was yet to meet Swinburne, was one of his earliest admirers, and later described that 'buoyant time of thirty years ago, when I used to read your early works walking along the crowded London streets, to my imminent risk of being knocked down'.[14] Swinburne's views were expressed in his *Hymn of Man* as 'Glory to Man in the highest! For Man is the master of things'.

In 1866 Hardy revealed to his sister, Mary, that it had been his serious intention to enter the Church. To this end, Horace Moule had sent him the *Students Guide to the University of Cambridge* (Moule's own university), but Hardy eventually decided that this 'notion was too far-fetched to be worth entertaining'. It would take three years, and then another three, and then almost another one, in order to get 'a title'[15] – which was a necessary prerequisite for those intending to enter the ministry.

The words of Hardy's poem, *The Impercipient* (subtitled 'At a Cathedral Service' and believed to have been written when he was in his twenties), indicate that this decision was the correct one, for the added reason that he had decided that the Christian faith was something he found impossible to embrace. This, Hardy reveals in his reference to worshippers:

That with this bright believing band
　I have no claim to be,
That faiths by which my comrades stand
　Seem fantasies to me …

It should also be mentioned that a few years previously, in 1858, the conflict between religion and science had been brought into sharp focus when Charles Darwin and Alfred Russell Wallace published a joint paper entitled *On the Tendency of Species to form Varieties*. The following year, *On the Origin of Species by Means of Natural Selection* was published by Darwin alone. Hardy, with his voracious thirst for knowledge, was familiar with this latter work, and 'had been among the earliest acclaimers' of it.[16]

Hardy now began sending poems, which he had recently written, to various magazines with a view to publication, only to have them rejected by their editors.

While in London, Hardy demonstrated that his love of music was as strong as ever, and took every opportunity to visit art galleries and the opera; neither of which had hitherto been available to him. Unfortunately, however, his health had deteriorated; perhaps from the polluted air of the metropolis (his lodgings fronted the River Thames, which was then little more than an open sewer). So, on the advice of Blomfield, he returned to Dorset in July 1867. Blomfield believed that this would be for convalescence. Yet Hardy had already been contacted by his former employer, Hicks of Dorchester, who told him that he, Hicks, was in need of an assistant to help with church restoration work.

Having returned to the house of his parents at Higher Bockhampton – where he regained his strength and health – Hardy resumed his habit of walking to work in Dorchester every day. This time, however, the work was of an irregular nature, and in his spare time Hardy wrote his first novel, *The Poor Man and the Lady*. This was read by Horace Moule, now a regular contributor to the *Saturday Review*, who must have liked it because he furnished Hardy with a letter of introduction to publisher Alexander Macmillan, to whom Hardy sent the manuscript on 25 July the following year. Anxious and impatient to hear Macmillan's opinion, he wrote again to the publisher on 10 September, saying that he, Hardy, had it in mind to write another story, but had not the courage to do so 'till something comes of the first'.[17]

Macmillan declined to publish the work, although he commented that much of it was 'admirable', and one scene in particular was 'full of power and insight'. He ultimately saw it as an excessive attack, by Hardy, on the upper classes, which were portrayed as 'heartless' in their dealings with the 'working classes'. These sentiments were echoed by John Morley, a friend of Macmillan to whom the latter had shown the work. Nevertheless, Morley did at least admit that the author 'has stuff and purpose in him'.[18]

Unwilling to take no for an answer, Hardy, in the December of 1868, made a brief visit to London to see Macmillan personally. The answer remained the same, but Macmillan did suggest that he approach Frederick Chapman of publishers Chapman & Hall. Hardy duly met Chapman the following day, left the work with him and returned to Dorchester.

He revisited London in January 1869, when the reply from Chapman & Hall finally arrived. They would publish *The Poor Man and the Lady*, but only if Hardy guaranteed to furnish them with the sum of £20 to cover any losses which the firm might incur. By the time March came, Hardy, instead of being sent the proofs of the book as he expected, was asked by Chapman & Hall to visit London yet again. Here he met George Meredith, who expressed the opinion that the book would be perceived as 'socialistic', or even 'revolution-ary'. As such, it would be liable to be attacked, on all sides, by conventional reviewers, and this might prove a handicap to Hardy in the future. Hardy should either rewrite the story or write another novel with a more interesting plot.[19]

What had prompted Hardy to make an assault on the nobility and squire-archy in this fashion? Was it simply that, as an Englishman, his sympathies naturally lay with the underdog? The 'establishment', as he was well aware, wielded immense power and bore down very heavily on those who dared to cross the boundaries which it had laid down. A classical example of this was the case of the six Dorset farm labourers – the so-called 'Tolpuddle Martyrs' – whose 'crime' had been to swear an illegal oath. This they had done in an attempt to organise and thus defend themselves against the progressive reduction of their wages from eight, to seven, and then to a threatened six shillings per week: an insufficient sum with which to support themselves and their starving families. For this, they had been sentenced in 1834 to be transported to Australia and Tasmania. Hardy was no doubt aware that their trial had taken place in Dorchester, even though this had occurred six years prior to his birth. He may also have been influenced both by the heroic work of Horace Moule's father, the Revd Henry Moule, who as vicar of Fordington struggled to improve the lot of the poor of his parish, particularly during the cholera epidemic of 1854, and by Moule's son Horace, who was an ardent socialist.

Despite George Meredith's adverse comments, Hardy, in April 1869, sent the manuscript of *The Poor Man and the Lady* to Smith, Elder & Company, who also rejected it. In December 1870, with dogged determination, he sent it to Tinsley Brothers, only to be offered terms for publication by them which were unacceptable to him.

John Hicks died in the winter of 1868/69. In April 1869 Hardy was asked by G.R. Crickmay – a Weymouth architect who had purchased Hicks' practice – if he would assist him in continuing with the work on church restorations. To this, Hardy agreed, and in July he commenced work at Crickmay's office in Weymouth.

Having found lodgings in Weymouth at 3 Wooperton Street, Hardy was able to avail himself of the amenities which the town provided. For him, pleasant summer diversions included listening to the town band playing waltzes (newly composed by Johann Strauss); bathing each morning, and rowing in the bay each evening. He also joined a dancing class to learn the quadrille. It was at about this time that he formed an attachment to his cousin Tryphena Sparks, a student teacher from Puddletown who was eleven years his junior, he even went as far as to buy her a ring.

By the time winter arrived, Hardy had completed the work set for him by Crickmay. Nonetheless, he chose to remain at Weymouth where he would commence work on a new novel entitled *Desperate Remedies*. In February 1870, however, he returned to the peace and quiet of his home at Bockhampton in order to concentrate more fully on the manuscript. Chapman & Hall's reader, George Meredith, had criticised *The Poor Man and the Lady* for the weakness of its plot. Hardy, therefore, resolved that the plot *of Desperate Remedies* would be nothing less than sensational.[20]

Within a week, Crickmay was in touch again, requesting that he depart as soon as possible for Cornwall, in order 'to take a plan and particulars of a church I am about to rebuild there'.[21] This was a reference to the church of St Juliot near Boscastle, on Cornwall's north coast. This visit to Cornwall was one which would change the life of the young Hardy dramatically and irrevocably.

# 3

# Emma: A Successful Author

## St Juliot: *Desperate Remedies*

Hardy's journey from Weymouth to Cornwall, on Monday 7 March 1870, involved him rising at four in the morning, catching the train at Dorchester station and changing several times before reaching the station at Launceston. For the remaining 16 miles he was obliged to hire a pony and trap, and by the time he arrived at St Juliot rectory, it was dark. Here, at the front door, a dazzling apparition met his eyes: a female with a rosy, Rubenesque complexion, striking blue eyes and auburn hair with ringlets reaching down as far as her shoulders.

Emma Lavinia Gifford, like Hardy, was aged 29. Born in Plymouth, she was the daughter of solicitor John Attersoll Gifford and his wife, also Emma (*née* Farman), and the youngest but one of a family of five. Brought up in a fine house not far from Plymouth's seafront or 'Hoe', Emma was educated privately at a school run by 'dear, refined single ladies of perfect manners',[1] and she was accustomed to mingling with 'the élite of the town'.[2] So how did she come to be living in this remote part of north Cornwall?

Prior to Emma's birth in 1840, her wealthy paternal grandmother, Helen Gifford (*née* Davie), a widow since 1825, had come to live with her family. According to Emma, Helen 'considered it best that he [Emma's father, John] should give up his profession which he disliked, and live a life of quiet cultivated leisure'.[3] However, John Gifford's name continued to appear on the Law Institution's list of registered solicitors up until the year 1851 (but not thereafter), and the census for that year gives his profession as 'Attorney at Law'. When Helen died in 1860, John (along with Helen's other offspring) inherited a portion of her estate. John and his family then relocated in June of that year to Bodmin in Cornwall, and John subsequently took his late mother's advice, retired from legal practice and became a 'Fundholder' instead – one who lives off the income from his investments.[4]

Here in Cornwall, Emma's elder sister, Helen, obtained a post first as a governess (in which capacity she was succeeded, for a brief period, by Emma), and then as companion to an elderly lady at Tintagel on the coast. There, Helen met her husband-to-be, the Revd Caddell Holder, MA Oxon, rector of St Juliot, the repair of whose church was the objective of Hardy's visit.

The Revd Holder was born on the Caribbean island of Barbados, where his father was a judge, and was educated at Trinity College, Oxford. When he married Helen, on 10 September 1868 at Bodmin parish church, he was aged 67, and she only 31. (This was Holder's second marriage; his first wife Ann having died three years previously.) When Holder took his new wife back to his home, Emma accompanied them. At the rectory of St Juliot, Emma would help her sister with 'house affairs' and also pay visits to the 'parish folk' (that is, her brother-in-law's parishioners).[5] Her spare time was spent riding her pony Fanny, painting in watercolour, sketching and gathering wild flowers. On Sundays she played the harmonium and 'conducted the church music'.[6]

It so happened that when Hardy arrived on the scene, the Revd Holder was suffering from an attack of gout. His wife was attending her husband and it was therefore Emma who received the visitor.

According to a circular, issued from St Juliot rectory in March 1869, the church, which dated from Saxon times:

> Has for many years been in a ruinous condition, and no service has been held in it for more than two years, the Parishioners being under the necessity of using the National School Room for the celebration of Divine Service, which in every respect is quite unfit for the purpose.
>
> The tower threatens to fall and is in a highly dangerous condition; the Roof, Floor and a large portion of the Walls of the Nave are too dilapidated for any partial repairs, and render the interior unhealthy for the congregation … With the exception of the walls of the South Aisle and Porch, an entire rebuilding will be necessary, the estimated cost of which is about £900.
>
> The Patron of the living, the Rev. R. [Richard] Rawle [vicar of Tamworth, Staffordshire] has promised to give the sum of £700 towards the Restoration, on condition that the further sum of £200 be raised within the present year.[7]

The arrival of architect Hardy was therefore a matter of great interest and excitement in the parish, for now, at last, long-awaited plans for the church could be put into operation.

The evening of Hardy's arrival, said Emma, was 'lovely ... after a wild winter'.[8] She also recalled that Hardy 'had a beard' and was wearing 'a rather shabby great coat'. A blue paper protruded from his pocket which proved to be, not a plan of the church, but the manuscript of a poem he had written.[9] Emma states that on his first visit to the church, 'the architect ... [Hardy] stayed a few days rather longer than first intended'.[10]

Two days after his arrival, Hardy, accompanied by Emma and her sister, visited Boscastle (2 miles down the valley from St Juliot), Tintagel (legendary birthplace of King Arthur) and the quarries of Penpethy, to seek slate for the roofing of the church. Next day, Hardy and Emma walked, unchaperoned, on the cliff tops. She loved the 'beautiful sea-coast, [and] the wild Atlantic Ocean rolling in, with its magnificent waves and spray', and declared that she and Hardy could scarcely have had a more romantic meeting.[11]

On the fourth day Hardy returned home. He later summed up just how deeply his own romantic instincts had been aroused by his meeting with Emma in a poem entitled *When I Set Out For Lyonnesse* (this being the poetical name for the county of Cornwall), and, in particular, in the poem's final verse:

> When I came back from Lyonnesse
> With magic in my eyes,
> All marked with mute surmise
> My radiance fair and fathomless,
> When I came back from Lyonnesse
> With magic in my eyes!

It seemed Hardy had found the woman of his dreams. From then on he returned to St Juliot every few months, taking the opportunity to visit other local beauty spots with Emma, including the beautiful Valency Valley. (The word 'valency' is believed to derive from the Cornish 'melin-jy', meaning 'mill house'.)

To return to Hardy's literary endeavours, George Meredith had demanded that his next novel contain more of a plot and, sure enough, he obliged.

However, in *Desperate Remedies*, the fact that there are effectively two stories going on – first a romance and then a murder – makes not inconsiderable demands on the reader. The story is as follows:

On the death of their father (who is already a widower), Owen Graye and his younger sister Cytherea leave the Midlands for Budmouth (Weymouth). Here they find lodgings and Owen takes up the post of assistant to a local architect. On an excursion by paddle steamer to Lulworth Cove, Owen misses the boat back. This enables Cytherea to become better acquainted with her brother's friend and colleague Edward Springrove (who is head draughtsman in Owen's office), who has joined the steamer for the return journey. Edward and Cytherea fall in love, but a problem arises. Edward is, in fact, already engaged to be married to his cousin.

Cytherea obtains employment as lady's maid to Miss Aldclyffe of Knapwater House, whose first name also happens to be Cytherea. By now, Edward Springrove, who lives at nearby Knapwater Park, has broken off his previous engagement and has become engaged to Cytherea. Miss Aldclyffe forms a deep, emotional attachment to Cytherea (reminiscent of Julia Martin and Hardy).

Miss Aldclyffe appoints Aeneas Manston to be her steward at Knapwater House, for reasons which only become apparent later. Although he is a married man, Manston is attracted to the young Cytherea. When he becomes enraged by the taunts of his drunken wife, he strikes her and she dies instantly. He leads everyone to believe that she has perished in a fire, but in fact he has hidden her body in the oven of a disused brew house. He is now free to marry Cytherea. Manston is a musician and when he plays some 'saddening chords' to Cytherea on the organ, she agrees to marry him instead of Springrove, even though she does not love him.[12] In this way she avoids being a burden to her brother Owen, who is not in good health.

When suspicion is aroused that Mrs Manston is still alive, Manston, to avert speculation, persuades another woman to impersonate her. However, a poem of Manston's is discovered in which he has described the colour of his wife's eyes as 'azure', whereas his 'new' wife – his deceased wife's imper-sonator – has eyes of 'deepest black'.

As Manston is in the act of recovering the body of his real wife and burying it, he is observed. He flees, but not before attempting to persuade Cytherea to run away with him, in the midst of which endeavour he is apprehended by Edward Springrove. Manston is detained in the county jail, where he confesses to his crime before hanging himself.

The plot is further complicated by the fact that Cytherea turns out to be the daughter of a man whom Miss Aldclyffe once loved. It is also revealed that when Miss Aldclyffe was aged 17, she was 'violated' by her cousin, a military officer, and the child born as a result of this untoward event was Aeneas Manston.

On her deathbed, Miss Aldclyffe confesses to Cytherea that the reason she appointed Manston as her steward was to bring him close to Cytherea; it being her dream that Cytherea, the daughter of the man she loved, and Manston, her own natural child, be married. Finally, all ends happily for Cytherea when she marries Springrove, now a qualified architect.

Hardy contrived for his novel *Desperate Remedies* to end happily, at least as far as Cytherea and Springrove were concerned. And surely, having himself fallen in love with Emma Gifford, he hoped that his own love affair would come to a similarly agreeable conclusion.

In March 1870 Hardy sent the manuscript of his second novel, *Desperate Remedies*, to Macmillan, who declined to publish it (in the same way that he had previously declined to publish *The Poor Man and the Lady*). John Morley (now editor of the *Fortnightly Review*) was particularly vitriolic about *Desperate Remedies*, saying that the story was 'ruined by the disgusting and absurd outrage which is the key to its mystery: the violation of a young lady at an evening party, and the subsequent birth of a child'. In his opinion, this was 'too abominable to be tolerated as a central incident from which the action of the story is to move'.[13]

Notwithstanding this setback, the novel was accepted on 6 May 1870 by Tinsley Brothers, on condition that Hardy paid them the sum of £75 – a great deal of money for a struggling architect who possessed only £123 in the entire world. Another condition was that Hardy made some minor alterations and completed the final chapters (of which he had hitherto sent them only a précis). It is likely that these alterations included a toning down of the 'violation' scene. The final wording agreed for this scene was that Miss Aldclyffe, when 'a young girl of seventeen, was cruelly betrayed by her cousin, a wild officer of six and twenty'.

Hardy's anxious search for a publisher was finally over. What had motivated him to carry on with his writing in spite of having had so many rejections? Undoubtedly, his creative instincts were nurtured by his having read so much of other people's work, and it was therefore only natural that now he should want to emulate these other writers by getting his own name into print. If they could leave their mark on the world of English literature, then why could not he?

⌒

On 16 May 1870 Hardy returned to London, where he assisted Blomfield and another architect, Raphael Brandon – an exponent of the English Gothic – and also spent time with Horace Moule who was in the capital at the time.[14] In August he visited Cornwall and was reunited with Emma, with whom he enjoyed a visit to King Arthur's Castle, Tintagel. The decrepit tower and north aisle of St Juliot church was now deliberately razed to the ground, prior to its rebuilding, and when the foundation stone of the new tower was laid, it was Emma who had the honour of laying it. The pews, the Saxon north door and the chancel screen were all discarded, but, fortunately, not before Hardy had made detailed drawings of them. Crickmay and Hardy did, however, succeed in preserving many of the windows, the altar, the granite font and the Elizabethan altar rails.

As the relationship between Hardy and Emma progressed from one of 'acquaintance' to one of 'affection',[15] she found him 'a perfectly new subject of study and delight, and he found a "mine" in me'.[16]

As a keepsake to ameliorate the pain of their long separations, Emma gave Hardy a lock of her hair. Subsequent visits by him would see the pair talking 'much of plots, possible scenes, tales [presumably for stories], and poetry and of his [Hardy's] own work'.[17] Said Emma: 'After a little time I copied a good deal of manuscript [of Hardy's] which went to-and-fro by post, and I was very proud and happy doing this, which I did in the privacy of my room, where I read and wrote also the letters [to and from Hardy].'[18]

⌒

On 25 March 1871 *Desperate Remedies* was duly published, anonymously, in three volumes. The book received excellent reviews in the *Athenaeum* and in the *Morning Post*, but it was vilified by the *Spectator* magazine, which saw it as an 'idle prying into the ways of wickedness', and also objected to it being published anonymously. Moule advised Hardy to ignore such criticism and, in an effort to counter it, reviewed *Desperate Remedies* himself for the *Saturday Review*. Unfortunately, however, there was a six-month delay before Moule's article was published.

## Under the Greenwood Tree

*Under the Greenwood Tree*, written when Hardy was aged 31, was to be his second published novel. In it, he did what many aspiring writers do: he wrote about what he knew best – in this case, his childhood.

The alternative title to *Under the Greenwood Tree* was *The Mellstock Quire*: 'Mellstock' being the collective name for the hamlets of Higher and Lower Bockhampton, the village of Stinsford and their surroundings. The 'Quire' refers to the choir of Stinsford Church, both instrumental and vocal. As for the names of his characters, Hardy obtained them from a study of the tombstones in Stinsford churchyard. John Morley, who had read Hardy's *The Poor Man and the Lady*, had commented in regard to that novel that 'the opening pictures of Christmas Eve in the tranter's house are really of good quality'. Drawing strength from this, Hardy decided to begin his new novel with the tranter's Christmas party.

The themes of the novel are twofold: the love of Dick Dewy (an honest yeoman) for Fancy Day (a certified teacher), and the destruction of the quire, brought about by the advent of a new vicar, the Revd Maybold – who, of course, is a facsimile of the real-life Revd Arthur Shirley, vicar of Stinsford. Dick proposes to Fancy and she accepts his offer. Nonetheless, she has a momentary flirtation with Farmer Shiner; then accepts a second proposal of marriage from the new vicar. Finally, she confesses to Maybold that she has acted hastily, and she and Dick get married amidst celebratory dances – under the greenwood tree – to the music of the quire.

Alongside this romance runs the story of the quire, whose members number such colourful characters as the tranter, the shoemaker and the simpleton. Having fallen asleep during a church sermon, they awake and, believing themselves still to be at the local dance which they had attended the night before, spring into life and play not a hymn, but a jig. Episodes like this show the lighter, vibrant side of Hardy's character, and reveal his keen sense of humour. Subsequently, however, and for reasons soon to become apparent, Hardy's works would assume a more serious, sombre and introspective dimension.

The quire have played their music since time immemorial; their previous vicar having left them undisturbed, allowing them to participate in the choosing of the hymns and never troubling them with a visit 'from year's end to year's end'. Now, they have to endure the Revd Maybold who never allows them 'a bit o' peace'. When Maybold announces that the musicians are to be replaced with an organ, they see it as a catastrophe; yet they resolve to fall gloriously 'with a bit of a flourish at Christmas', rather than be 'choked off quiet at no time in particular'.

In view of the real-life trauma which the Revd Shirley had brought to the Stinsford choir, it must have given Hardy enormous pleasure and satisfaction to have Fancy Day turn down the proposal of marriage by the Revd Maybold in favour of Dick Dewy.

Hardy sent the manuscript to Macmillan, who would probably have published it but for a misunderstanding. When the manuscript was returned to him, Hardy was of a mind to give up writing altogether, but was persuaded by a letter from Emma to persevere with it as she felt sure that authorship was his true vocation. In this, she demonstrated an unselfish side to her nature; after all, a career in architecture would have provided greater security for herself and Hardy in the event of them one day marrying.

In the spring of 1872, Hardy returned again to London with the aim of furthering his architectural career. He found work with a Mr T. Roger Smith, Professor of Architecture at the Royal Institute of British Architects, and assisted in the design of schools for the London School Board.

Horace Moule, in a chance meeting with Hardy, also advised him to continue with his writing; one reason being that in the event of his eyesight deteriorating, at some time in the future, and thus halting his architectural career, then this would provide him with an alternative occupation.

By another coincidence Hardy encountered Tinsley, who asked him whether he had any other manuscripts for him to look at. Hardy accordingly sent him, in April 1872, the manuscript of *Under the Greenwood Tree*. This was duly published two months later in June. The book was reviewed favourably by both the *Athenaeum* and the *Pall Mall Gazette*. On the strength of this, Tinsley asked Hardy to write a story for his *Tinsley's Magazine*, to be serialised over a period of twelve months. (In Victorian times, to be published in a popular magazine provided a lucrative source of income for an aspiring new writer.) To this end, Hardy took a break from work and commenced his next novel, *A Pair of Blue Eyes*, which was inspired by his visit to Cornwall and his meeting with Emma, two and a half years previously.

Meanwhile, on Thursday 11 April 1872, the newly restored church of St Juliot was reopened, although neither Hardy nor Crickmay attended the ceremony. Morning and afternoon services were held. At the former, there was a much more numerous congregation than could have been expected, considering the busy season and the scattered population of this agricultural district. In the afternoon the beautiful building was filled with a devout audience.

It was reported that many clergymen from other parishes round about were also in attendance, including the Revd Henry M.A. Serjeant of St Clether – a village situated 7 miles from St Juliot – of whom more will be said shortly.[19] The 'Statement of Receipts ... on the Restoration of St Juliot Church, 1871–2'[20] makes for interesting reading:

| RECEIPTS | £ | s. | d. |
|---|---|---|---|
| Revd. C [Caddell] Holder | 55 | 19 | 6 |
| Mrs [Helen] Holder | 5 | | |
| Lady Molesworth | 25 | | |
| Capt. [Cecil] Holder [son of Caddell] | 1 | 1 | 0 |
| Bishop of London | | 10 | |
| Miss [Emma] Gifford | | 10 | |
| Mrs [Emma] Gifford [wife of John A. Gifford] | | 10 | |
| T. Hardy, Esq. | | 10 | |
| Mr H. Jose | | 10 | |
| Mr J. Jose | | 10 | |
| W. [Walter] E. Gifford, Esq. [Emma's brother] (London) | | 5 | |
| Miss Gifford [again Emma] by sale of sketches | | 8 | 10 |
| Collected at opening services | 11 | 2 | 1 |
| On next Sunday | 1 | 0 | 0 |
| Proceeds of luncheon and tea | 14 | 15 | 6 |

Emma's father was conspicuous by his absence. The editor of the *Royal Cornwall Gazette*, however, could not hide his displeasure at the 'restoration' and the fact that:

> Many old architectural features in the original building ... are now destroyed and swept away for ever, adding another unmistakable specimen of Vandalism to what has already taken place at Tintagel, Lesnewth, and Forrabury.[21]

## Hostility: *Near Lanivet*

In August 1872 Hardy made another visit to Cornwall, this time to Kirland House on the outskirts of Bodmin Town, where Emma's parents, the

Giffords, were now living. It is likely that the purpose of this visit was for Hardy to ask Emma's father, John Attersoll Gifford, for permission to marry his daughter. Strictly speaking, this was not necessary as both parties were of age. Nevertheless, it was the convention of the times.

In the event the visit was not a happy one, and this is reflected in a poem which Hardy later wrote entitled *I Rose and Went to Rou'tor Town* ('Rou'tor' being his name for Bodmin). The poem purports to express the views of a female; a thin attempt at disguise by Hardy, for the sentiments expressed are undoubtedly his. It commences with a sense of cheerful anticipation:

> I ROSE and went to Rou'tor Town
>> With gaiety and good heart,
>> And ardour for the start …

It continues:

> When sojourn soon at Rou'tor Town
>> Wrote sorrows on my face …

And it ends in bitterness:

> The evil wrought at Rou'tor Town
>> On him I'd loved so true
>> I cannot tell anew:
> But nought can quench, but nought can drown
> The evil wrought at Rou'tor Town
>> On him I'd loved so true.

Hardy was subsequently questioned about this poem by writer Vere H. Collins.[22] What is 'the evil wrought at Rou'tor Town', asked Collins; to which Hardy replied: 'Slander, or something of that sort.' In other words, Emma's father, who was violently opposed to any future attachment between Hardy and his daughter, was slanderously abusive to Hardy on the occasion in question.[23] It is possible that Gifford was drunk, for as Emma states:

> He married my mother after the death of her sister – a lovely golden haired girl of eighteen to whom he was engaged, shortly to be married … [immediately after whose death] he drank heavily, and in after life never a wedding, removal, or death occurred in the family but he broke out again.[24]

Gifford would subsequently refer to Hardy as 'a low-born churl who has presumed to marry into my family'.[25]

Faced with this setback, how the cautionary words spoken to him by his mother must have echoed in Hardy's mind, when she had warned him of the figure which 'stands in our van (path) with arm uplifted, to knock us back from any pleasant prospect we indulge in'. Also, the effect on Hardy, with his sensitive nature, was to reinforce his pre-existing feelings of inferiority with regard to himself. So how was he to express his outrage and frustration about the way he had been treated by Emma's father, and about the rigid class distinctions which pervaded Victorian society of which he was now a victim? Why, in the best way he knew how – through his writings.

Having extricated himself from this unpleasant interview with Gifford, Hardy subsequently relocated to St Benet's Abbey, near Lanivet, the home of Captain Charles Eldon Serjeant[26] and his wife Jane, who were friends of Emma's. The captain was the first cousin of William Henry Serjeant, son of the curate of St Clether. Emma had formed a deep attachment to William, as will shortly be seen, but he had died seven months earlier in January 1872, at the young age of 23.

It is likely that Emma joined Hardy during his brief sojourn at St Benet's Abbey in August 1872, and that it was then, notwithstanding the hostility of Emma's father, that the couple became engaged. They also visited the Holders at St Juliot, where they received a more agreeable reception than they had at Kirland House.

Hardy went back to London, but quickly decided to return to the tranquillity of his family home at Bockhampton in order to give *A Pair of Blue Eyes* his full attention. An invitation from Professor Smith to revisit the capital was refused, despite the cordial relationship which existed between them.

☞

Hardy's visit to Cornwall in August 1872 prompted him to write another poem (which was subsequently published as part of his *Moments of Vision* collection):

**Near Lanivet**

THERE was a stunted handpost just on the crest,
   Only a few feet high:
She was tired, and we stopped in the twilight-time for her rest,
   At the crossways close thereby.

She leant back, being so weary, against its stem,
    And laid her arms on its own,
Each open palm stretched out to each end of them,
    Her sad face sideways thrown.

Her white-clothed form at this dim-lit cease of day
    Made her look as one crucified
In my gaze at her from the midst of the dusty way,
    And hurriedly 'Don't,' I cried.
I do not think she heard. Loosing thence she said,
    As she stepped forth ready to go,
'I am rested now. – Something strange came into my head;
    I wish I had not leant so!'

And wordless we moved onward down from the hill
    In the west cloud's murked obscure,
And looking back we could see the handpost still
    In the solitude of the moor.

'It struck her too,' I thought, for as if afraid
    She heavily breathed as we trailed;
Till she said, 'I did not think how 'twould look in the shade,
    When I leant there like one nailed.'
I, lightly: 'There's nothing in it. For *you*, anyhow!'
    – 'O I know there is not,' said she …
'Yet I wonder … If no one is bodily crucified now,
    In spirit one may be!'

And we dragged on and on, while we seemed to see
    In the running of Time's far glass
Her crucified, as she had wondered if she might be
    Some day. – Alas, alas!

Almost half a century was to pass before Hardy confided to author, critic and writer of his biography *Thomas Hardy*, Harold Child, that the 'the strange incident' related by him in the poem 'really happened'.[27] He also admitted to his friend, Florence Henniker, that the poem was 'literally true'.[28] And finally, he told his friend, the poet, author and critic, Edmund Gosse, that the scene described 'occurred between us [himself and Emma] before our marriage'.[29]

It seems that the signpost ('handpost') which stood on the hill reminded Emma of Calvary, and the cross on which Jesus Christ was crucified. But why did she then choose, to Hardy's horror, to mimic Christ and his posture on the cross? And why afterwards did she ask him, again to his horror, if it was possible for a person to be crucified in spirit, rather than in body? Given the time and context in which the poem was written – that is, shortly after Hardy's visit to Kirland House, and his unfortunate interview with Emma's father – its meaning is not difficult to deduce.

When Christ was crucified he was making atonement for the sins of the world. Emma, as a devout Christian, would therefore have regarded crucifixion as a punishment for sin, and it was because of her own feelings of guilt that she chose, on that gloomy evening spent with Hardy, to mimic Christ on the cross. Possible sources of this guilt are as follows. In promising herself to Hardy, Emma had gone against the express wishes of her father, who regarded the young architect as 'a low-born churl'. But even more serious was the fact that she did not love Hardy: her thoughts were not with him, but with another, and for this reason she had no intention of ever having a sexual relationship with him. Extraordinary as this latter statement may seem, evidence of its veracity will be produced in due course.

This being the case, why did Emma consent to marry Hardy? According to a reliable source, it was because her sister Helen, wife of the Revd Caddell Holder, 'was trying to marry her younger sister … to any man who would have her'. Also, Emma 'was nearly thirty then &nd the sisters had violent quarrels'.[30]

# 4

# Emma Inspires a Novel

## *A Pair of Blue Eyes*: Death of Horace Moule

Hardy would set his novels in an area which included the counties of south-west and central-southern England, which he called 'Wessex' (after a previous Saxon kingdom of that name), but he invented his own names for the real-life places which existed within this region. For example, 'Knollsea' is Swanage; 'Casterbridge' is Dorchester; 'Weatherbury' is Puddletown; 'Budmouth Regis' is Weymouth.[1]

As for the content of his novels, Hardy, as already mentioned, once told his friend Edward Clodd that 'every superstition, custom, &c., described therein may be depended on as true records of the same – & not inventions of mine'.[2] This fact is borne out by a surviving notebook of Hardy's which contains extracts collected from *The Dorset County Chronicle*, which was a primary source for the plots of many of his novels, together with extracts of histories and biographies which he had studied. However, Hardy also had a habit of blending into the fabric of his novels some of his own experiences, and in this, his third published novel, *A Pair of Blue Eyes*, was to be no exception. To begin with, it is surely no coincidence that Emma Gifford, with whom Hardy had fallen in love, had eyes of blue.

In *A Pair of Blue Eyes*, the reader is brought face to face with a drama involving love, betrayal and death; played out in the equally dramatic countryside of Cornwall. It was published in May 1873 by Tinsley Brothers, when Hardy was aged 32.

The story centres around two friends, who unbeknown to one another fall in love with the same woman. The one, Stephen Smith, is an architect (as, of course, was Hardy) who is sent to Cornwall to work on the restoration of a church. Here he meets Elfride Swancourt, daughter of the parson, and falls in love. This, of course, is Hardy himself, reliving, vicariously through 'Smith', his own journey to Cornwall and his first meeting with Elfride (Emma). Furthermore, Smith's father (like Hardy's) is a stonemason who lives not in Dorset, but near to Elfride's home.

Smith's friend, Henry Knight, also an admirer of Elfride, is a writer, reviewer, barrister and Smith's former mentor. Knight is therefore reminiscent of Hardy's friend Horace Moule, who in 1862 was admitted to the Middle Temple. This begs the question, if 'Smith' represents Hardy, and 'Knight' represents Moule, did Moule in real life also fall in love with Emma? The answer is no. In fact, Moule and Emma never met.[3]

Another parallel between the novel and Hardy's own life may be that, just as Smith was at pains to conceal the fact that he formerly had a lover, so Hardy may have been anxious lest Emma find out about his own former attachment to his cousin Tryphena Sparks. As for Elfride's mortification at Knight's scathing review of a 'novelette' which she has written, this is surely a reflection of Hardy's hurt at having his own works criticised and rejected.

In *A Pair of Blue Eyes*, Hardy beguiles the reader with the elegance of his prose and the richness of his vocabulary. For example, here are to be found words like 'diaphanous' and 'parallelepipedon'. There are delightful descriptive passages, such as when candlelight falls on Elfride and transforms her hair 'into a nebulous haze of light, surrounding her crown like an aureola'. He also makes skilful use of imagery, as when Smith 'drew himself in with the sensitiveness of a snail'; 'Time closed up like a fan before him'; 'one ray was abstracted from the glory about her head'; and 'feet' played about under Elfride's dress 'like little mice'. (It takes but little discernment to realise that these references to the hair and feet of Elfride were inspired by Emma.)

There are references in the novel which reveal just how familiar Hardy was with the authors Shakespeare and Catullus; with the Psalms; with painters Holbein and Turner; with Raphael's *Madonna della Sedia*, and with 'Dundagel' (the ancient name for the Cornish village of Tintagel). He also demonstrates his attention to detail, as for example when he is describing the so-called 'cliff without a name' (near 'Castle Boterel' – Boscastle), which he compares to others such as Beachy Head, St Aldhelm's, St Bee's, and the Lizard. And he is aware of the significance to the earth's history of fossils, and in particular a type known as 'trilobites'.

That Hardy is in touch with the land and its people – as is to be expected from one born in the country and steeped in its ways – is revealed when he writes of how 'labouring men' are able to tell the time of day 'by means of shadows, winds, clouds, the movements of sheep and oxen, the singing of birds, the crowing of cocks, and a hundred other sights and sounds which people with watches in their pockets never know the existence of …'

He is familiar with 'hydatids' – a disease of sheep caused by tapeworm larvae which affects the animals' brains and causes them to walk 'round and round in a circle continually'. The elegance of his style is shown by this description of the sea:

> And then the waves rolled in furiously – the neutral green-and-blue tongues
> of water slid up the slopes, and were metamorphosed into foam by a careless
> blow, falling back white and faint, and leaving trailing followers behind.

He also writes in an informed way about such places as Naples, Greece, Berlin, and even India, despite not having visited them.

There is to be found much humour and wit in *A Pair of Blue Eyes*. For example, in English history it is a well-known fact that there were only two King Charles' – I and II. However, the driver of the dog-cart in which Smith is travelling believes that there was also a King Charles III. To which Smith replies sceptically: 'I don't recollect anything in English literature about Charles the Third.' When the driver goes on to mention a Charles the Fourth, Smith retorts: 'Upon my word, that's too much!'

'Why?' asks the cab driver, after all, 'there was a George the Fourth, wasn't there?'

After the death of Lady Luxellian, wife of the squire, the mourning letters are seen to have 'wonderful black rims … half-an-inch wide'. Was this too excessive, asks inn proprietor Martin Cannister dryly? Was it really possible for people to feel grief to the extent of 'more than a very narrow border'?

These two examples alone are sufficient to demonstrate Hardy's keen sense of humour; but did he ever laugh? Writer, critic and acquaintance of his, Desmond MacCarthy, affirms that he did laugh, but that 'his laughter made no sound. As is usual with subtle people, his voice was never loud, and a gentle eagerness, which was very pleasing, showed his manner when he wanted sympathy about some point.'

On the other hand, says MacCarthy, Hardy 'would instantly recoil on being disappointed'.[4] Another acquaintance of Hardy's, Dorset-born publisher Sir Walter Newman Flower, states that when Hardy was amused, 'A happy smile would flick across his face like a flash of summer lightning. He would inwardly chuckle: he would relate a humorous happening he had known, and rejoice in it.'[5]

In any novel the plot is of fundamental importance, so how, in *A Pair of Blue Eyes*, did Hardy craft the story so as to keep the reader interested, right up until the final page? The answer lies in the character of Knight, who in many ways is similar to his creator. Knight is a man animated by 'a spirit of self-denial, verging on asceticism', whose imagination had been 'fed ... by lonely study', and whose emotions had been 'drawn out ... by his seclusion'. Knight's 'introspective tendencies' have 'never brought himself much happiness'. As for Elfride, the object of Knight's desire, his inflexibility demands that he should be 'the first-comer'. In other words, she should have had no other lovers prior to him, for he simply cannot tolerate an 'idol' who is 'second-hand'. Surely this is precisely how Hardy saw himself in respect of Emma.

Conflict, of course, is at the heart of all novels, and it is to be found in *A Pair of Blue Eyes* when Knight begins to suspect that he is not, in fact, Elfride's first love. There are clues along the way which alert Knight as to this possibility. Elfride is in the company of Knight when she rediscovers an earring which had previously been lost when in the company of Smith. This earring had been given to her by a lover to whom she had been informally engaged. Knight and Elfride later find themselves in a cemetery, sitting together on a tombstone, when he discovers that this is the tomb of Felix Jethway, Elfride's first love.

Elfride says she would like to give Knight 'something to make you think of me during the autumn at your chambers'. When he suggests a particular potted dwarf myrtle tree of hers, she demurs, and presents him with a different one; whereupon he guesses that the tree which he had originally chosen was given to her by a former lover.

Knight recognises a likeness to Elfride in faces drawn by his friend, Smith, as designs for proposed images of saints and angels to be created in stained glass. Finally, Felix Jethway's mother sends Knight a letter telling him the full story of Elfride's previous attachments, including the one to Smith. Again, Hardy is using 'Knight' to reflect his own feelings – in this case, feelings of anxiety and jealousy, for (as will be seen) he was aware that Emma had at least one suitor in Cornwall before he himself arrived on the scene.

The final twist-in-the-tail comes when Knight and Smith find themselves journeying together from London to Cornwall, each to claim Elfride for his own; not realising that the coffin containing her dead body is also travelling with them.

*A Pair of Blue Eyes* gives the author the opportunity of presenting some of his own personal views about women. It is his opinion, for example, that Smith's 'failure to make his hold [on Elfride's heart] a permanent one was [because of] his too timid habit of dispraising himself' to her, because such self-denigrating behaviour on his part 'inevitably leads the most sensible woman in the world to undervalue him who practises it. Directly domineering [of the woman] ceases in the man, snubbing begins in the woman.' Hardy also states that it is an 'unfortunate fact the gentler creature [the woman] rarely has the capacity to appreciate fair treatment from her natural complement [her male spouse]'.

Suppose for a moment that what Hardy is really doing here is voicing his own thoughts in regard to Emma. He feels that he is not appreciated, and wonders if instead of being self-deprecating to her, which gives her the opportunity to snub him, he should be more assertive, in which case she might have more respect for him. It also implies that Emma has adopted the same supercilious attitude to Hardy as her father has done. And suppose that Hardy was of the same opinion as 'Knight', who regards women as something of an unknown quantity, and declares it to be a 'trick' to read truly 'the enigmatic forces at work in women at given times'.

Hardy's criticisms are not reserved only for the female sex. 'What fickle beings we men are!' says Knight to Smith. 'Men may love strongest for a while, but women love longest.'

The difficulties encountered by one who falls in love with another from a higher social class, and the consequent feelings of social superiority or inferiority which the rigid class structure existing in Hardy's day could engender, was a theme which would occupy Hardy greatly throughout his life. This was an issue which he had addressed in his first (unpublished) novel, *The Poor Man and the Lady*. Perhaps it was Hardy's youthful infatuation with the aristocratic Julia Martin that had first put the idea into his head that he might one day marry a 'lady'. And when, three years later, he met Emma Gifford, the issue would confront him head on. 'Fancy a man not being able to ride!' says Elfride scornfully to Smith, when he sorrowfully confesses that he does not go horse riding. (Emma rode a pony called Fanny, whereas Hardy himself did not ride.)

'Did you ever think what my parents might be, or what society I originally moved in?' enquires Smith of Elfride, before revealing to her that his father is a 'cottager and working master mason'. 'That is a strange idea to me,' Elfride replies, 'but never mind, what does it matter? I love you just as much.'

To Elfride's father, the Revd Swancourt, however, it *does* matter. Says Swancourt, scornfully, on discovering his daughter's attachment to Smith: 'He a villager's son; and we, Swancourts, connections of the Luxellians. What shall I next invite here, I wonder?' If his daughter were to marry Smith, then even though he was an architect, Elfride would always be known thereafter as 'the wife of Jack Smith the mason's son, and not under any circumstances as the wife of a London professional man'. In Swancourt's experience, it was always the 'drawback' and 'not the compensating factor' which was talked of in society.

The Revd Swancourt's reservations were confirmed when he observed that Smith did not care about 'sauces of any kind'. Said he: 'I always did doubt a man's being a gentleman if his palate had no acquired tastes.' After all, did not the presence of an 'unedified palate' indicate 'the irrepressible cloven foot of the upstart'? Why, the Revd might have lavished a bottle of his '[18]40 Martinez' – of which he had only eleven bottles left – on 'a man who didn't know it from eighteenpenny'.

As for Elfride's stepmother, she is obliged to rebuke Elfride for using the word 'gentlemen' in what she considers to be the wrong context. 'We have handed over "gentlemen" to the lower middle class, where the word is still to be heard at tradesmen's balls and provincial tea parties,' said she haughtily. It was now 'Ladies and MEN', always! Again, in reality, these voices are those of Emma's father John Gifford and his wife.

Why did Hardy choose to include such details of his personal life in a novel? Partly because this was his modus operandi, but also out of anger. He had asked Emma's father, in all good faith, for the hand of his daughter, and instead of being welcomed into the Gifford family, John Gifford had chosen to humiliate him. So how could Hardy express his disgust? Through his writings, where not he but his fictitious character, Stephen Smith, becomes the victim of social snobbery. And Hardy was determined to have the novel published, come what may, even if this meant offending Emma, who would inevitably read it, if she had not done so already.

To summarise, the idea that Hardy used *A Pair of Blue Eyes* as a debating chamber in which to mull over his own private thoughts about women in general, and Emma in particular, and the problems attendant on who falls in love with a person of higher social standing, may at first appear fanciful; but as the novel progresses, it becomes more and more apparent that this is *exactly* what he is doing.

The first instalment of *A Pair of Blue Eyes* appeared in *Tinsley's Magazine* in September 1872, and in May 1873 the novel was published by Tinsley Brothers in three volumes.

In June 1873 Hardy visited Cambridge where he met his friend Horace Moule, and the two of them visited Kings College Chapel, from the roof of which they could see Ely Cathedral 'gleaming in the distant sunlight'.[6]

(Whatever doubts Hardy may have had about the dogma of Christianity, he was still in love with its ritual, its imagery and the splendours of its architecture.) Sadly, this was to be the pair's last encounter. Hardy visited St Juliot on two occasions during 1873; the second time at Christmas.

On 21 September 1873, in his rooms at Queens College, Cambridge (where he was employed as a Poor Law inspector), Horace Moule took his own life. He had befriended Hardy; encouraged him with gifts of books and intellectually stimulating conversations; set him on the road to socialism, and shielded and defended him when his books were denigrated by other critics. But for years Moule, a taker of opium and a heavy drinker, had battled against severe depression and suicidal tendencies, and at the end of the day, Hardy's great friend and comrade had been unable to overcome his problems. What was it that had brought the two of them so closely together? Perhaps in Hardy, Moule recognised a kindred spirit: a person, like himself, of great sensitivity, who saw enormous suffering in the world and found it hard to bear.

Moule's body was brought back to Fordington for burial in consecrated ground. This was possible, because although it was normally considered a crime for a person to commit suicide, the jury had returned a verdict of 'temporary insanity'. Hardy was nonplussed and wrote, quoting Psalm 74: 'Not one is there among us that understandeth any more.'

## Far from the Madding Crowd

In December 1872, scholar and critic Leslie Stephen, who had been impressed by his reading of *Under the Greenwood Tree*, asked Hardy to provide a story suitable for serialisation in the *Cornhill Magazine*, of which he was editor. Stephen, a philosopher and man of letters, was also editor of the *Dictionary of National Biography*. A year later, Hardy would meet him in person and the two would become lifelong friends.

Accordingly, having completed *A Pair of Blue Eyes*, Hardy set out to write *Far from the Madding Crowd*, in which he ventured beyond the world of his own personal experiences and instead used as the basis of the plot a story told to him by his cousin Tryphena Sparks. It tells of a woman who has inherited a farm, which contrary to the tradition of the times she insists on managing herself. However, Hardy does not neglect to include his favourite theme – that of a man of humble means but nevertheless honourable, steadfast and industrious, who finds himself in the seemingly impossible position of having fallen in love with a woman above his station. This, of course, is a reflection of his inferiority complex in respect of Emma.

The novel is set in and around Puddletown ('Weatherbury'), and it is said that during the writing of it, when Hardy remembered to carry a pocket notebook, 'his mind was [as] barren as the Sahara [Desert]'. And yet when he did not, and ideas came thick and fast, he was obliged to search for 'large dead leaves, white chips [of wood] left by the wood cutters or pieces of stone or slate that came to hand' on which to write.[7]

Gabriel Oak, known as 'Farmer Oak', is the lessee of a sheep farm on which he keeps 200 sheep. One day, he encounters an attractive young lady riding in a cart. She approaches a toll gate but refuses to pay the gatekeeper the full fare requested. Oak offers to make up the difference, which is tuppence. When he receives no thanks for his pains, he considers the young lady to be vain.

However, he is determined to make her his wife, and to this end he calls at her house with the gift of a lamb. 'I am only an every day sort of man,' he tells her, self-deprecatingly, but he has a 'nice, snug little farm', and when they are married, he promises to work 'twice as hard as I do now'. Music is introduced into the story, when Oak tells Bathsheba Everdene – for that is her name – that if she marries him, she shall have a pianoforte 'in a year or two', and he, for his part, will practise on the flute and play to her in the evenings. He will love her, he says, until he dies.

Oak's offer is refused. Bathsheba says she does not love him, and throws in the fact that she is better educated than he; she advises that he find someone to provide him with the money with which to stock a larger farm. 'Then I'll ask you no more,' says Oak. Another disaster befalls Oak, when an over-zealous sheepdog chases his flock over a precipice.

In the hope of finding work, Oak journeys to Casterbridge to attend a 'hiring fair' – where workers would assemble in the hope of being taken on by an employer – but without success. He then travels onward by waggon to Shottsford, where another hiring fair is being held. En route, he hears the waggoner discussing a woman, evidently a farmer, whom he describes as a 'very vain feymell [female]' who can 'play the peanner [piano]'. Oak deduces, correctly, that this woman is none other than Bathsheba.

Having alighted from the waggon, Oak sees a hayrick which is on fire. This is an opportunity for the author, Hardy, in his description of burning hayricks, to display his deep knowledge of country matters. He states that in such an eventuality: 'the wind blows the fire inwards, the portion in flames completely disappears like melting sugar, and the outline is lost to the eye.' By the judicious placement of tarpaulins around the base of the stack to stop the draught, and with the application of water, Oak saves the day. His actions do not go unnoticed, and the lady farmer (who, as it happens, is Miss

Bathsheba Everdene), agrees to employ him as her shepherd. A deputy is required to assist Oak – the person chosen being 'Young Cain Ball'.

'How did he come by such a name as Cain?' enquires Bathsheba. The answer: because his mother was not 'a Scripture-read woman', and believing that it was Abel who killed Cain, instead of the other way round, a mistake was therefore made at his christening. As always, the Bible is never far from Hardy's thoughts.

Bathsheba catches her farm bailiff stealing barley; she dismisses him, but instead of seeking a replacement, swears that she will attend to everything herself. At the same time, Fanny Robin, the youngest of her servants, goes missing. In fact, impatient to be married, she has gone to see her 'young man', Sergeant Troy of the militia.

Bathsheba buys a Valentine's Day card, thinking to send it to a child, but instead sends it as a prank to Farmer Boldwood, a bachelor who has a neighbouring farm. The words imprinted on its seal read 'Marry Me'. Boldwood shows the card to Oak, who tells him that the handwriting on it is Miss Everdene's.

Fanny Robin's plans to marry Sergeant Troy encounter a hitch when she mistakenly goes to the wrong church. Meanwhile Boldwood, who has taken the sending of the Valentine card seriously, proposes marriage to Bathsheba. She refuses him on the grounds that she does not love him. Furthermore, she admits to him that the sending of the Valentine card was 'wanton' and 'thoughtless' on her part. When she asks Oak his opinion on the matter, he gives it to her in no uncertain terms. The act, says he, was 'unworthy of any thoughtful, and meek, and comely woman'. Leading a man on whom she did not care for was 'not a praiseworthy action'. (He had previously described her behaviour as 'coquettish'.) Bathsheba is incensed by Oak's criticism of her and she orders him to leave the farm. Oak is quickly recalled, however, when his services are required to attend to some sheep which have become bloated and sick after breaking down the fence and feeding off a field of clover.

Boldwood reappears at the shearing supper, held in Bathsheba's great barn, where there is much music and merriment. When farm labourer Joseph Poorgrass is asked to sing, he retorts, 'I be in liquor, and the gift is wanting in me', but he obliges nonetheless.

One night, when Bathsheba is taking a final look around her farm, she encounters Sergeant Troy, and her skirt becomes entangled in his riding spur. 'I wish it had been the knot of knots, which there's no untying,' he says, on catching sight of her beautiful face. Troy tells Bathsheba she is beautiful, something Farmer Boldwood had never done; and this she regards as a fatal omission on the latter's part. Bathsheba meets Troy again at the haymaking, at which he has come to assist. He gives her a gold watch which had belonged to his father. He then helps her with her bees, and gives her an exhibition of sword play. Here, in describing the various 'infantry cuts and guards', Hardy again shows his knowledge and attention to detail.

When Oak warns Bathsheba of the dangers of becoming involved with one such as Troy, she reacts by dismissing him, once again, from the farm. She confesses to her maid Liddy that she loves Troy 'to very distraction and agony'. When Boldwood discovers this he is distraught. Despite her feelings for Troy, Bathsheba decides to travel to Bath where he is currently staying and 'bid him farewell' – that is, end her relationship with him. Troy, on his return, encounters Boldwood, who encourages him to marry Fanny Robin. However, when Boldwood sees how much Bathsheba appears to love Troy, he changes his mind and exhorts Troy instead to marry Bathsheba. Troy then informs Boldwood that he and Bathsheba are already married – she having changed her mind once more and the ceremony having taken place in Bath.

At the harvest supper and dance, when all the employees are the worse for drink and a storm blows up, Oak, with Bathsheba's help, manages to save the precious hayricks once again. Bathsheba confesses to Oak that when she had visited Troy in Bath, he had emotionally blackmailed her by saying that he had seen a woman more beautiful than her, and therefore could not be counted upon unless she 'at once became his'. Through 'jealousy and distraction' she had married him. As her husband, Troy, now demands money from Bathsheba for gambling purposes.

Bathsheba becomes suspicious when they encounter a poor woman en route to the Casterbridge workhouse whom Troy appears to know. It is Fanny Robin. Troy promises to meet her and bring her money in two days time. He confesses to Bathsheba that this is the woman he was intending to marry before he met her. Bathsheba realises that her romance with Troy is at an end. When news comes that Fanny Robin has died, Bathsheba sends a waggon to Casterbridge to collect her coffin.

On the return journey with the coffin, driver Joseph Poorgrass, who 'felt anything but cheerful' and wished he had some company, calls at an inn, where Oak finds him so drunk that he himself is obliged to drive the waggon for the remainder of its journey. 'All that's the matter with me,' says Poorgrass, 'is the affliction called a multiplying eye.' This reference to double vision, brought on by drink, is Hardy's rustic humour at its best.

It is now too late for the funeral to take place so it is postponed until the following day. Meanwhile, the coffin is kept at Bathsheba's house in a sitting room next to the hall.

While awaiting her husband's return, Bathsheba, who suspects that Fanny Robin has had a baby, allows her curiosity to overcome her; she prises open the coffin lid. Her worst fears are realised when she finds two bodies inside: one of an infant child, and the other of Fanny. Troy returns, sees the situation, kisses the corpse and tells Bathsheba: 'This woman is more to me, dead as she is, than ever you were, or are, or can be.'

Troy, miserable after the death of Fanny Robin, chooses to disappear from the scene, and Bathsheba believes him to be dead – he having left his clothes on a beach, prior to going for a swim from which he does not return. In reality he has found employment at a sheep fair in an 'entertainment', in which he takes the part of highwayman Dick Turpin.

Boldwood finally extracts from a most reluctant Bathsheba a promise that she will marry him in six years time, provided that Troy has not returned. But Troy does return, making himself known at a party held by Boldwood one Christmas Eve, at which Bathsheba is in attendance. As Troy summons her, and seizes her arm, Boldwood reacts by shooting him dead.

Oak, meanwhile, has decided to emigrate to California. Bathsheba is dismayed at this news. The wheel has turned full circle and now it is she who wants him. This causes Oak to change his mind and move, instead, to a small farm in the locality. Would Bathsheba allow him to love her, win her and marry her, even though, as he puts it, 'I've danced at your skittish heels ... for many a long mile, and many a long day'.

'But you will never know,' she replies.

'Why?' he asks.

'Because you never ask.'

Finally, after a rollercoaster ride to which both humour and tragedy are essential ingredients, the coquettish Bathsheba and the long-suffering but steadfast Oak resolve their differences and the couple marry to the sound of cannon fire and numerous musical instruments, including drum, tambourine, serpent, tenor viol and double bass. Such a happy ending is also, undoubtedly, what Hardy the author desires for himself and Emma.

In respect of *Far from the Madding Crowd* (which Leslie Stephen helped him to edit), Hardy had the satisfaction of being asked by a publisher for a manuscript, rather than having to endure the painful process of seeking a publisher out as previously. He is now at his best, as, confidently and without inhibition, he portrays the life and landscape of his beloved Wessex. The novel was serialised between January and December 1874 in the *Cornhill Magazine* and, on the strength of Hardy having been paid the sum of £400 by its publishers, Smith, Elder & Co., he and Emma could now afford to marry.

# 5

# Marriage

Hardy and Emma were married on 17 September 1874. Hardy was living in lodgings at Westbourne Park, Paddington, London, at the time, and the ceremony was held in the local church of St Peter. Emma's uncle, Dr Edwin Hamilton Gifford, canon of Worcester Cathedral, officiated; the only other people present being Emma's civil servant brother, Walter E. Gifford (born 1842), and Sarah Williams, the daughter of Hardy's landlady, who signed the register as a witness.[1]

This is curious, because it was common practice then, as it is now, for a bride-to-be to be married in her own parish (Emma's parents were currently living in Bodmin). Alternatively, had Emma's brother-in-law, the Revd Holder married them, then his church of St Juliot was near enough to Bodmin for Emma's parents to have attended the ceremony without difficulty.

The absence of Hardy's parents from the wedding ceremony is also noteworthy (after all, his father Thomas II was well used to visiting his son in London), as is the absence of his sisters – Mary in particular, to whom he was closest – and his brother Henry. Could it be that the antipathy to the couple's union came not just from the Giffords but also from Hardy's mother? From Jemima's point of view, she had gone to great lengths to educate her son, now an aspiring and talented young architect living in London, and she might reasonably have expected him to avail himself of all the opportunities that the capital had to offer. Now, he was throwing himself away on a nonentity of a girl from rural Cornwall, who was actively undermining her (Jemima's) efforts by encouraging her son to give up his chosen career and embark on the much more hazardous course of becoming a writer. Despite the opposition, from whatever quarter, the couple decided to go ahead with the wedding.

After a few days spent at the Palace Hotel, Queensway, London, and then in Brighton on the south coast, the newly-weds embarked on their honeymoon (September to October 1874), heading for the Continent; to Rouen, Paris and Versailles. (Emma could write, and no doubt speak, fluent French.)[2] In Paris they visited Notre Dame Cathedral, the Louvre Museum and the Tuileries Gardens – all that remained of the seventeenth-century Tuileries Palace which was destroyed in 1871. Emma kept a diary in which she made some rather contemptuous comments about the Parisian 'working classes', who were 'very short and small altogether – pigmies in fact – men and women – the old women very ugly and dark'. These remarks were not at all in keeping with Hardy's sentiments, which were always to champion the cause of the disadvantaged. Apart from this, there is little sentiment in Emma Hardy's diary of events: instead, a detailed description of bedrooms, streets, children, domestic animals and, in particular, hotel menus.[3]

For Hardy, ever anxious to see both life and death in the round, no visit to Paris would be complete without a visit to the city's mortuary (La Morgue). According to Emma, who accompanied him, they saw 'Three bodies – [the] middle one pink – Their clothes hanging above them'. She found the experience 'Not offensive but repulsive', which was not altogether surprising.[4] The visit to the Paris mortuary had led to speculation that Hardy may have had a tendency to necrophilia (a morbid, and in particular an erotic, attraction to corpses). This was probably not the case, and the likelihood is that his motives were two-fold: he was curious, but also hoped to discover new material which he could incorporate into his novels. As Sir Newman Flower explained, Hardy 'was drawn towards Tragedy, not by any macabre interest, but by his confusion as to why these things should be. [The] implacability and mercilessness [of] life in punishment'. The way in which life appears to punish certain unfortunate individuals for no apparent reason were, said Flower, matters which affected Hardy deeply and caused him to be 'stricken inwardly'.[5]

They returned to England on 1 October 1874, Emma recording in her diary: 'Dirty London. Very wet.'

Hardy and Emma found lodgings for a time in Surbiton, Surrey, from where Hardy wrote to novelist Katherine Macquoid giving his views on 'whether women of ordinary types should or should not be depicted as the heroines of novels'. Yes, women were 'quite worthy enough in nature', he said, but all too frequently they did not 'exhibit that nature true and simply'. Again, this is a reflection of Hardy's bemusement with the female sex. Nonetheless, he considered that Bathsheba Everdene of *Far from the*

*Madding Crowd* was 'not devoid of honesty', and declared that 'no satire on the [female] sex' was intended by him in his portrayal of the imperfections of his heroines. Instead, he was more concerned in his art with 'picturesqueness' than with 'perfect symmetry'.[6]

One day, Emma's father, John Gifford, arrived unexpectedly at their Surbiton lodgings, which was curious considering he had not attended their wedding. Emma mentioned the visit in her diary but gave no explanation for it.[7] The couple subsequently relocated to lodgings in Newton Road, Bayswater, London.

Meanwhile, public demand for *Far from the Madding Crowd* was so great that its publishers, Smith, Elder & Co., requested that Hardy produce another novel for them – doubtless music to his ears.

⌒

Hardy was still living in London when he commenced the writing of *The Hand of Ethelberta – A Comedy in Chapters* featuring Rouen and Paris, places he had recently visited with Emma. His first novel, *The Poor Man and the Lady*, had been rejected on the grounds that it portrayed the upper classes as being uniformly bad. He now decided to write a light-hearted satirical comedy about them. However, as a person who loved solitude, he was beginning to find living in the capital a strain, and he found it difficult to accept the advice given to him by Anne, daughter of novelist William Thackeray (and sister-in-law of Leslie Stephen), that 'a novelist must necessarily like society'. According to poet Henry Newbolt (later Sir Henry):

> [Hardy] had apparently a strong feeling that a writing man should spend most of his leisure in solitude … much as he used to do in the days when he had not yet attracted the attention of the public. [However] When success comes to a writer (Hardy thought) he generally follows the opposite course – he accepts invitations and takes a place in society; he changes his habits and tastes, till he has almost lost the thread of his own life and is no longer the only begetter of his work; then his critics revise their judgement, and his public drops away, because they think they have been deceived in him, and now find him to be after all no wizard, but a manufacturer for the market, like the rest.

And when Newbolt attempted to 'put the other side of the case', Hardy enquired of him:

Do you find that it *gives* you anything, this going to lunch with great people? I have found most of them like farmers' folk – they have nothing to say – nothing worth calling conversation.[8]

When, in early 1875, Hardy sent the introductory chapters of his new novel to his publisher, the immediate reaction was that this was no comedy in the accepted sense of the word, and he was advised to abandon the subtitle. In May he wrote to Leslie Stephen, agreeing with this proposal and explaining his purpose in writing the novel. The story, he said, 'would concern the follies of life', rather than 'the passions'. He would tell it 'in something of a comedy form, all the people [characters] having weaknesses at which the superior lookers-on smile, instead of being ideal characters'.[9]

In the book's preface he went into more detail. Describing the narrative as 'somewhat frivolous', he said he had undertaken the delicate task of exciting 'interest in a drama' in which 'servants were as important as, or more important than, their masters'. He had reversed the 'social foreground' so that the 'drawing room was sketched, in many cases, from the point of view of the servants' hall'.[10] For a novel written in the mid-Victorian era, this was certainly an innovative approach.

In March 1875 Leslie Stephen, who had long since taken over from the late Horace Moule as Hardy's mentor and confidant, summoned him to witness his signature on a deed. Stephen, once a Fellow and Tutor of Trinity Hall, Cambridge, had been ordained with a view to becoming a parson. However, in 1862, finding that his religious faith had ebbed away, he had resigned his tutorship and moved to London. Now, he informed Hardy that he had belatedly decided to renounce Holy Orders. Stephen confided to Hardy that he had 'wasted' too much time on 'systems of religion and metaphysics', and instead had become fascinated by 'the new theory of vortex rings'.[11] This was a reference to the views of François Comte (the French philosopher and mathematician), who advocated 'humanism', believing that man had passed through the theological phase to that of the 'positive' in which science had taken the place of theology and philosophy. Hardy, too, had made a study of the works of Comte, and this renunciation of faith by Stephen, his dearest friend, would undoubtedly have led him to question further his own religious beliefs.

On 12 July 1875 Emma recorded in her diary: 'Left London for Bournemouth.' Three days later she and Hardy were in Swanage, where they found lodgings at West End Cottage on the south side of the town, adjacent to the downs and overlooking Swanage Bay. The cottage belonged to Joseph Masters, a former sea captain. Now an invalid, Masters regaled the couple with fascinating stories of the sea. This would be the first of many sojourns which Hardy and Emma would make to various locations in Dorset.

Here in Swanage, Hardy continued with the writing of *The Hand of Ethelberta*, while Emma made sketches of boats, bathing machines and a cliff-side stone quarry. In her diary she described a trip by 'steamer' to the Isle of Wight and a picnic at Corfe Castle, where she and Hardy were joined by his sisters Mary and Katharine, and by his brother Henry. 'A splendid day,' said Emma.[12] Any tensions between the two families, for the younger generation at least, appear for the time being to have been resolved.

The heroine of *The Hand of Ethelberta*, Ethelberta Chickerel, is the daughter of a butler; she hopes that if she can get some poems which she has written published, then this will enable her to support her brothers and sisters, and her infirm mother. In this ambition, however, she is to be disappointed.

Ethelberta is a free spirit whose ambition is to enter an intellectual society and at the same time pursue her writing. This she can achieve by marrying a man of means who will indulge her in her vocation. Accordingly, she marries the son of the gentleman of the house in which she is employed as a governess, but he dies, leaving her a widow at the age of 21. Her aim now is to retain her position in society, which she does by concealing her lowly origins and marrying Lord Mountclere. Although she becomes a successful author, she dislikes the trumpeting of 'drawing room' success – just as Hardy, a man of modesty, does in real life.

When Ethelberta brings her brothers, Dan and Sol – who are builders – up from the country to her London home, Sol chastises her for 'creeping up among the useless lumber of our nation that'll be the first to burn if there comes to a flare'. Perhaps here Sol had in mind the French Revolution of 1789 and the purging of the aristocracy which followed it. Sol's words may also be a reflection of Hardy's own strength of feeling and indignation towards the upper classes, as portrayed in his first (unpublished) novel *The Poor Man and the Lady*, and an indication that such sentiments of his have by no means been quenched.

Despite the presence of her brothers, Ethelberta, in her new position as the wife of Lord Mountclere, feels both estranged from her own kith and kin, and also disloyal to them on this account. Here, Hardy is once again articulating his own particular problem, viz. that of a person such as himself migrating from a lower social class to a higher one, such as that occupied by Emma.

This is also a story about 'town' versus 'country'; written by one who has decided to abandon living in London in favour of living in the countryside, and having tasted both, there is no doubt which of the two Hardy prefers. This is not least because in his experience, country people are the more loyal, honest, generous and colourful; as well as being healthier.

In March 1875 George Smith, head of Smith, Elder & Co., accepted *The Hand of Ethelberta* for serialisation in the *Cornhill Magazine*. For Hardy, the work represented a complete departure from what he had previously written, and he admitted that the 'migratory circumstances' of the novel (a reference to the many different locations in which the action takes place) 'were deemed eccentric' on its first publication.[13]

This was not one of the most successful of Hardy's novels: for of all his talents, writing satire was not one of them. So what had persuaded him to depart from a winning formula and 'forsake the farm for the drawing room'? According to Hardy's American acquaintance and admirer, Rebekah Owen, this was because of the adverse criticism that *Far from the Madding Crowd* had received.[14]

In the year following his marriage to Emma, Hardy wrote a curious poem entitled *We Sat at the Window*. It is dated 'Bournemouth 1875', and its second and final verse reads as follows:

We were irked by the scene, by our own selves; yes,
For I did not know, nor did she infer
How much there was to read and guess
By her in me, and to see and crown
   By me in her.
Wasted were two souls in their prime,
And great was the waste, that July time
   When the rain came down.

A second poem, which is equally curious, and which was written in the same year at Durlston Head near Swanage, is entitled *To a Sea Cliff*. Its final verse reads thus:

> He slid apart
> Who had thought her heart
> His own, and not aboard
> A bark, sea-bound …
> That night they found
> Between them lay a sword.

Both these poems, which portray deep unhappiness on the part of 'me' in the first and 'he' in the second, were written when Hardy was on vacation with Emma. What did the poems mean? Given Hardy's propensity for incorporating details of his personal life into his writings, it is impossible to escape the conclusion that they refer to him and Emma. But could it really be true that all his hopes and dreams in respect of his 'love from Lyonnesse' had evaporated so soon? And why did Hardy choose the particular word 'sword' to describe the divide? Was this a word which had some special significance? The answer to these questions would be revealed by Hardy himself over the course of the succeeding decades.

By the time *The Hand of Ethelberta* was published, in April 1876, Hardy and Emma had moved to lodgings in Yeovil, Somerset, while they sought more permanent accommodation. In May they travelled once more to the Continent: this time to Holland, and to Germany where the cathedrals of Cologne and Mainz proved to be of great interest to the 36-year-old architect-turned-writer. As for Emma, her diary records that she paid great attention to the religious paintings of the 'masters' in the 'Picture Gallery at Antwerp' and to the religious iconography on display in the local churches.[15]

## Sturminster Newton: *The Return of the Native*

On 3 July 1876 Hardy and Emma found lodgings at 'Riverside Villa' which overlooked the River Stour at Sturminster Newton; here they would remain for almost two years. It was at 'Riverside Villa' that Hardy wrote poems and allowed his fertile imagination to be fired by the local legends, superstitions and folklore of the region – his fund of knowledge, of course, for further stories. That Christmas of 1876 they stayed at Bockhampton, and this was evidently the first time that Hardy's parents met Emma.

On Coronation Day 1877 (28 June) – marking the coronation of Queen Victoria thirty-nine years previously – there was a holiday with games and dancing. In October Hardy visited Bath, where he was joined by his father Thomas II, who had travelled up from Dorchester by train. They went to the theatre and Thomas II 'took the waters', which they both hoped would alleviate the rheumatic condition from which he was suffering. That December, true to form, Hardy accompanied the local coroner to an inquest on a boy who was believed to have been poisoned, which in the event proved not to have been the case.

Meanwhile, the couple's hopes for a child remained unfulfilled; a fact made more poignant when they discovered that their former maidservant – who had eloped with her lover – had herself become pregnant.

It was at Sturminster Newton that Hardy wrote his next novel, *The Return of the Native*, set on the great and mysterious Egdon Heath on the periphery of which lay the Hardys' family home at Bockhampton. Hardy's description of the heath is one of the most wonderfully evocative passages in the English language:

> To recline on a stump of thorn in the central valley of Egdon, between after-noon and night, as now, where the eye could reach nothing of the world outside the summits and shoulders of heath-land which filled the whole cir-cumference of its glance, and to know that everything around and underneath had been from prehistoric times as unaltered as the stars overhead, gave ballast to the mind adrift on change, and harassed by the irrepressible New. The great inviolate place had an ancient permanence which the sea cannot claim. Who can say of a particular sea that it is old? Distilled by the sun, kneaded by the moon, it is renewed in a year, in a day, or in an hour. The sea changed, the fields changed, the rivers, the villages, and the people changed, yet Egdon remained.

The story concerns Eustacia Vye, a 19-year-old who lives with her grand-father on the heath, which she says is 'my cross, my shame, and will be my death'. Her desire is 'To be loved to madness' for only this will 'drive away the eating loneliness of her days'.

Eustacia has formed a romantic attachment to Damon Wildeve, a failed engineer who is now an innkeeper. Wildeve, however, has agreed to marry not her, but Thomasin who lives with her aunt, Mrs Yeobright. Thomasin is also loved by Diggory Venn, the reddleman (one who deals in red ochre – a pigment used by farmers in preparing sheep for market). With Thomasin's interests at heart, Venn intervenes, unselfishly, to persuade Eustacia to relinquish her hold on Wildeve in order that the latter may marry Thomasin without impediment – which he does:

> Dismissing his regrets Venn determined to aid her [Thomasin] to be happy in her own chosen way. That this way was, of all others, the most distressing to himself, was awkward enough: but the reddleman's love was generous.

Mrs Yeobright's son Clym now returns from Paris where he has been in the employment of a diamond merchant. Dissatisfied with this work, he proposes to give it up in favour of a more worthy, though less well paid occupation: that of becoming 'a schoolmaster to the poor and ignorant [at] Budmouth [Weymouth], to teach them what nobody else will'.

Eustacia now turns her attention to Clym, whom she sees as a future husband, but perhaps more importantly, as a passport to a more romantic life. 'To be your wife and live in Paris would be heaven to me,' she says. Clym's mother disapproves, not only of her son abandoning his career to become a teacher, but also of his growing attachment to Eustacia, who is commonly believed to be a witch. Despite his mother's opposition, Clym leaves home and he and Eustacia marry. As a result, Clym becomes estranged from his mother.

Subsequently, Clym begins to suffer from failing eyesight which necessitates him abandoning any idea of teaching and forcing him to become a humble cutter of furze (gorse, which was used for fuel). For Eustacia, this means the end of any dream she might have had of escaping the boredom of the heath.

Wildeve, although he has since become a married man, has by no means abandoned his attachment to Eustacia. When he calls on her at her home, while Clym is asleep and therefore unaware of his presence, there is a knock at the door. It is Clym's mother, who has decided to seek reconciliation with her son. But Clym does not awaken and Eustacia chooses not to answer the door, even though she is aware who is there. On the way home, Mrs Yeobright is bitten by an adder and dies, but before she does so, she tells a small boy, Johnny Nunsuch, that she is 'a broken-hearted woman, cast off by her son'.

Eustacia tries to conceal the whole occurrence from Clym but he discovers the truth; whereupon she returns to her grandfather. After a period of time, Clym writes a letter to Eustacia proposing that they reunite, but it arrives too late: Eustacia has already fled with Wildeve.

Wildeve is drowned, however, while trying to rescue Eustacia from a stream near a weir, while Clym and Venn – both of whom are also involved in the attempted rescue – survive. Finally, the now-widowed Thomasin marries Venn, the faithful reddleman, who has watched and waited patiently as events have unfolded. Says she, 'he has been kinder to me than anybody else', and therefore, 'I must marry him if I marry anybody'. And this she does, notwithstanding the fact that, in her words, Venn was not quite 'gentleman enough'.

*The Return of the Native* contains descriptions of local topography and customs, both of which were dear to Hardy, including the ancient tumulus of Rainbarrow; a chorus of rustic musicians; and the 'mummers' (play actors), who from time immemorial had re-enacted epic plays like *St George*, featuring such characters as The Turkish Knight, The Doctor and The Valiant Soldier for the amusement of the local populace. There were also allusions to witchcraft, as when Eustacia was stabbed with a needle by Susan Nunsuch on the occasion of Thomasin's wedding.

A criticism made of *The Return of the Native* was that the primary aim in life of its heroine, Eustacia, appeared to be to gratify her sensual passions. True, she did, and her attempt to achieve such gratification is a fundamental part of the story.

In the character of Venn (as with that of Gabriel Oak in *Far from the Madding Crowd*), Hardy reaffirms his belief that in the battle to win a prospective partner, qualities such as loyalty, steadfastness and kindness deserve to prevail.

Mrs Yeobright describes Eustacia as one who is 'lazy and dissatisfied' and in no way a suitable partner for her son Clym. And he, for his part, bitterly regrets the pain which he has caused his mother by marrying her. 'If my mother were reconciled to me and to you I should, I think, be happy quite,' says Clym to Eustacia. 'Something must be done to heal up this ghastly breach between my dear mother and myself.' Hardy subsequently refers to the 'chasm in their lives which Clym's love for Eustacia had caused'.[16] This, of course, begs the question: was Hardy's mother Jemima similarly pained by her son's marriage to Emma, and did Hardy himself feel regret or even guilt on this account? And did he, like Clym Yeobright, long for reconciliation with his mother before it was too late? If so, then perhaps this reconciliation came when Hardy and Emma spent the Christmas of 1876 with his parents at their home at Bockhampton.

In the novel, Clym finally finds 'his vocation in the career of an itinerant open-air preacher and lecturer on morally unimpeachable subjects'. In fact, the word preacher is misleading, for it was said of him that: 'He left alone creeds and systems of philosophy, finding enough and more than enough to occupy his tongue in the opinions and actions common to all good men.' Here, Hardy gives an intimation of his own disenchantment with the Christian faith.

By early 1878, Hardy had reluctantly come to the conclusion that in order to succeed as a writer, it was necessary for him to live in, or near, London. For this reason, on 22 March of that year the couple relocated to the capital. On 4 November *The Return of the Native* was published by Smith, Elder & Co.

# 6

# A Plethora of Novels

*The Trumpet Major*: Illness: Wimborne

Now lodging with Emma in Upper Tooting, London, Hardy immersed himself once more in the life and culture of the capital. He was elected to the Rabelais Club (which held literary dinners every two months), and also to the exclusive Savile Club for gentlemen. Time was spent at the Grosvenor Gallery studying and admiring sculptures and paintings. He also witnessed the final performance of actor Henry Irving, in a scene from Shakespeare's *Richard II* at the Lyceum Theatre. Hardy's love of the theatre may have had its origins in the strolling players whom he saw in and around Dorchester when he was a boy.

Needless to say, Hardy kept in touch with his native Dorset, where, in August and September of 1878, he renewed his acquaintance with poet William Barnes, and with Charles W. Moule, brother of the late Horace.

In August 1879 Hardy and Emma visited Hardy's parents at Bockhampton. They also stayed for a time in Weymouth, where Hardy's mother visited them and accompanied them on a drive to Portland.

Hardy was now moving in the upper echelons of London society, where among the people he met were Sir Percy Shelley, son of the poet Percy Bysshe Shelley; poet, educationalist and writer Matthew Arnold; poet Robert Browning; Poet Laureate Lord Tennyson (who said that of Hardy's novels he liked *A Pair of Blue Eyes* best); novelist and cartoonist George du Maurier; and painter Sir Lawrence Alma-Tadema. He also attended the Epsom races for Derby Day.

Ever since his boyhood, when he had discovered a magazine on the subject at his home in Bockhampton, Hardy had been fascinated by the Napoleonic Wars. He would also have been aware that his grandfather, Thomas I, as a volunteer militiaman, had travelled with his regiment to Weymouth to prepare for the threatened invasion by Emperor Napoleon I of France.

Four years previously, in June 1875 (the 18th of that month being Waterloo Day, commemorating the Duke of Wellington's victory in 1815 over Napoleon in the Battle of Waterloo), Hardy and Emma had visited Chelsea Hospital and heard real-life accounts of the battle – from men who had fought in it. On another excursion to the Continent with Emma, in 1876, he had visited Waterloo and explored the battlefield. And, of course, nearer to home, he would often have seen the local 'redcoats' – based at their barracks in Dorchester – exercising their horses on the downs.

Hardy availed himself of any opportunity to immerse himself in matters Napoleonic, as when he attended the funeral of the exiled Prince Louis Napoleon (only son of Emperor Napoleon III), who had been killed, paradoxically, while fighting for Britain in the Zulu War. The prince's body was duly brought back to England for burial at Chislehurst in Kent. It therefore seemed inevitable that Hardy would write a novel set during this period of history, and with this in mind he visited the British Museum and also read C.H. Gifford's *History of the Napoleonic Wars* in order to acquaint himself with the full facts. Relevant information was also to be found in parish records and from inscriptions on local tombstones.

*The Trumpet Major* is set in those anxious times when an invasion of England by the forces of Napoleon seemed imminent. The story is about two brothers: John Loveday (the Trumpet Major) and Robert, a sailor. Sons of the miller, the brothers are rivals for the hand of village beauty Anne Garland. Anne vacillates as to which one she really loves, and finally, it is the less deserving Robert whom she chooses. Meanwhile, John, reliable and self-sacrificing, sails under Admiral Lord Nelson and Captain Hardy (Thomas Hardy's alleged ancestor) in the warship *Victory*, only to meet his death in Spain in the Peninsular War.

Included in the story is the visit of King George III to Weymouth amidst a fanfare provided by the 'quire' of fiddlers, violoncellists, trombonists and drummers. There is also mention of the local Dorchester 'strong beer' – a subject always close to Hardy's heart which he describes thus: 'It was of the most beautiful colour that the eye of an artist in beer could desire; full in body, yet brisk as a volcano: piquant, yet without a twang; luminous as an autumn sunset; free from streakiness of taste; but finally, rather heady.'[1]

⌒

On 11 February 1880 Hardy wrote to the Revd Handley Moule – at that time Fellow of Trinity College, Cambridge (who was another of the brothers of his late friend Horace) – concerning the recent death of his father, the Revd Henry Moule, vicar of Fordington. Hardy, for many years, had regarded himself as a parishioner of Henry Moule (even though, technically speaking, this was not the case), and had referred admiringly to the 'energies' which the vicar had brought 'to bear upon the village'. Here, Hardy would have especially remembered the Revd Moule's heroic efforts on behalf of the local population during the cholera epidemics of 1849 and 1854.

⌒

Hardy stated that of all his novels, *The Trumpet Major* was the one 'founded more largely on testimony, oral and written, than any other'. It was published by Smith, Elder & Co. on 26 October 1880.

In November 1880, on a visit to Cambridge, Hardy attended the 5 p.m. service at Kings College Chapel. It was in Cambridge that he fell ill. On his return to London a surgeon was summoned to determine why Hardy was experiencing acute abdominal pain. The diagnosis was internal bleeding. By now, Hardy had already written the early chapters of his next novel, *A Laodicean*, to be serialised in *Harper's Magazine* with illustrations by George du Maurier. He was now, on account of his illness, 'forced to lie in bed with his feet higher than his head for several months'.[2] For this reason, the only way he could complete his manuscript was by dictating it to Emma, who nursed him through this episode. The process of dictation was completed on 1 May 1881, by which time Hardy was able to leave his sickbed and venture outdoors once again.

Due to Hardy's illness, he and Emma had been obliged to ask for an extension to the lease of their house in Upper Tooting. Having previously been torn between London and Dorset, they now decided to return to the country. In future, they would visit the capital for a few months only each year. A return to Dorset, they hoped, would not only be beneficial to Hardy's health, but would also provide inspiration for him in his future writing. Accordingly, they relocated to Wimborne, to a house named 'Llanherne'.

In retrospect, it seems likely that Hardy had suffered a prolonged attack of biliary colic, a condition in which a small concretion ('stone') becomes temporarily lodged in the duct which drains bile from the liver into the gut. This would account for his jaundice, as observed by Edmund Gosse, who visited him at the time.[3] (Renal colic, also caused by a stone, is another possibility. However, this might well have manifested itself by haematuria (blood in the urine) or by Hardy actually passing the stone, of which there is no mention.)

In July 1881 Hardy and Emma, in company with Hardy's younger sister Katharine, visited the ancient British stronghold of Badbury Rings, and also Kingston Lacy (seat of the Bankes family). Hardy pointed out Charborough on the journey (the home of Mrs Drax), in the grounds of which stood a tall tower – which subsequently reappeared in one of Hardy's novels, as will be seen.[4] In August the couple travelled extensively in Scotland where they visited castles and lochs, and Hardy sketched. On their return they attended a ball given by Lady Wimborne at Canford Manor.

## A Laodicean

Hardy undoubtedly derived the title of his next novel, *A Laodicean*, from the Biblical book of Revelation, where the phrase 'lukewarm in religion, like the Christians of Laodicea' is to be found.[5] These words apply equally well to the heroine of the story, Paula Power.

Paula's father purchases Castle de Stancy from the ancient de Stancy family, but he permits one of the members of that family, Charlotte, who is now penniless, to continue to live there as a friend for Paula. The hero is George Somerset, an architect, music lover and poet. Other characters include Captain William de Stancy, Charlotte's brother, who hopes to marry Paula and thereby reclaim the ancestral home; William Dare, de Stancy's illegitimate son; and James Havill, also an architect, who competes with Somerset in drawing up plans for the restoration of the castle.

Paula adores the 'romantic and historical', considers the castle to be wonderful, and even wishes that she was one of the ancient de Stancy family who had built it all those years ago. But whereas de Stancy can offer Paula a pedigree and a title to go with it, Somerset, who is also a suitor of Paula, reminds her that there is another nobility, one of 'talent and enterprise', and he cites such creative geniuses from the past as Archimedes, Newcomen, Watt, Telford and Stephenson. In fact, Paula's father is himself an engineer and builder of railways. Finally, it is Somerset who wins the day, and he and Paula become man and wife.

A favourite device which Hardy used in his novels was that of two men each vying for the hand of the same woman. This was a legacy from the time when he was courting Emma; for when he first met her at St Juliot, another rival for her hand[6] (who was known to be a farmer) was already on the scene. As Somerset pleads his case with Paula, so one may imagine Hardy pleading his case with Emma and asking her to ignore his humble origins and judge him on his merits.

What was the identity of this rival to Hardy for Emma's hand? A clue is given by Hardy in his poem *The Young Churchwarden* (part of his *Moments of Vision* collection), which reads as follows:

When he lit the candles there,
And the light fell on his hand,
And it trembled as he scanned
Her and me, his vanquished air
Hinted that his dream was done,
And I saw he had begun
    To understand.

When Love's viol was unstrung,
Sore I wished the hand that shook
Had been mine that shared her book
While that evening hymn was sung,
His the victor's, as he lit
Candles where he had bidden us sit
    With vanquished look.

And originally attached to this poem (and subsequently crossed out) was a note which read: 'At an Evening Service/August 14. 1870.' So where was Hardy on this occasion? The answer appears in a note which he wrote in his copy of the Prayer Book, next to the 73rd Psalm, which reads: 'Lesnewth, Evening Prayer, Aug. 14, 1870' – a reference to the village of Lesnewth, situated ¾ mile from St Juliot and its church of St Michael & All Angels.[7]

Henry Jose was the son of William Jose and his wife Ann, who farmed 64 acres of land at Trebiffin, situated ¾ mile south of St Juliot, across the Valency Valley in the parish of Lesnewth.[8] Five years younger than Emma, Henry, in August 1870, was aged 25. A clue that Henry was the person in question was provided by his great-nephew, Walter Henry Jose, whose father had once told him that 'Uncle Henry had a great fancy for Emma Gifford'.[9] Another clue is given by Emma herself when, referring to 'the Cornish working orders', whom in general she disliked, she affirmed that:

> Only one stands out amongst them with worth of character and deep devotion, though rather dumb of expression, a man gentle of nature, musical, christlike in guilelessness, handsome of face and figure, David-like farming his own land: he never married and told after I had left [the area] of his disappointment, and attraction on first seeing me.[10]

And what clinches the matter is that Henry (in addition to being a farmer like his father) was indeed, at the time in question, a churchwarden at Lesnewth's church of St Michael & All Angels.[11] Finally, as Emma stated, Jose remained unmarried; he died in March 1928 aged 83.

Hardy's poem, therefore, refers unquestionably to himself, Emma and Henry Jose. But instead of being joyful that he had emerged victorious in the battle for the hand of Emma, the poem is one of deep regret. For by the time it was written (which was some time after the occasion to which it refers), the love between its author (Hardy) and the subject of his love (Emma) had become 'unstrung'. Furthermore, as the second verse of the poem indicates, Hardy is now regretting that he, and not the 'young churchwarden' (Jose), had been the 'victor' in the battle for Emma's affections. So what was the story behind this sad fact? All would be revealed in due course.

Henry Jose's younger brother Digory also did not marry. (His elder sister Jane Pearse Jose, however, married Richard Prout of Peventon.) Had Hardy not been assigned to St Juliot by architect Crickmay in the March of 1870, then it is possible that Emma would have married Jose, despite his more lowly position in society, and that Hardy would have married someone else. How different his life might then have been.

Other poems of Hardy's are less easy to decipher. Sometimes he deliberately alters the time when a particular event happens; at other times, he transposes the male and female roles, or disguises the location in which the scene is set. Nevertheless, in virtually everything he ever wrote, subsequent to his first meeting with Emma, there are allusions not only to his love for her, but also to their problematical relationship.

Hardy divulged that his novel, *A Laodicean*, contained 'more of the facts of his own life than anything else he had ever written'.[12] This, as will be seen, became an increasing tendency with him in the succeeding novels and poems which he produced.

The novel also shows that far from being entrenched in the past, Hardy was quite willing to recognise and embrace the advances of science, as long as the effect was not to enslave the people, drive them off the land or destroy the landscape. Threshing and ploughing machines driven by steam traction engines were therefore *not* welcome. In *A Laodicean*, that 'old chestnut', the subject of infant baptism, is revived; church minister Mr Woodwell being the reincarnation of Frederick Perkins of Dorchester – the real-life Baptist minister and father of the two youths with whom Hardy used to have deep discussions on the subject in his younger days.

The novel appeared in *Harper's Magazine* between December 1880 and December 1881, and was published in December 1881 by Sampson Low of London.

On 26 April 1882, during a stay in London, Hardy attended the funeral of Charles Darwin whose book *The Origin of Species* he had embraced and long admired, and which had posed serious philosophical questions for him when he had first read it many years previously.

In September 1882 Hardy and Emma set out on a journey which took them to three counties. As they travelled from Axminster in Devon to Lyme Regis in Dorset, Hardy noticed how: 'The horse (pulling the coach) swayed [and] leant against the pole … his head hung like his tail. The straps and brass rings of the harness seemed barbarously harsh on his shrinking skin.' Throughout his life, a concern for animals was one of Hardy's trademarks. Emma would apparently have intervened had it not been for the 'anger of the other passengers, who wanted to get on [to their destination]'.[13] In early October the pair set out once more, this time for France, where they explored Paris and visited that city's Louvre Museum and its Luxembourg Museum of Art.

The Revd Holder, rector of St Juliot and husband of Emma's sister Helen, died in November 1882, aged 79. He had always been on friendly terms with Hardy, whom he was in the habit of regaling with amusing stories.

Holder had also permitted Hardy to read the lesson at church services when he himself had been 'not in vigour'.[14] He was buried (presumably) in the churchyard at St Juliot in the same grave as his first wife Ann.[15] Hardy himself designed his memorial plaque.

## *Two on a Tower*: 'The Dorsetshire Labourer'

The novel *Two on a Tower* deals ostensibly with the subject of astronomy, but beneath the surface lies a more powerful and compelling theme. This theme, which Hardy describes in the Preface, was 'the outcome of a wish [of his] to set the emotional history of two infinitesimal lives against the stupendous background of the stellar universe'.

To achieve this, a knowledge of astronomy was necessary, and Hardy therefore sought permission from the astronomer royal to visit the Royal Observatory at Greenwich. In particular, he required an answer to the following question: was it possible to site a telescope with which to study the stars in an old tower, despite the fact that the tower in question had not been built for the purpose? In his mind was the great eighteenth-century tower which, as previously mentioned, stood in the grounds of Charborough Park near Wimborne, Dorset.

In the story, the aristocratic Lady Viviette Constantine, believing that her husband Sir Blount has died in Africa and that she is now a widow, falls in love with curate's son and budding astronomer Swithin St Cleeve, who is considerably younger than herself. She provides him with astronomical instruments and sets him up in a tower on her estate, which he uses as an observatory.

Hardy now inserts the proverbial spanner in the works. Having married Swithin and become pregnant by him, her ladyship discovers that her late husband, Sir Blount, although now dead, was actually still alive at the time of her second marriage, and because of this fact, her marriage to Swithin is invalid. Anxious to avoid adversely affecting Swithin's career as an architect, and in order not to jeopardise his inheritance from his uncle, Lady Constantine now marries the Bishop of Melchester. Meanwhile, Swithin goes abroad to pursue his studies.

By the time Swithin returns, the bishop has died. He realises that he no longer loves Lady Constantine, who is now 'worn and faded', but nonetheless proposes to her a second time. Overwhelmed with joy at her reunion with him, she dies in his arms.

*Two on a Tower* was published by Sampson Low in late October 1882.

⌒

In 1883 an article written by Hardy, entitled 'The Dorsetshire Labourer', was published in *Longman's Magazine*. Such a person as the labourer, said he, was hitherto personified as having an image of:

> uncouth manner and aspect, stolid understanding, and snail-like movement [who spoke with a] chaotic corruption of regular language, that few persons … consider it worth while to enquire what views, if any, of life, nature, or of society, are conveyed in these utterances. He hangs his head and looks sheepish when spoken to, and thinks Lunnon [London] is a place paved with gold. Misery and fever lurk in his cottage. He has few thoughts of joy, and little hope of rest.

For Hardy, a champion of his Dorset heritage whose sentiments lay always on the side of the poor and the oppressed, this was an over-simplification. He pointed out that the language of the Dorsetshire labourers was, in fact, an agglomeration of English as taught at the National Schools which they attended, and the 'unwritten, dying, Wessex English that they had learnt from their parents'. Far from being uniformly joyless and dull, some were happy, many serene and a few depressed. Some were clever 'even to genius, some stupid, some wanton, some austere'. Their political views were equally varied and it was therefore a mistake to roll them all together into one. It was also a mistake to think that the 'grimiest families' were the poorest.

Years later, in March 1902, in a letter to author Henry Rider Haggard, Hardy developed his theme still further. Up until about 1855, he said, the labourers' condition was one of great hardship. For instance, he had heard when young of a 'sheep-keeping boy' (whose father's wages were a mere 6*s* a week) who had died of hunger; at autopsy the boy's stomach was found to contain nothing but undigested, raw turnip. Since then, matters had improved, noted Hardy. Now, it was not unusual to see a cottage with carpeting; with brass rods going up the staircase to keep the carpet in place. A piano might be found within and a bicycle by the doorway. At night, a paraffin lamp was available.

While these changes were welcome, others were not. The life-hold principle of tenancy, which had given the cottager security of tenure for three generations – a period of up to 100 years – had now been replaced by weekly, renewable agreements, leading to great insecurity. 'The Damocles' sword which hung perpetually over the poor, said Hardy, 'is the fear of being turned out of their houses by the farmer or squire'. For example, if an honest man's daughter were to have an illegitimate child, or if he or his wife took to drink, then this provided grounds for the family's instant eviction. For this and other reasons there was now a massive migration into the towns, which were not 'fraught with such trying consequences' as was the case in the villages. And because the labourer was forced to relocate himself to wherever a job was available, the effect on his children was deleterious. Said Hardy, in 'shifting from school to school … their education could not possibly progress with that regularity which is essential to their getting the best knowledge in the short time available to them'.[16]

As for the village, the loss of its labourers and their families meant that it declined 'into eternal oblivion'. There was now no longer 'continuity of information', with the result that 'Names, stories, and relics' of a place were now speedily forgotten.[17]

# 7

# Dorchester: Max Gate

In June 1883 the Hardys moved to Dorchester, to lodgings in Shire Hall Lane. Two months later, accompanied by Edmund Gosse, they attended a church service at Winterborne Came, conducted by clergyman, poet and Hardy's former teacher, William Barnes. (Barnes had retired from school mastering two decades earlier in 1864, when he had been offered the living of Winterborne Came-cum-Whitcombe – the rectory of which stood not half a mile from Max Gate.)

Unable to find a house in Dorchester, Hardy purchased a plot of land from the estate of the Duchy of Cornwall, situated a mile out of town to the east, on the road to Wareham. Here, he would build a house of his own; or rather design it and arrange for his brother Henry to construct it. The dwelling would be called 'Max Gate': the name being derived from that of the inhabitant of a nearby toll gatehouse, a Mr Mack. During the digging out of the foundations for Max Gate, some Romano-British graves containing urns and skeletons were discovered.

In June 1884, the day after Hardy's 44th birthday, he went to see a performance of the circus in nearby Fordington Field. That month and the following found the couple again in London, meeting artists and writers, including the painter Edward Burne-Jones. In July Hardy, having returned to Dorset, visited the Dorchester Assizes, and in August he attended a performance of Shakespeare's *Othello*, performed in the town by strolling players. August also saw Hardy and his brother visiting the Channel Islands, taking the steamer from Weymouth. In December he attended the New Year's Eve bell-ringing ceremony at Dorchester's church of St Peter, where he observed that the tenor bell was worn and its 'clapper battered with its many blows'.[1]

Early in 1885 Hardy was invited to Eggesford, Devon, by his friend Lady Portsmouth, who together with her husband encouraged Hardy and Emma to move to Devonshire to be near them. Emma would have gone willingly, Hardy records, as this was the county of her birth. However, it was impracticable as the Dorchester house was now nearing completion.[2]

On 19 April Hardy completed the writing of his novel *The Mayor of Casterbridge*. It had taken at least a year, during which time he had been 'frequently interrupted'.[3]

*The Mayor of Casterbridge* was, in Hardy's own words, 'more particularly the study of one man's deeds and character', and in this way it differs from his other novels.[4] That man is Michael Henchard – a powerful, dominating person who towers above the other characters in the novel but, nonetheless, is ultimately 'defeated by his own defects'.[5]

Henchard, a journeyman (hired workman) hay-trusser, arrives at Weydon Fair in search of work. Here, while out of his mind through drink, he puts his wife Susan, together with their child Elizabeth Jane, up for auction. Mother and daughter are 'bought' by a wandering sailor called Newson. When he emerges from his drunken stupor, Henchard bitterly regrets his action and vows to abstain from drink for a period of twenty years. He settles in Casterbridge (Dorchester) where he prospers as a corn merchant and ultimately becomes the town's mayor.

Years later, Susan appears in Casterbridge. She believes her husband Newson to be drowned and is therefore in need of support for herself and her daughter. She and Henchard are reunited and they remarry, but Henchard does not realise, and Susan does not apprise him of the fact, that their original daughter, Elizabeth Jane, is dead and this Elizabeth Jane is, in fact, her daughter by Newson. On a previous business visit to Jersey, Henchard had met one Lucetta Le Sueur, whom he intended to marry. He writes to inform her that this is now no longer possible.

When a young and able Scotsman, Donald Farfrae, arrives on the scene, Henchard appoints him as his business manager. However, jealous of Farfrae's success and of his popularity in the town, Henchard subsequently dismisses him. Susan dies, but leaves a letter for her husband informing him of the truth about Elizabeth Jane. Henchard, who knew no better at the time, has already told Elizabeth Jane that it is he who is her father and not Newson, as she had previously understood.

Lucetta arrives from Jersey and takes Elizabeth Jane on as her companion. But instead of paying court to the widower Henchard, Lucetta transfers her affections to Farfrae, which makes the former even more jealous of the Scotsman. Henchard threatens Lucetta with revealing the truth about her former attachment to him, and thereby blackmails her into promising that she will marry him. He comes to grief, nevertheless, when sitting as a magistrate he is exposed in court as a one-time wife-seller. His credibility is now lost, leaving Lucetta free to marry Farfrae, which she does. The weather now takes a hand.

In Hardy's own words, 'the home Corn Trade ... had an importance that can hardly be realised'.[6] The entire population depended on the harvest and 'after mid summer they [the farmers] watched the weather-cocks as men waiting in antechambers watch the lackey'.[7] With this in mind, Henchard purchases enormous quantities of grain. If the weather is bad and the harvest poor, as he believes, then the price of grain will rocket. However, the sun shines, the harvest is an excellent one, the price plummets and he becomes bankrupt. And the final indignity for him is when Farfrae purchases his former house.

When a certain 'Royal Personage' passes through Casterbridge and Henchard makes a foolish exhibition of himself, Farfrae – now mayor of the town in Henchard's stead – is forced to intervene. Henchard challenges Farfrae to a fight to the death, but relents, having got the Scotsman at his mercy. Henchard also relents about making use of some love letters once sent to him by Lucetta (who is now pregnant by her husband), and instead of taking revenge on her and Farfrae, he agrees to return them to her. The plan misfires and the love letters become public knowledge. The shock of witnessing the townspeople parading an effigy of herself and Henchard through the streets causes Lucetta to miscarry and die.

When Newson reappears, having 'come back from the dead', Henchard lies to him and tells him that Elizabeth Jane is also dead; although Newson subsequently discovers the truth. Henchard then disappears from the scene, revisiting Casterbridge only briefly for Elizabeth Jane's marriage to Farfrae. He then dies in an abandoned house in the presence of his former employee, Abel Whittle.

Described as a 'smouldering, volcanic fellow', Henchard's pattern is 'to cheat himself of success, companionship, happiness, love'. He is 'a confusing mixture of good and evil', but despite his 'negative qualities', he also possesses 'courage, generosity' and 'forthrightness'.[8] This is a man 'driven by inner destructive forces beyond his comprehension and control'.[9] In short, Henchard illustrates the Darwinian Theory of Evolution (with which Hardy was familiar), in that being unable to adapt, he is therefore incapable of surviving. Also, Henchard's bitter experiences in life bear out the notion held by Hardy's mother, Jemima, that there is always a figure standing in our path to 'knock us back'. In this case, the figure was Henchard himself.

As usual with Hardy, *The Mayor of Casterbridge* is rooted in fact. There was a case in real life of a man selling his wife, and a 'Royal Personage' – namely Prince Albert – did actually visit Dorchester in July 1849.

There is usually a rock solid and utterly dependable character in each of Hardy's novels, and in this case it is Elizabeth Jane, who continues to demonstrate her concern for Henchard, despite all, right to the bitter end. If Hardy had ever had a daughter, how he would have loved her to be like Elizabeth Jane.

*The Mayor of Casterbridge* was published on 10 May 1886 by Smith, Elder & Co.

～

April 1885 found the Hardys again in London, viewing paintings at the Royal Academy and attending a party given by Lady Carnarvon, wife of the 4th Earl, at which they met Conservative politician Lord Salisbury. When June came, it was time to transfer the furniture from their Dorchester lodging house to their new house, Max Gate: described as an unpretentious, red-brick structure of moderate size, standing on a 1½-acre plot of land. Hardy was soon to plant in excess of 2,000 trees around it. This would afford greater privacy, together with protection from gales. One of the first visitors to Max Gate was Scottish novelist Robert Louis Stevenson, who was then living in Bournemouth in a house called 'Skerryvore'. In the drawing room of Max Gate, Hardy would write his next novel, *The Woodlanders*.

A 'careful observer' described Hardy at this time as being 'below the middle-height' (he was actually 5ft 7in tall), of 'slight build', with a 'pleasant, thoughtful face, exceptionally broad at the temples and fringed by a beard'. He always wore a moustache and his eyes were 'a clear, blue-grey'.[10]

In October 1885 William Barnes related to Hardy how, when Prince Louis Napoleon of France was resident in England, he had visited the Darner family at nearby Winterborne Came House. Hardy had already written one book set in Napoleonic times – *The Trumpet Major*. One day, his fascination with the period would lead him to write another: *The Dynasts*.

The termination of the year 1885 made Hardy 'sadder than many previous New Year's Eves have done'. He asked himself whether the building of Max Gate was 'a wise expenditure of energy', but hinted that there may have been darker forces at work which had undermined his spirits.

86

In London once again, in the spring and summer of 1886, he spent time in the British Museum's Reading Room, and attended the House of Commons where the Home Rule Bill for Ireland was being debated. In May he describes meeting a 'Hindu Buddhist' who spoke English fluently, was remarkably well educated and was a 'coach' of the Theosophical Society (which professes that knowledge of God may be gained by intuitive insight into the nature of the divine). He went to his club, observed criminal trials at the law courts, and with Emma attended dinners at various private houses to which they had both been invited.

October 1886 found Hardy in an aggrieved frame of mind, and he wrote to Edmund Gosse describing how he had suffered previously at the hands of certain critics; in particular, the 'anonymous' ones who chose not to reveal their names. The 'crown of my bitterness', he says, 'has been my sense of unfairness in such impersonal means of attack'. Such attacks mislead the public into thinking that there is 'an immense weight of opinion' behind the criticism, which one such as he, Hardy, can only oppose with his 'own little solitary personality'.[11] Two months later, he makes use of this word again in a letter to journalist William H. Rideing, in which he says: 'My life when a boy was singularly uneventful & solitary.'[12] But he does admit that there is a positive side to the 'slow, meditative lives of people who live in habitual solitude', for such lifestyles render 'every trivial act … full of interest'.[13]

That same month, William Barnes died at the age of 85.

## The Woodlanders

It was in the study above the drawing room at Max Gate that Hardy wrote *The Woodlanders*. However, the plot caused him considerable anxiety and he complained of a 'sick headache' and 'a fit of depression' in which he seemed to be 'enveloped in a leaden cloud'.[14]

In *The Woodlanders*, many of Hardy's favourite themes resurface. They include the problems encountered when two persons of different social status fall in love, and when two men compete with one another for the hand of one woman, together with the problems men and women may have of understanding one another. Hardy also stresses that qualities such as loyalty, devotion and steadfastness in a male suitor, ought always to triumph over wealth, property and title.

In the novel's preface, Hardy explains that the book is principally concerned with 'the question of matrimonial divergence, the immortal puzzle [of] how [a couple are] to find a basis for their sexual relation[ship]'. But why did Hardy use the word 'sexual' – an excessively daring one by the standards of the time – when he might have preferred, instead, 'matrimonial relationship'? From one of the foremost wordsmiths of the day, this surely was no accident, and use of the word 'sexual' undoubtedly reflected his own preoccupation with the subject.

In the preface to *The Woodlanders*, Hardy explains how a problem may arise when a person 'feels some second person to be better suited to his or her tastes than the one with whom he has contracted to live'. This may be viewed on the one hand as the 'depravity' of an 'erratic heart'. But on the other hand, no thinking person, concerned with the question of 'how to afford the greatest happiness to the units of human society during their brief transit through this sorry world', would be content to let the matter rest here. How are these statements to be interpreted, as far as Hardy's own personal life is concerned?

Hardy had fallen in love with Emma, perhaps at first sight; he had returned from Lyonnesse with 'magic' in his eyes; he had courted her over four and a half long years, and now here he is in the preface to The Woodlanders, and only a dozen years after his wedding, admitting in so many words that he regrets the whole affair and wishes that he had married somebody else. (It should be stressed that whatever Hardy's thoughts were about other women, he remained faithful to Emma all his life.)

Finally, in the preface to the novel, Hardy makes mention of the religious aspect of marriage. Is it to be seen as a divinely sanctioned 'covenant' – 'What God hath joined together' – or simply as a secular 'contract' between two people?

The story of *The Woodlanders* begins with estate-owner Mrs Charmond demanding to have the locks of hair of Marty South – a poor girl who is assistant to Giles Winterborne, cider-maker and forester. Her objective is to make a wig out of it for herself. Straight away, an upper-class person is behaving as if she owns the body, if not the soul, of one whom she considers to be beneath her.

Timber merchant George Melbury has a daughter, Grace, to whom he has provided a good education. Giles Winterborne is devoted to Grace, and it has always been assumed that one day the two of them will marry. However, Grace's father intervenes and tells her that she is worthy of someone better, 'a man who can take you up in society, out into the world'.

An incident which reveals Hardy's impish sense of humour occurs when Giles invites the Melburys to a 'gathering', at which Grace discovers a slug in her 'leaves of winter-green'. When the guests have departed, Giles' servant reassures his master that the slug was well cooked. Says he: 'I warrant him well boiled. God forbid that a live slug should seed on any plate of victuals that's served by Robert Creedle!'

Edred Fitzpiers arrives on the scene to take up the position of local doctor. When Giles forfeits some properties which he owns and becomes less eligible on this account, Melbury points his daughter in the direction of Dr Fitzpiers.

Mrs Charmond's carriage and Giles' waggon meet head to head in the lane. When Giles is unable to reverse, Mrs Charmond sees this as insubordination and spitefully announces that she intends to demolish his cottage as part of a road-widening scheme – another typical example, to Hardy's mind, of the callous behaviour of which the upper classes are capable. (*The Woodlanders* also contains a detailed description of man traps: spring-loaded devices made of iron, designed with teeth to lacerate the flesh and crush the bones; they were used by gamekeepers on country estates to catch poachers. Although the use of such devices had largely died out by the mid-nineteenth century, Hardy would have seen them as yet another example of oppression – barbaric brutality, in fact – by those who should have known better.)

Grace and Fitzpiers duly marry, but when he tells her that it is not appropriate for them, as a couple, to associate with such lowly people as her brothers, she tells her father that she feels the doctor is ashamed 'of us, of me'. When Grace discovers that Fitzpiers is a liar, and that he has been philandering with Mrs Charmond, she and her father realise that the marriage has been a great mistake. However, Melbury doubts that his daughter will be permitted to divorce Fitzpiers because, says he: 'Your husband has not been cruel enough. The law will leave you as Mrs Fitzpiers, 'till the end of the chapter [her life].'

Here, Hardy shows his distaste for legal statutes which condemn those such as Grace to lives of misery.

Fitzpiers accompanies Mrs Charmond to the Continent. When he returns, looking for Grace, she leaves home and flees to Giles' hut. Giles, mindful of her reputation as a married woman, spends several nights sleeping outdoors in the open, whereupon he succumbs to a sickness and dies. He is mourned by Grace, and by Marty South who also loved him. At Grace and Fitzpiers' final meeting, the doctor, now contrite, asks Grace what she feels for him. 'Nothing' is the answer.

Hardy completed *The Woodlanders* on 4 February 1887 and recorded in his diary that he felt relieved at having done so.[15] This relief surely reflects the fact that, vicariously through the characters of the novel, he has brought the problems of his own marriage out into the open, which is a catharsis for him. And as his emotions finally boil over, what he writes – albeit in measured tones – is an expression of frustration, anger, bitterness and regret, engendered in him by years of marriage to Emma.

Surprisingly, and despite all their differences, Hardy and Emma left Dorchester on 14 March 1887 for London, en route to Italy. Here, they visited the cathedrals of Pisa and Milan, the Colosseum in Rome and the graves of the poets Shelley and Keats; all indicative of Hardy's reverence for both good architecture and poetry. Venice was the city which he appears to have enjoyed the most. In Florence they visited the tomb of Elizabeth Browning, poet and wife of Robert, who had died in 1861. They also visited Lucy Baxter, daughter of Hardy's former mentor, the late William Barnes, who had settled in Florence after her marriage.

Emma, in her (surviving) diaries, reveals some of the tensions which existed between herself and Hardy at this time. Referring to her husband, she says: 'Tom very vexed. Dyspeptic before and worse now' – 'Tom has taken another little stroll by himself' – 'Tom … had an altercation [with the father of a family] about seats' (this was on the train journey from Italy to Paris, where Emma admitted to siding with the father of the family in question against her husband). When she says, 'Little shoe-black [presumably a reference to a child whose job it was to polish the shoes of visitors] persistent at Forum [in Rome] Sunday morning, [I] broke my umbrella beating him off', this may be construed as the sign of her contempt for what she described as the 'working orders'. Hardy, no doubt, would have been horrified and disgusted by her behaviour in this respect.[16]

## Wessex Tales: A Group of Noble Dames

Back in London in the spring of 1887, Hardy and Emma trod the well-known path to society gatherings, and again met the poet Robert Browning, with whom they discussed their recent holiday in Italy. Queen Victoria's Golden Jubilee took place on 28 June and they went to see the procession which included vast numbers of royalty.

In August 1887, in a letter to Edmund Gosse, Hardy told of the weeks and months of 'despondency' which he had experienced 'in byegone years', the most recent bout being 'several years ago'. This he attributed to his 'stomach' and eating habits, but alluded to the fact that other factors may have been involved. In the autumn, Hardy was toying with ideas for plots for his forthcoming epic drama, *The Dynasts*. Meanwhile, his reading of the poets and the Classics continued unabated.

In the spring of 1888, Hardy and Emma again sojourned in London before returning to Paris; this time to the Salon, to the races at Longchamps, and to an exhibition of drawings and paintings by French writer Victor Hugo.[17] On their return, Hardy called upon Lady Portsmouth and, being always one with an eye for a pretty female face or figure, remarked upon how well her ladyship's 'black, brocaded silk' fitted her.

On 4 May 1888 Hardy's *Wessex Tales* – a collection of short stories – was published by Macmillan. They included *The Three Strangers*, in which the hangman meets his victim-to-be (an escaped convict) in a shepherd's cottage; *The Withered Arm*, where a woman invokes magic to cure a malady; and *A Tradition of Eighteen Hundred and Four*, where Napoleon (with whom Hardy was always fascinated) is engaged in a reconnaissance of the Wessex countryside. In *The Distracted Preacher* Hardy makes use of anecdotes told to him by his grandfather, Thomas I, in regard to smuggling on the 'Wessex' coast.

In mid-July Hardy and Emma return to Dorchester, where Hardy makes a note of interesting stories he has heard for possible inclusion in future novels. Examples include the tale of a man who took 'casts of the heads of executed convicts', and that of a young lady who got married wearing 'a dainty pair of shoes' – these shoes had been previously thrown at her by another man, a shoemaker, whose love she had spurned; he had made them for her as a present.

In London in 1889 Hardy was fascinated by Turner's use of light at an exhibition of his paintings at the Royal Academy. He also compared the techniques of Botticelli and Rubens in their depiction of the 'flesh', vis-à-vis the 'soul'; the fact that both these men were portrayers of the female form par excellence would not have been wasted on him. As always, he and Emma attended church services, concerts, plays and, of course, society events.

In a letter to poet and essayist John Addington Symonds in April, Hardy asks 'whether we ought to write sad stories, considering how much sadness there is in the world already'. He concludes that the justification for doing so is that 'the first step towards cure of, or even relief from, any disease (is) ... to understand it'. This may then provide an escape from the worst forms of sadness in real life.[18] This may be interpreted to mean that for Hardy, the writing of novels and poems with a sad theme acted as a catharsis in respect of his unhappy life with Emma.

At the end of July 1889, the Hardys returned to Max Gate, where Hardy settled into the daily routine of writing what would be his next novel: *Tess of the D'Urbervilles*. This was not, however, to be a straightforward project. The first two magazines to which he sent the manuscript rejected it on the grounds that it was 'improper', and it was only after Hardy had laboriously edited it, removing parts or all of various chapters, that it was finally accepted by the editor of the weekly newspaper *The Graphic*.

Hardy, despite the labour of writing, still found the time and energy to record his thoughts and feelings on those subjects which he found intriguing; for example, religion. He had been searching for God for fifty years, he confessed, 'and I think that if he had existed I should have discovered him'.[19] He also found time to write to Hugh Thackeray Turner, secretary to the Society for the Protection of Ancient Buildings, objecting to the proposed demolition of the church in the village of Stratton, near Dorchester; in his view, 'some judicious repair' was all that was necessary.[20]

At Easter 1890, Hardy visited the grave of William Barnes at Winterborne Came. In May, when he and Emma were again in London, he sent the manuscript of *A Group of Noble Dames* to *The Graphic*, which agreed to serialise it. This was a collection of short stories – for the background of which Hardy drew heavily on *The History and Antiquities of the County of Dorset* by the Revd John Hutchins (first published in 1774). For the plots of the stories, however, he relied on 'the lips of aged people in a remote part of the country, where traditions of the local families linger on, & are remembered by the yeomen & peasantry long after they are forgotten by the families concerned'.[21]

A year later, *A Group of Noble Dames* was published, in book form, by Osgood, McIlvaine & Co. of London.

What did the critics have to say about *A Group of Noble Dames*? In the words of one, it was a 'pageant of disastrous marriages, confessed and unconfessed adulteries, complicated illegitimacies, sudden deaths, suspected crimes [and] bizarre cruelties ... among the Wessex gentry of some generations back'.[22]

At the end of June 1890, Hardy said he was 'getting tired of investigating life at music halls and police courts', which appears to have been his principal preoccupation during that season in London. Attendance at the latter would probably have provided material for his stories, as well as satisfied his somewhat morbid curiosity; whereas the beautiful actresses and dancers with their 'lustrous eyes and pearly countenances', which he would have seen at the former, would doubtless have afforded him light relief and titillation.

When, in that year of 1890, Emma's father John Gifford died, Emma left London to attend his funeral in Devon. Hardy did not accompany her. Thereafter, Hardy generously arranged an annuity for Emma's niece and nephew, (Ethel) Lilian (Attersoll) Gifford and her brother Gordon. That August, Hardy and his brother Henry went on a visit to Paris together.

⸙

It may have afforded Hardy some amusement to consider that he, an outspoken critic (through his writings) of the upper classes, was now coming into contact more and more not only with London society, but also with the gentry of Dorset. For example, in January 1891 he attended a ball given by Mrs Brinsley Sheridan (a descendant of Irish dramatist Richard Brinsley Sheridan) at her home, Frampton Court, Frampton, near Dorchester. To this, Emma arrived on horseback; horse riding being a favourite pastime of hers.

In the spring of 1891 Hardy was elected to the Athenaeum (a London gentlemen's club), from the balcony of which he saw the German emperor, Wilhelm II, pass by.

Despite his literary success, Hardy was still unable to afford a second home in London, and he and Emma were obliged to find rented accommodation for their annual spring sojourns in the capital. At a luncheon at Mary Jeune's (Lady St Helier, wife of a distinguished judge) in July, Hardy mentions sitting between 'a pair of beauties', the one with 'violet eyes' being 'the more seductive', while the other was 'more vivacious'.[23]

In September Hardy and Emma visited Scotland and many of the places depicted by Sir Walter Scott in his novels. In November he gave his opinion on whether eminent men of letters should be awarded national recognition. The problem, as he saw it, was that while 'the highest flights of the pen [by an author] are mostly the excursions and revelations of souls unreconciled to life, [the] natural tendency of a government [was] to encourage acquiescence in life as it is'.[24]

In that year of 1891, Emma's mother died. It is not known if Emma attended the funeral.

## Tess of the D'Urbervilles

When Hardy began a new book, it was his habit firstly to select a brand new pencil with which to write it, and secondly to relocate to a different room in the house. So, for *Tess of the D'Urbervilles*, he moved out of his old study and into a new one, situated at the rear of Max Gate with a window facing west.

The story commences with Parson Tringham, antiquary, addressing Jack Durbeyfield, a 'haggler', as 'Sir John', and informing him that he (Durbeyfield) was descended from the 'ancient and knightly family of the D'Urbervilles'. (It will be recalled that the Hardys liked to think of themselves as being descended from the ancient 'le Hardy' family of Jersey.) Hardy describes Jack as a 'slack-twisted fellow' whose 'times [of work] could not be relied on to coincide with the hours of requirement' – another example of Hardy's wit.

When Durbeyfield's wife informs her husband that a great lady by the name of D'Urberville is living at nearby Trantridge (Pentridge, near Cranborne), they decide to send their daughter Tess to pay the family a visit, with the purpose of claiming kinship to them.

At the D'Urbervilles, Tess meets Alec, the young man of the house, who confesses to her that his family are not genuine 'D'Urbervilles' but that they obtained the title of this 'old, extinguished family' simply by purchasing it. Nevertheless, Alec's mother offers Tess a job managing her poultry farm. The old lady is deeply attached to her fowls and, despite being blind, is able to recognise each one of them individually by their comb, beak and claws.

On hearing from Tess that her family's horse has died, Alec generously provides them with a replacement. He then takes advantage of Tess while she is sleeping, forcing himself upon her. She falls pregnant, and after being mistress to him for a period of four months, she returns home to have his baby. When the vicar arrives to baptise the infant, Tess's father forbids it – his family having suffered such disgrace. When the child dies, Tess informs the vicar that she herself had previously baptised it. Nevertheless, the vicar refuses to allow it a Christian burial. Here, Hardy is venting his anger against prejudice and religious dogma.

Tess then finds employment with Farmer Crick, described as a 'kindly man who has his own pew in church'. Among his employees is Angel Clare (Hardy having obtained the name 'Angel' from a memorial plaque in Stinsford church), a parson's son who wishes to become a farmer. When in the dairy the butter refuses to set, this is taken to mean that someone is in love – Hardy's appreciation of folklore – and in this case the loving couple are Tess and Angel. Angel proposes to Tess, she accepts and they marry.

When Angel confesses to having had a brief relationship with an older woman, Tess forgives him. However, when, despite her mother warning her against it, Tess confesses to having had a similar relationship with Alec, which resulted in the birth of a child, now deceased, Angel takes this as proof that she is the 'the belated seedling of an effete aristocracy' and departs for Brazil. Tess returns home. She now has to endure jeering and being referred to as a 'trollope'. Here is Hardy railing against hypocrisy.

Tess now endures great hardship working in the fields, uprooting turnips and feeding wheat into the threshing machine which works, remorselessly, from dawn to dusk. Meanwhile, she resists the overtures of Alec, who tells her that had he known her circumstances he would have done his duty by the child. Aware that Tess's father is ill and that her family are liable to be evicted, Alec offers his help, but is again rejected. Alec also offers to marry Tess, but she declines because she does not love him. Finally, Jack Durbeyfield dies and the family is rendered homeless.

Angel returns from Brazil to find letters of desperation from Tess which have not been forwarded. He goes looking for her, eventually finding her in Sandbourne (Bournemouth). He asks her forgiveness, but she tells him it is too late. Tess is now living with Alec, who has been good to her family and won her back to him. A distraught Angel catches the train home, only to have Tess jump into the carriage and join him. She has murdered Alec.

The couple flee; Angel determined to save her from the forces of the law. However, at the 'pagan temple' of Stonehenge she is captured.

⁓

In *Tess of the D'Urbervilles*, Hardy's heroine's brief dalliance with Alec sets her on a course of destruction, culminating with her being hanged for murder at Wintonchester (Winchester). Her second 'mistake' was being honest. She wanted to have no secrets from Angel, who must know the truth about her past.

Tess showed immense qualities of endurance in resisting Alec, who, by pro-posing marriage, offered her an easy escape from a life of toil and hardship.

But she did not love him and remained true to Angel, even though he had forsaken her. The forces which crushed Tess were enshrined by an establishment which condemned adultery and 'bastardy'. For this, Tess was punished by being jeered at and by being denied a Christian burial for her child. The impact of this on her life would not have been so catastrophic had it not been for Angel's intolerance in assessing her 'lapse' to be of greater significance than his. In short, Tess was literally hounded to death by the combined harshness of the establishment and the bigotry of those around her.

The notion that they are descended from a distinguished family leads the Durbeyfields to ruination, as they make desperate but futile efforts to live up to the 'knightliness' of their ancestors. As for Hardy, the fact that this is a recurring theme implies that what he perceived as his lack of 'pedigree' was a source of deep regret to him. This, of course, is a paradox, in one who invariably championed the cause of the lower orders of society.

Tess provided Hardy with a vehicle for yet another outburst against the victimisation of the weak and oppressed, perpetrated by the upper classes and enforced by a callous and impersonal legal system. Tess acknowledges this, in an almost masochistic way, when, having struck Alec on the mouth, she invites him to punish her. 'Whip me, crush me,' she cries. 'I shall not cry out. Once victim, always victim, that's the law.' And the scene where Tess is hanged was, for Hardy, reminiscent of a similar scene: the hanging of Elizabeth Brown at Dorchester, which he had witnessed personally in the year 1856 when he was 15.

*Tess of the D'Urbervilles* was published in late November 1891 by Osgood, McIlvaine & Co. The novel became a talking point throughout the land and was quickly translated into several languages, including Russian. Despite this, many libraries refused to stock it. Its review in *The Quarterly* was to offend Hardy deeply. The article, he said, was smart and amusing, but at the expense of truth and sincerity. 'If this sort of thing [criticism] continues,' he said, there would be 'no more novel writing for me'.[25]

On 20 July 1892 Hardy's father died. Like Horatio in Shakespeare's *Hamlet*, he had in his lifetime taken suffering and fortune 'with equal thanks'. His last request had been for a drink of water from the well, which led him, when he had tasted it, to say: 'Now I know I am at home.' He was buried in Stinsford churchyard, and it was Hardy himself who designed his tombstone. From then on, the family business was continued by Hardy's brother, Henry.

That October also saw the death of Tennyson, whose funeral in Westminster Abbey Hardy attended.

The following May, in 1893, Hardy and Emma visited Ireland, where in Dublin they met Florence Henniker (sister of Lord Houghton, the Lord Lieutenant, and wife of Arthur Henniker-Major, an army officer). Although Florence was fifteen years Hardy's junior, the pair were to strike up a long friendship and correspondence. The Hardys were also present in the Irish capital for Queen Victoria's Birthday Review, held on the 24th of that month.

June 1893 found Hardy in Oxford, at a time when commemoration proceedings were taking place to honour the university's founders and benefactors; the purpose of the visit was to gather material for his next novel, which would be entitled *Jude the Obscure*. In August Hardy and Emma spent some time in Wales. In November he wrote two poems, and on Christmas Eve at Max Gate he and Emma received carol singers who, with their lanterns, stood under the trees and sang to the accompaniment of a harmonium.

# 8

# *Jude the Obscure*

In February 1894 a collection of Hardy's short stories was published by Osgood, McIlvaine & Co. under the title *Life's Little Ironies*. The Hardys again rented accommodation in London, taking their servants with them and spending the spring in their customary way, viz. attending dinners, plays and the theatre.

At this time Hardy was still engaged in his never-ending quest to understand women; Emma in particular. This much is clear from certain annotations which he made in the margins of a book of short stories entitled *Keynotes*, by George Egerton, given to him by Florence Henniker. Beside a passage in the book which describes 'the eternal wilderness, the untamed, primitive, savage temperament that lurks in the mildest, best woman', Hardy remarked: 'This if fairly stated is decidedly the UGLY side of a woman's nature.' And where *Keynotes* refers to man's 'chivalrous, conservative devotion to the female idea he has created, [which] blinds him, perhaps happily, to the problem of her complex nature', Hardy asks if the conclusion is that 'REAL woman is abhorrent to man? hence the failure of matrimony?' If so, this is a desperately negative view of the female sex on Hardy's part, but it should be remembered that he was a man of limited experience where women were concerned, and his conclusions were based almost entirely on his relationship with Emma.[1] Meanwhile, an idea was developing in his mind for a novel in which the problem of male/female relationships would be explored in full.

Hardy had 'jotted down' the plot for what was to become *Jude the Obscure* in 1890.[2] Two years later, he visited the village of Great Fawley in Berkshire, from where his maternal grandmother, Mary Head, who had experienced a miserable life as an orphan, had originated. The hero of the story, Jude Fawley, would derive his name from this village. The novel was to be serialised, commencing in November 1894 in *Harper's Magazine*, but only after certain changes were made at the insistence of the publisher. Hardy then restored the work to its original version – an exhausting process – before its publication in book form a year later, in November 1895, again by Osgood, McIlvaine & Co.

In *Jude the Obscure*, the plot develops in Hardy's characteristic style, taking innumerable twists and turns as he throws not one, but a sackful of proverbial spanners into the works (or paths) of his 'characters'.

Following the death of his parents, Jude Fawley is brought up in the village of Marygreen by his great-aunt, Miss Drusilla Fawley. Drusilla urges Jude to persuade his schoolmaster, Mr Phillotson (who had advised Jude to 'read all you can'), 'to take 'ee [Jude] to Christminster [Oxford] wi' un [him], and make a scholar of 'ee'. With this suggestion Jude is entirely in accord; Christminster, in his eyes, being a romanticised world where scholars work in the rarefied atmosphere of high academia. Here, Hardy the author is fully in tune with his hero: a sound education is something they both value. Before Jude has the opportunity to fulfil his dream, however, he is tricked into marrying Arabella Donn, the daughter of a pig breeder.

Jude had been taught by his schoolmaster to 'be kind to animals and birds', and when his and Arabella's pig has to be slaughtered, he is broken-hearted. After the pig's death he mourns the creature: a scene in which Hardy manages to convey, simultaneously, a sense of both pathos and humour – even though it is obvious that the author's sympathies are entirely with Jude and the pig. This, Hardy makes clear when he admits to having deliberately introduced this episode into the novel, in order for it to 'serve a humane end in showing people the cruelty that goes on unheeded under the barbarous *régime* we call civilization'.[3]

Arabella deserts Jude and goes to live in Australia. Jude now moves from Marygreen to Christminster, where he obtains employment as a stonemason, continuing with his studies in his spare time. Here, he meets his cousin, Sue Bridehead.

Jude longs to use his talents and to have them recognised, whereas Sue prefers to be unconventional – a free spirit. Sceptical of religion, Sue sees the saints as the stuff of legend rather than reality, and sees Christminster as a place where intellect is pushing one way and religion the other, 'like two rams butting each other. The medievalism of Christminster must be

sloughed off,' she declares, 'or Christminster itself will have to go.' This statement reflects Hardy's own inner struggle to reconcile what his intellect is
telling him on the one hand, with Christian dogma on the other.

Jude's ambition at Christminster is to study at the university, but he finds
himself thwarted by the university authorities. He is a stonemason, therefore he cannot be a scholar; not officially at any rate. In this, Hardy was not
writing from personal experience (he appears not to have made any serious
attempt to enter university, despite the encouragement of Horace Moule),
but was making the general point that university was a 'closed shop' for all
but the privileged few.

Jude introduces Sue to Phillotson, whom she subsequently marries.
However, the marriage ends acrimoniously, and Phillotson, seeing how
unhappy she is, and out of 'natural, straightforward humanity', agrees to
give her freedom and a divorce. She returns to Jude. For his act of compas-
sion, Phillotson is dismissed from his post as schoolmaster.

Jude receives a letter from Arabella to say that she has remarried. She also
tells him that, unbeknown to him, she has borne his child; a son, 'little Jude'
– or 'Juey' – to whom she wishes Jude to give a home, a proposal to which
both he and Sue agree. Jude finds himself falling in love with Sue, but there
are problems here also, for she has a natural aversion to marriage. At one
point, the couple get as far as the registrar's office, before Sue says to Jude:
'Let us go home, without killing our dream.'

There comes an event which brings Jude and Sue's failure to marry
into sharp relief. He is employed by the church to inscribe a stone tablet
with words from the Ten Commandments, which include: 'Thou shalt
not commit adultery.' When he is recognised as one who is committing
this very sin himself, he is told that his services are no longer required.
Subsequently, for the very reason that he and Sue are unmarried and
therefore 'living in sin', the couple, along with their children, now three in
number including Juey, are turned out of the lodgings which they occupy
in Christminster.

When Commemoration Day (which Hardy calls 'Remembrance Day')
dawns, and the university remembers its former founders and benefactors,
Jude sees it more as 'humiliation day', for despite all his knowledge, gained
from long years of study, he is still regarded as an outsider.

The ultimate tragedy occurs when Juey, Jude's son by Arabella, hangs
Jude's two children by Sue and then hangs himself; which Sue regards as a
judgement from God. She returns to Phillotson, remarries him, and finally
submits to his desires because 'it is my duty'. Meanwhile, Jude is tricked into

marrying Arabella for a second time, shortly after which he becomes seriously ill and dies.

*Jude the Obscure* contains an important clue as to the real reason why Hardy chose not to become a clergyman. The reason he gave at the time was that it would have involved him in a prolonged period of study, but surely, for a scholar such as he, this would have presented no problem. In this novel, however, when Jude Fawley kisses Sue Bridehead, he experiences all the pleasure of that moment of intimacy. He realises how 'glaringly inconsistent' it would be for him to pursue 'the idea of becoming ... a servant of religion', when that religion (in this case Christianity) regards sexual love 'at its best as a frailty, and at its worst a damnation'.

## Jude: A Story of Male/Female Disharmony

In the book's preface, Hardy describes *Jude the Obscure* as a 'tragedy of unfulfilled aims'. Intended for men and women of 'full [adult] age', it was an attempt, he said, to confront the issue of:

> the fret and fever, derision and disaster, that may press in the wake of the strongest passion known to humanity [physical attraction and sexual desire]; to tell, without a mincing of words, of a deadly war waged between flesh and spirit.[4]

Hardy begins the novel with a quotation from the book of Esdras in the Apocrypha:

> Yea, many there be that have run out of their wits for women, and become servants for their sakes. Many also have perished, have erred, and sinned, for women.

Those who read *Jude the Obscure* at the time it was published may be forgiven if they failed to realise that in reality, the problematical male/female interpersonal relationships discussed therein relate to Hardy himself and Emma. However (as will be seen), when the full story of the Hardys' marriage finally emerges, it becomes clear that this was absolutely the case.

It would be a mistake for the reader to assume that in the novel it is the hero, Jude Fawley, who invariably voices the true thoughts of Hardy, for sometimes his thoughts are expressed by Sue Bridehead, or even by one of the more minor characters. It is therefore interesting to 'unscramble' the story in an effort to discover the meaning, of the plot within the plot. Firstly, however, it is important to note that the novel begins with a caveat, namely Jude's great-aunt Drusilla's dire warning to him about the consequences of matrimony. Said she:

> Jude, my child, don't *you* ever marry. Tisn't for the Fawleys to take that step any more. The Fawleys were not made for wedlock: it never seemed to sit well upon us. There's sommat in our blood that won't take kindly to the notion of being bound to do what we do readily enough if not bound.

Drusilla subsequently apprises Jude of the various tragedies that have befallen his forebears, including his own parents. And after Drusilla's death, Jude tells Sue that his great-aunt had once told him that the Fawleys 'particularly … members of our family … made bad husbands and wives. Certainly we made unhappy ones.' Drusilla's friend, Mrs Edlin, reinforces this idea when she tells cousins Jude and Sue about certain mishaps which their common ancestors had experienced. 'They was always good-hearted people … wouldn't kill a fly if they knowed it, but things happened to thwart 'em.' This leads Sue to say, despairingly: 'It makes me feel as if a tragic doom overhung our family, as it did the house of Atreus [a tragic family from Greek mythology].'

*Of Love*
When Jude first sets eyes on Sue:

> the emotion which had been accumulating in his breast as the bottled-up effect of solitude and the poetized locality he dwelt in, insensibly began to precipitate itself on this half-visionary form; and he perceived that for whatever his obedient wish in a contrary direction, he would soon be unable to resist the desire to make himself known to her.

Subsequently, instead of regarding Sue as a cousin, he comes to admit that his interest in her is 'unmistakably of a sexual kind'. Yet, as far as love is concerned, he feels that his relationship with her is one-sided, for, referring to himself, he declares: 'I, who love you better than my own self, – better – O far better than you have loved me!' If only she would say that she loved him 'a quarter, a tenth, as much as I do you' then he would 'be content'.

'Sue, you are not worth a man's love!' he tells her, in exasperation. 'Sue, sometimes when I am vexed with you, I think you're incapable of real love.'

Sue, nevertheless, sees matters entirely differently. In respect of Phillotson, she explains to Jude that 'sometimes a woman's *love of being loved* gets the better of her conscience, and though she is agonized at the thought of treating a man cruelly, she encourages him to love her while she doesn't love him at all'. To which the horrified Jude replies: 'You simply mean that you flirted outrageously with him, poor old chap, and then repented, and to make reparation, married him, though you tortured yourself to death by doing it?'

'Well – if you put it brutally – it was a little like that,' says Sue. Her love for Jude began similarly, she said, 'in a selfish and cruel wish to make your heart ache for me without letting mine ache for you'. But she does admit that eventually she did come to love him truly.

## Marriage

Presenting matters from the male standpoint, Jude tells Sue: 'People go on marrying because they can't resist natural forces [presumably, sexual attraction], although many of them may know perfectly well that they are possibly buying a month's pleasure with a life's discomfort.'

And he expresses his impatience to marry Sue by telling her: 'I've wanted you to be [my wife], and I've waited with the patience of Job, and I don't see that I've got anything by my self-denial.'

This can only be interpreted in one way – that their relationship is, at Sue's insistence, a platonic one. Sue, for her part, feels that she rushed into her marriage to Phillotson without proper consideration. Says she: 'Before I married him I had never thought out fully what marriage meant, even though I knew. It was idiotic of me – there is no excuse. I was old enough, and I thought I was very experienced. So I rushed on.'

And when she left Phillotson for Jude, she was extremely nervous at the prospect of remarriage, having a 'dread', as she told him, 'lest an iron contract should extinguish your tenderness for me, and mine for you, as it did between our parents'. She goes on to say:

If a marriage ceremony is a religious thing, it is possibly wrong; but if it is only a sordid contract, based on material convenience in householding, rating, and taxing  ...– which it seems to be – why surely a person may say, even proclaim upon the housetops, that it hurts and grieves him or her? [For once one is] contracted to cherish ... [the other] under a Government stamp ... Ugh, how horrible and sordid.

Instead of being bound by a 'dreadful' marriage contract, the whole essence of a relationship, in her view, should be one of 'voluntariness'. For this reason, having got as far as the registry office with Jude, she declares: 'An irrevocable oath is risky. Then, Jude, let us go home without killing our dream!'

## Sexual Incompatibility

Jude describes Sue as 'such a phantasmal, bodiless creature, one who – if you'll allow me to say it – has so little animal passion in you, that you can act upon reason in the matter when we poor unfortunate wretches of grosser substance can't'.

As for Sue, when she was married to Phillotson, who was about twenty years her senior, she declared that:

> Though I like Mr Phillotson as a friend, I don't like him – it is a torture to me to – live with him as a husband! I suppose you'd call it – a repugnance on my part. What tortures me so much is the necessity of being responsive to this man whenever he wishes, good as he is morally! I wish he would beat me, or be faithless to me, or do some open thing that I could talk about as a justification for feeling as I do! But he does nothing.

Phillotson discovers Sue sleeping in a 'clothes-closet' under the staircase, instead of sharing the marital bed with him. When he attempts to enter the closet by wrenching open the door, 'she sprang out of her lair, great-eyed and trembling' and implored him to 'go away'. Sue requests that she be allowed to leave Phillotson and go to Jude, even though she does not love him. But, 'if you won't let me go to him, will you grant me this one request – allow me to live in your house in a separate way?'

Phillotson agrees for the two of them to sleep in separate bedrooms. However, when one evening he enters her bedroom inadvertently, she demonstrates her physical aversion to him once again when she 'sprang out of her lair and implored him [once again] to go away'. On a third occasion, when Phillotson accidentally enters the room that his wife is occupying, Sue's reaction is to leap out of the window, even though her bedroom is on the first floor. Said Phillotson:

> She jumped out of the window, so strong was her dread of me! Though as a fellow-creature she sympathizes with me, and pities me, and even weeps for me, as a husband she cannot endure me – she loathes me – there's no use mincing words.

Finally, he speaks of Sue's 'unconquerable aversion to myself as a husband. Even though she may like me as a friend, 'tis too much to bear [any] longer.' He therefore agrees that she may return to Jude.

Sue admits to Jude that she has been 'so cold' to Phillotson, but, despite everything, she tells the schoolmaster that she will continue 'with so much pleasure' to copy manuscripts for him at any time, should he require it.

The reason that Sue gives for her coldness to Phillotson is a curious one. For her to live on 'intimate terms' with him, she declares, would be regarded by herself as 'adultery, in any circumstances, however legal'. She had said as much on her wedding night when, having been handed a pretty nightgown to wear, she cried, as she tore it to pieces. 'It is adulterous! It signifies what I don't feel … It must be destroyed!' He had told her that her action had hurt him, and reminded her that she (in the marriage ceremony) had 'vowed to love me'.

Sue becomes introspective, and asks Jude:

Are there many couples, do you think, where one dislikes the other for no definite fault? Wouldn't the woman be very bad-natured if she didn't like to live with her husband; merely because she had a personal feeling against it – a physical objection – a fastidiousness, or whatever it may be called – although she might respect and be grateful to him? I am merely putting a case. Ought she to try to overcome her pruderies?

When Jude again professes his love for Sue, she admits that she has kept him at 'a distance'. Nonetheless, she does not like to be thought of as a 'cold-natured, sexless creature'.

'The marriage laws', said Hardy in a postscript to *Jude the Obscure*, written sixteen years after its publication in April 1912, were 'used in great part as the tragic machinery of the tale'; his own opinion being that 'a marriage should be dissolvable as soon as it becomes a cruelty to either of the parties – being then essentially and morally no marriage'.[5]

## The Real Meaning of *Jude the Obscure*: its Aftermath

In the preface to *Jude the Obscure*, Hardy explains the reasons why he has written the novel. It was, he said, 'simply an endeavour to give shape and coherence to a series of seemings [apparent, but perhaps not real, occurrences], or personal impressions'.[6] In other words, he is writing about his personal experiences in an effort to make sense of them. This begs the question, just how much does *Jude the Obscure* reflect the author's own life?

When Jude's great-aunt Drusilla warned that the Fawley family 'was not made for wedlock', it may be assumed that it was Emma's family which Hardy had in mind. After all, his own parents had, by all accounts, a harmonious relationship with each other, and as for his siblings, none of them were married. On the other hand, as Hardy was doubtless aware, several of Emma's relatives had mental health problems (an account of which will be given shortly). Thus, when 'Sue Bridehead' acknowledges the fact that 'a tragic doom' overhangs her family, this was equally applicable to the family of Emma; at least as far as certain members of it were concerned. Hardy may also have had in mind Emma's family's 'truly horrible home', her father John Attersoll Gifford's 'drunken ravings', and the fact that he once 'chased [Emma's] mother into the street in her nightgown'.[7]

Only with hindsight, and with a full knowledge and recognition of just how traumatised Hardy was by his marriage to Emma, is it possible to be confident about the following working hypotheses in respect of *Jude the Obscure*.

When Jude first sets eyes on Sue he clearly falls head over heels in love with her, and experiences an 'unmistakeably … sexual' attraction to her. However, he feels that he in return has received only a fraction of the love from Sue that he gave to her. Hardy felt exactly the same way about Emma. Just as Sue had behaved in a 'selfish and cruel' way by encouraging Phillotson to make advances to her, simply because she had fallen in love with a 'love of being loved', so Emma had behaved in a similar way towards Hardy. When Jude became frustrated at having waited 'with the patience of Job' for Sue to become his wife, Hardy was deliberately mirroring the fact that the reason why his courtship to Emma lasted for four and a half long years, was that she had feared the marriage contract, just as Sue did.

The following possibilities must also be considered: that Emma felt the same way as Hardy's fictitious character Sue Bridehead, who confessed that the idea of falling in love held a greater attraction for her than the experience of love itself; that Emma, like Sue, derived a perverse pleasure from seeing her admirers break their hearts over her; that Emma felt the same physical revulsion for Hardy that Sue had felt for Phillotson; and that just as Jude regarded Sue as 'phantasmal', 'bodiless' and 'cold', so Hardy saw Emma in the same light.

What of Sue Bridehead's belief that to make love to Phillotson, her husband, would, for the reason that she did not love him, be to commit adultery? Did Emma feel the same way towards Hardy, and if so, was this irrational belief of hers a manifestation of a delusion on her part? (Emma's manuscript *What I Think of My Husband* may have shed more light on the matter, had Hardy not chosen to destroy it.) And finally, as with Phillotson and Sue, did Hardy regard his marriage to Emma as 'a cruelty' and 'morally no marriage' at all?

Did Hardy simply pluck the notions expressed by Sue and Jude in *Jude the Obscure* out of thin air, or were they based on his own bitter experiences? And was the writing of the novel in reality an attempt on his part to try to understand the differences between himself and Emma, in the desperate hope that these difference might be resolved?

Those who remain sceptical, and regard the similarity between the lives of Jude Fawley and Sue Bridehead and those of Hardy and Emma as being purely coincidental, should ask themselves this: why, having been obliged to endure criticism over other works of his, in particular *Tess of the D'Urbervilles*, did Hardy risk provoking the critics further by choosing the subject of sex in a relationship, as a primary theme, in a novel which he intended to place before both them and the notoriously prudish Victorian public? And why did he risk finally and irrevocably antagonising Emma, whom he must have guessed would read the novel, and in so doing realise exactly why he wrote it? (Unlike Hardy's other novels, this was one which she had not previously had access to.)

Sue enquires, in a moment of reflection: 'Is it wrong, Jude, for a husband or wife to tell a third person that they are unhappy in their marriage?'[8] Hardy came very close to doing just that, when, on 20 November 1895 (the very day of the novel's publication), he wrote to 'a close friend' to tell him more about the characters of Jude and Sue; in reality it was of himself and Emma that he spoke.[9]

Although Hardy's sympathies lay primarily with Jude and Phillotson, he bent over backwards to present Sue's (Emma's) point of view also. And he subsequently elaborated on this in a letter to Edmund Gosse. One of Sue's reasons for fearing the marriage ceremony, said Hardy, was that she was afraid that it would be:

breaking faith with Jude to withhold herself [from having sexual intercourse with him] at pleasure, or altogether, after it; though while uncontracted, she feels at liberty to yield herself as seldom as she chooses. This has tended to keep his [Jude's] passion as hot at the end as at the beginning, & helps break his heart. He has never really possessed her as freely as he desired.[10]

This may be seen as an admission by Hardy that he is broken-hearted, after years of frustration, and a confirmation by him that his marriage to Emma was never consummated.

To the above hypotheses a final caveat must be added. Hardy, in *Jude the Obscure*, was voicing his opinion as to why Emma did not love him as he deserved, and why she refused to make love to him. Whether the reasons for this, given vicariously by Jude and Sue, are the correct ones, or whether Emma had different reasons for adopting the attitude towards Hardy that she did, can never be known with certainty, given the fact that the majority of her private writings and correspondence was destroyed. What appears not to be in doubt, however, is that she did *not* love Hardy in a physical and demonstrative sense, and that she did *not* have a sexual relationship with him. However, some further light will be shed shortly on Emma's attitude in this respect.

What is surprising is that, despite everything, the couple maintained an outward veneer of normality, in that Emma continued to travel with Hardy and to attend social functions with him.

In June 1894, in an article published by the *New Review*, Hardy was prompted to ask whether young women should be informed of the facts of life *prior* to marriage, instead of being left to discover them afterwards. The inference here is that had Emma been apprised of precisely what the act of sexual intercourse entailed, she would not have consented to marry Hardy, which would have saved them both much anguish. And Hardy is scarcely able to contain his sense of bitterness and disillusionment when he goes on to enquire whether marriage was 'such a desirable goal for all women as it is assumed to be'. Or was it the truth that that particular institution had 'never succeeded in creating that homely thing: a satisfactory scheme for the conjunction of the sexes'.[11]

The 'earthquake' which followed the publication of *Jude the Obscure* was of an even greater magnitude than that which had followed *Tess of the*

*D'Urbervilles*. In January 1896 Hardy complained that the novel had been misinterpreted, in that the theme of 'the doom of hereditary temperament and unsuitable mating in marriage' had been taken as an attack on that institution in general. He also denied that the book was in any way immoral.[12] The following month he complained of 'fearful depression' and a 'slight headache'.[13]

That section of the press which greeted *Jude the Obscure* with outrage and disgust now chose to ignore Hardy and his works. As for the Bishop of Wakefield, he announced that he had thrown the novel into the fire. Hardy reacted to this news by remarking, dryly, that 'theology and burning' had been associated for many centuries, and supposed that 'they will continue to be allies to the end'.[14]

(In a postscript to *Jude the Obscure*, written some years later, Hardy made further comments on the novel and on its reception by the public and the critics: an experience which, he declared, completely cured him of any further interest in novel writing.)

Despite everything, Hardy and Emma continued with their routine of travelling up to London, where during the 1896 season they met with such people as Susan, Countess of Malmesbury (a writer); the Duchess of Montrose; Theresa, Lady Londonderry, and the author Henry James. August found the couple at Stratford-upon-Avon, where they visited places associated with William Shakespeare. September saw them in France and in Belgium where Emma, who had by now given up horse riding, purchased a bicycle which she imported into England. When Hardy revisited the site of the Battle of Waterloo, he doubtless had in mind the epic drama *The Dynasts*, which he was about to write. It was based on the mighty struggle between the French army, commanded by Emperor Napoleon Bonaparte, and the British army, commanded by the Duke of Wellington. In June he wrote from London to his sister Katharine, offering to obtain for her 'pianoforte pieces', or 'dance music', from the music publisher Chappell.[15]

In October 1896 Hardy once more vented his spleen against the critics:

To cry out in a passionate poem that the Supreme Mover ... [which he believed controlled all earthly happenings, and which he would shortly allude to in *The Dynasts*] must be either limited in power, unknowing, or cruel – which is obvious enough, and has been for centuries ... [would] set all the literary contortionists jumping upon me, a harmless agnostic, as if I were a clamorous atheist.[16]

In his characters, plots and locations, Hardy was the master of disguise. But for once he is found out. In the words of Emma's nephew, Gordon Gifford, she 'strongly objected to this book [*Jude the Obscure*], and, I think, the outlook of some of the characters depicted therein'.[17] Clearly, Emma had recognised herself in the novel, and felt that she had been portrayed in a poor light. Consequently, after its publication, the rift between herself and Hardy grew wider than ever.

By now, because his marriage was defunct in all but name, Hardy felt that in having *Jude the Obscure* published he had nothing to lose as far as Emma was concerned. He therefore forged ahead regardless, and having remained silent for so long, vented all his pent-up frustrations, bemusement, bitterness and anguish, which, no doubt, was to some extent a catharsis for him.

Just prior to his death, Jude uttered these words from the Book of Job:

Let the day perish wherein I was born, and the night in which it was said, There is a man child conceived.

Let that day be darkness; let not God regard it from above, neither let the light shine upon it. Lo, let that night be solitary, let no joyful voice come therein.

Why died I not from the womb? Why did I not give up the ghost when I came out of the belly? ... For now should I have lain still and been quiet. I should have slept: then had I been at rest.

Was this how Hardy himself felt? Did he now regret that at his birth, when he was thought to be dead, the vigilant nurse, realising that he was still alive, had intervened to save his life? It is a possibility which has to be faced and, if true, it is impossible to read the above lines from Job without feeling unutterably sorry for Hardy.

Why, in view of the trauma that he had suffered, did Hardy not simply walk away from Emma and petition for a divorce? There were several possible reasons: one was pride – in that he wished to avoid a scandal, which may have led to him being ostracised by society and shunned by his publisher; also, he still felt responsible for Emma's welfare, and he could not bear the thought of the upheaval which this would entail, including the disruption to his writing. The over-riding reason, however, may have been that, as will be seen, the vision of Emma as he had once perceived her – the beautiful woman who had transfixed him, perhaps at first sight – had not left him, and it never would. And he would spend the remainder of his days in bewilderment, searching for his lost Emma, and hoping against hope that the vision would return.

The meaning of the two previously mentioned poems, which Hardy wrote in the year 1875, now becomes all too painfully obvious, for it is clear that the words 'Wasted were two souls in their prime' (from *We Sat at the Window*), and 'Between them lay a sword' (from *To a Sea Cliff*), clearly apply to himself and Emma. The poems also confirm that Emma's failure to respond to his sexual advances was a problem for Hardy, right from the very onset of their married life.

# 9

# Hardy Reveals Himself in Novels & Poems

## *The Well-Beloved*

Although *The Well-Beloved* (originally entitled *The Pursuit of the Well-Beloved*) was published by Osgood, McIlvaine & Co. in March 1897, the bulk of it was written before the publication of *Jude the Obscure*. This is a novel which stretches both imagination and credulity, but is successful in that it introduces the reader to a concept which he or she may be subconsciously aware of, but may not have hitherto heard articulated. That is, the idea that a person may fall in love, and continue to do so throughout his or her life, not with a particular being, but with a notion of perfect beauty: what Hardy called 'The Well-Beloved', which may temporarily reside in an actual person, but is fleeting and soon transmigrates to inhabit somebody else.

The story is set on the Isle of Slingers (Portland Island in Dorset), and its hero is the 20-year-old Jocelyn Pierston, who is a sculptor. Pierston's 'well-beloved' was:

> perhaps of no tangible substance, [but rather] a spirit, a dream, a frenzy, a conception, an aroma, an epitomised sex, a light of the eye, a parting of the lips. He [Pierston] loved the masquerading creature wherever he found her, whether with blue eyes, black, or brown.[1]

For Pierston, the 'well-beloved' is first 'embodied' in Avice Caro, a boyhood sweetheart. The couple become engaged, but by this time the embodiment has transferred itself to Marcia Bencomb, a local beauty. However, before he can propose to her she leaves him, and he finds a new incarnation of the 'well-beloved' in high-society widow Nichola Pine-Avon. Twenty years later, Avice dies and Pierston returns to the island for her funeral. Here he meets her daughter, Ann Avice (Avice II), and realises that the embodiment has transferred itself to her. Avice II has had her own experience of 'well-beloveds', having already experienced no less than fifteen male embodiments herself. Unfortunately for Pierston, it transpires that she is already married.

Another twenty years pass and Pierston duly falls in love with Avice II's daughter, Avice III. She, on learning of his former attachments not only to her own mother, but also to her grandmother, leaves him for a younger man, who is the stepson of Pierston's former 'well-beloved' Marcia Bencomb. Pierston admits that whenever he grapples with the reality of the 'well-beloved', 'she's no longer in it', so he is unable to 'stick to one incarnation' even if he wishes to.[2] Finally, Pierston marries his second 'well-beloved' Marcia Bencomb, who by this time is an invalid.

The theme of *The Well-Beloved* is that a person's preconceived idea of the perfect partner may locate itself in one real-life person, before transferring to another, and then another, and so forth: also, that 'all men are pursuing a shadow, the Unattainable' (and here he was no doubt thinking of himself). This, he hoped, might 'redeem the tragi-comedy from the charge of frivolity'. In other words, Hardy did not wish to appear irresponsible by condoning flirtation and infidelity.[3]

Hardy, when he wrote this particular novel, clearly had in mind Portland Island: a long peninsula in South Dorset stretching several miles out into the sea, where stone is to be found of the finest quality for building and sculpting. But what he was principally concerned with, as a romantic person who since his youth had been easily prone to falling in love, was the concept of the passion a person feels for someone being able to migrate to somebody else.

It is not difficult to visualise how Hardy himself may have had the same experiences as Jocelyn Pierston. During his courtship to Emma, Hardy's 'well-beloved' would undoubtedly have found its embodiment in her. However, when severe and intractable problems arose in their relationship, such as have already been alluded to, Hardy's 'well-beloved' may have migrated, perhaps to one of the beautiful society women with whom he was constantly encountering when in London, whether at dinner parties, the theatre or music halls. Given his marital problems, it was only natural that he should look longingly at such women and think to himself, 'if only' and 'what if?' He may also have thought wistfully of the attractive young ladies whom he had known prior to meeting Emma.

Given that for Hardy his 'well-beloved' no longer resided in his wife Emma, and had migrated, then two of the likely candidates for its new embodiment were Florence Henniker, and the beautiful Lady Agnes Grove, author and daughter of General and the Honourable Mrs Pitt-Rivers.[4]

Former acquaintance of Hardy and member of the original 'Hardy Players', Norrie Woodhall, treats such a notion that Hardy was unfaithful to Emma with incredulity and disdain.[5] Nevertheless, the effort of controlling his emotions and (thwarted) desires was a truly superhuman one. Stoical is perhaps the word that describes him best. He had made his marriage vows and he would stick to them, come what may, and at whatever the cost to his own well-being.

In January 1897 Hardy wrote to Edward Clodd in scathing terms of how 'theology' had been responsible for the arrest of 'light and reason' for 1,600 years. So-called 'Christianity', he said, with its 'terrible, dogmatic ecclesiasticism', had 'hardly anything in common' with the 'real teaching of Christ'.[6] That same month he wrote to Florence Henniker expressing his admiration for the poet Percy Bysshe Shelley (1792–1822). Of all the men whom he (Hardy) would like to meet 'in the Elysian fields', he would choose Shelley, not only for his 'unearthly, weird, wild appearance & genius', but for his 'genuineness, earnestness, & enthusiasms on behalf of the oppressed'. Truly, Hardy believed himself to be a kindred spirit of that great poet.[7]

In 1897 the Hardys departed from their usual routine of renting accommodation in London, and instead opted to stay at Basingstoke, 50 or so miles away, and commute to the capital every few days. In June, the occasion of Queen Victoria's Diamond Jubilee, they travelled to Switzerland to escape the crowds. On their return they visited Wells and its cathedral, the ancient ruins of Stonehenge, and Salisbury, where they attended a service in the cathedral.

Hardy's prodigious efforts on the literary front did not prevent him from taking a keen interest in local architectural affairs. In September he was advising architect Hugh Thackeray Turner on necessary repairs and maintenance to the tower of East Lulworth church, and in October on the re-thatching and re-flooring of the White Horse Inn at Maiden Newton.[8] Hardy visited the latter site on a bicycle, and having therefore incurred no expenses, informed Turner that no repayment for his services was necessary. The writer Rudyard Kipling joined Hardy for some of his cycling excursions; the latter having purchased a new Rover Cob bicycle.[9]

The following year, 1898, saw Hardy, now aged 58, travelling ever further afield on his bicycle, visiting such places as Bristol, Gloucester and Cheltenham, sometimes in company with Emma – who also cycled – and at other times with his brother Henry. Often he would take his bicycle part of the way on the train. The advantage of possessing a bicycle, for literary people he said, was that they could travel a long distance 'without coming in contact with another mind – not even a horse's', and in this way there was no danger of dissipating one's mental energy.[10]

That February he wrote an amusing letter to Elspeth Thomson (sister of the artist Winifred Hope Thomson), thanking her for her 'charming Valentine' which made him feel young again. He said: 'I can just remember the time when written Valentines were customary – before people became so idle as to get everything, even their love-making, done by machinery!'[11]

In April Hardy wrote to Edmund Gosse to tell him of a local belief, 'still held in remote parts hereabout', that in the early hours of every Christmas morning, the farm cattle kneel down (as if in prayer).[12] The same month, an amusing letter was sent by Hardy to his sister Katharine. Ever one for a good story, he had enquired of a London 'omnibus conductor' how it was that young women, who rode their bicycles recklessly into the midst of traffic, did not meet with accidents? Came the reply: 'Oh, nao [no]; their sex pertects [sic] them. We dares not drive over them, wotever they do; & they do jist wot they likes … No man dares to go where they go.'[13]

In May Hardy went to see the body of Mr Gladstone, the former prime minister, which lay in state in Westminster Hall, close to the Houses of Parliament 'where his voice had echoed for 50 years'.[14] In July, in a letter to Florence Henniker, he described a visit to Gloucester Cathedral, where the Perpendicular style of architecture was invented. 'You can see how it grew in the old [medieval] masons' minds,' he said. In September he informed Florence that some Americans, who used to rent a house and 700 acres of shooting near Coniston in the Lake District, did so not in order to shoot, 'but *to keep the birds from being shot* – a truly charming intention'.[15]

A letter to William Archer, critic and journalist, revealed Hardy's total disillusionment with the critics. In his attempt, he said, 'to deal honestly & artistically with the facts of life', he was liable 'to be abused by any scamp who thinks he can advance the sale of his paper by lying about one'.[16] In a witty ending to a letter to Edmund Gosse in December, Hardy advanced the view that Gosse's poems lacked 'the supreme quality of their author being dead' or 'starving in a garret' – the implication being that if this were the case, the poems would be better appreciated.[17] Whoever said that Hardy lacked a sense of humour?

## Wessex Poems

In December 1898 a volume of fifty or so of Hardy's *Wessex Poems* were published by Harper & Brothers. In the main, they were written either in the 1860s, or more recently, after a long interval. They were generally well received; some were about the Napoleonic era, others were drawn from Wessex life. However, the most interesting were those which gave insight into Hardy's state of mind during this period.

In a large proportion of the poems which Hardy wrote the theme is lost love. Did he conjure up such poems out of nowhere? Or were they, as with his novels, based on real-life experiences? If so, then whose experiences were they: those of relatives, friends or acquaintances? Given the depth of feeling expressed by him in such poems, and their great number which runs into not tens, but *hundreds*, then this is hardly feasible. What *is* feasible is that virtually all of them allude to Emma, and this being the case, they reveal that his relationship with her was the stuff of which nightmares are made. For example, in *Neutral Tones* he refers to having learnt, since his youth, 'keen lessons that love deceives'. In *Hap* he specifically mentions 'suffering' and 'love's loss', and finds himself wondering if some divine power is the cause of it:

> If but some vengeful god would call to me
> From up the sky, and laugh:
> 'Thou suffering thing, Know that thy sorrow is my ecstasy,
> That thy love's loss is my hate's profiting!'

In *At an Inn* Hardy longs to put the clock back to a time (presumably) when he and Emma were in love:

> As we seemed we were not
>     That day afar,

And now we seem not what
   We aching are.
O severing sea and land,
   O laws of men,
Ere death, once let us stand
   As we stood then.

In *To Outer Nature* he reveals that the real-life Emma and what he originally imagined her to be were two completely different things:

Show thee as I thought thee
When I early sought thee ...

And then declares sorrowfully:

Thy first sweetness,
Radiance, meetness,
None shall re-awaken.

In *Revulsion*, however, not only does all hope appear to have been extinguished, but it has been replaced by a sense of overwhelming bitterness and disillusionment:

Let me then never feel the fateful thrilling
That devastates the love-worn wooer's frame,
The hot ado of fevered hopes, the chilling
That agonizes disappointed aim!
So I may live no junctive law fulfilling,
And my heart's table bear no woman's name.

In fact, the very title of the poem sums up Hardy's sentiments at this time. Finally, in *I Look Into My Glass*, Hardy, who is now elderly, expresses the fervent wish that his heart (that is, his desires and longings) had shrunk, in the same way that his aged 'wasting skin' had.

    The depth of sentiment expressed in these poems, and the repetitive and obsessional nature of their themes, leads to the inexorable conclusion that in them, the tormented Hardy is expressing his deepest sentiments with regard to his failed relationship with Emma.

## A New Century Dawns

In London as usual with Emma, in the spring of 1899, Hardy continued to fraternise with the literary set, and met with the poet A.E. Housman for the first time. That October he was present in Southampton on the occasion of the departure of troops for the South African War, and saw similar preparations being made by the battery stationed at Dorchester. These events inspired him to write several poems.

In June Hardy wrote from London to his sister Katharine, asking her to remember to instruct the local carpenter to erect a cupboard outside the door of the bedroom at Max Gate that used to be his study, and enclosed a diagram showing exactly where this cupboard should be located.[18] He was now writing frequently to Florence Henniker. In July he complained to Florence that one of the problems with life in the country was the unavailability of good music. In October he told her (referring to the South African War) how he deplored the fact that civilised nations had learnt no other way of settling disputes than 'the old and barbarous one'. In November he sent her his newly composed sonnet entitled *Departure* – referring to the soldiers leaving Southampton docks, bound for South Africa.[19]

The coming of the new century in 1900 saw Hardy as energetic as ever: cycling from Max Gate all the way to Portland Bill and back in one day – a distance of 20 miles, up hill and down dale. That February he expressed to Florence Henniker how he was enjoying studying the strategy and tactics of the current war, but also his horror at the fate of Boer general Piet Cronje, whose army, including its womenfolk, was currently trapped in a river bed (by British forces), and whose animals were being 'mangled'.[20]

In July Hardy apprised William Earl Hodgson, journalist and author, of his view that the (British) constitution 'has worked so much better under queens than kings', and recommended that 'the Crown should [therefore], by rights descend from woman to woman'.[21] (So much for any notion which might be entertained that Hardy had an inherent bias against women.) In October he expressed the opinion to Florence Henniker that the 'present condition of the English novel, is due to the paralysing effect of English criticism on those who would have developed it'.[22] He also enquired whether she had heard from her father, the colonel, currently serving in South Africa with the British army.

In the same month of October, Emma heard that her widowed sister Helen, now resident at Lee-on-Solent in Hampshire, had fallen ill. Emma left Max Gate immediately to go and care for her. Two months later, however, Helen died at the age of 63.

$$\approx$$

In April 1901 Hardy is to be seen mourning the death of a favourite cat which was 'mutilated by the mail train', even though the railway line was quarter of a mile distant from the house. This was Hardy's own cat – the first he had ever had – and he blamed himself for allowing it to stay out at night.[23]

A literary society called the Whitefriars Club did Hardy the honour of visiting him at his home in May. His mother, who was now aged 88, got to hear of the visit and was taken by her daughters, Mary and Katharine, in her wheelchair to view the carriages as they conveyed the society's members to Max Gate. How proud she must have felt of her now famous son.[24]

In November Hardy remarked that the army had taken possession of part of his beloved Egdon Heath – a place which until now 'has lain untouched since man appeared on the earth'.[25]

## Poems of the Past and Present

Hardy's *Poems of the Past and Present* was published in November 1901 by Harper & Brothers of New York. The poems cover a variety of subjects: war, other writers and poets (in particular Shelley and Keats), flowers, birds, Rome, Switzerland, and there is one humorous poem entitled *The Ruined Maid*. Just as many of the happenings described in Hardy's novels had their root in his own experiences, so the same pattern emerges in his poems, where his main preoccupation is his fraught relationship with Emma. And because the couple's problems remain unresolved, the outpouring of plaintive poems never ceases. (This continued to be the case, even after Emma's death.)

A poem which sheds light on Hardy's tortured mental state is *How Great My Grief*:

How great my grief, my joys how few,
   Since first it was my fate to know thee!
   – Have the slow years not brought to view
How great my grief, my joys how few,
Nor memory shaped old times anew,
Nor loving-kindness helped to show thee
How great my grief, my joys how few,
   Since first it was my fate to know thee?

Here, Hardy is complaining that although he has displayed love and kindness towards his wife, he feels that this has not been appreciated. Nevertheless, he has decided to accept his fate, despite the fact that the passage of the 'slow years' has brought no amelioration of his grief.

Similarly, in *I Said to Love*, he writes on the subject of love as follows:

It is not now as in old days
When men adored thee and thy ways …

And continues:

I said to him,
'We now know more of thee than then;
We were but weak in judgement when,
   With hearts abrim,
We clamoured thee that thou would'st please
Inflict on us thine agonies!

Having implied that it had been a misjudgement on his part to marry Emma, Hardy goes on to refer to 'iron daggers of distress', but says, resignedly, 'We are too old in apathy' to fear any further threats from 'Love'. The inference is quite clear. Hardy once longed for love, but is now totally disillusioned with the hand that fate has dealt him.

In *To Lizbie Browne* he laments the fact that he once lost the subject of the poem as a lover:

When, Lizbie Browne,
You had just begun
To be endeared
By stealth to one,

You disappeared
My Lizbie Browne.

And he continues:

You were a wife
Ere I could show
Love, Lizbie Browne.

In other words, soon after his meeting with her, Lizbie had gone off and married somebody else. In real life, Lizbie Browne is alleged to be the beautiful, red-headed daughter of a gamekeeper, who was known to Hardy in his youth. As for the inference of the poem, it is obvious. Hardy, in retrospect, feels that it was she he should have married. Instead, he let her slip, when he should have 'coaxed and caught' her, 'ere you [she] passed'.

## Hardy: A 'Time-Torn Man'

The poem *A Broken Appointment*, from his *Poems of the Past and Present* collection, for once relates not to Emma, but to Florence Henniker. In it, he describes himself as a 'time-torn man'. This raises the question: what were the likely adverse effects on the mental and physical health of one such as Hardy, who endured years of marital disharmony and enforced sexual abstinence? In a paper entitled 'How Does Marriage Affect Physical and Psychological Health? A Survey of the Longitudinal Evidence', Chris M. Wilson and Andrew J. Oswald of the Institute for the Study of Labor in Bonn, Germany, reviewed approximately 100 research papers on the subject, written between 1981 and 2005.

In regard to the possible benefits of marriage, Wilson and Oswald noted the following findings:

Marriage is a source of emotional and instrumental support. Emotional help seems to reduce the incidence of depression and mental illness, and may provide an important buffer against stress. Marriage can also enhance feelings of attachment and belonging, which are thought to affect mental health.[26] Individuals who value the permanence and importance of marriage have a larger reduction in depression and suffer more from marriage dissolution.[27] Marital harmony is associated with much better sleep, less depression and fewer visits to the doctor.[28] The married have higher levels of emotional support.[29]

The authors also point to the large number of studies which show that marriage increases longevity, and 'the longer the duration of a marriage the greater the gain'.[30] Conversely:

> Marital break-up has a large depressive effect. Compared to those continually married, the continually separated/divorced show significantly lower levels of mental health. A transition from marriage to separation or widowhood increases depression and unhappiness.[31]

(Hardy's marriage had effectively 'broken up', and he lived an increasingly separate life from Emma, albeit under the same roof. Therefore, he falls into the latter category.)

In regard to sexual intercourse, the study showed that: 'Married people have much more sex than other groups. Sexual activity is strongly and monotonically correlated with happiness. So more sex may be one reason why marriage raises psychological well-being.'[32]

Wilson and Oswald summarised the vast volume of literature which they reviewed as follows:

> Marriage makes people far less likely to suffer psychological illness.
> Marriage makes people live much longer.
> Marriage makes people healthier and happier.
> Both men and women benefit, though some investigators have found that men gain more.
> These gains are not merely because married people engage in less risky activities.
> Marriage quality and prior beliefs can influence the size of the gains.[33]

The authors also point to the fact that human beings with good friendship networks (including friendship with their respective spouses) can repel the simple common cold.[34] This suggests that marriage has a positive effect on the ability of the immune system to function well.

Wilson and Oswald's study merely confirms the obvious benefits to well-being of a loving and caring relationship (and this would undoubtedly apply equally well whether within marriage or without), even though the physiological basis of this is not fully understood. What *is* known is that during orgasm, experienced during sexual intercourse, endorphins are released which create a feeling of euphoria, and also have an analgesic effect. (Endorphins are substances produced by the pituitary gland which are related to the opiate morphine.) It should be noted that endorphins are also released during strenuous or prolonged physical exercise, such as cycling. Hardy was a keen cyclist and this activity was therefore undoubtedly beneficial to his health and well-being, even if it in no way compensated him for enforced sexual abstinence.

Additionally, it is known that being in an unhappy relationship creates excessive stress, which, in turn, may lead to tiredness, tension headaches, increased susceptibility to infections, high blood pressure and peptic ulcers, as well as anxiety, tearfulness, irritability, insomnia, loss of appetite and lassitude. One way of obviating such stress would be to remove its cause, which for Hardy would have meant seeking a divorce from Emma and embarking on a new relationship. This, however, he felt unable to do, for reasons already discussed. Alternatively, it might have helped him to discuss his feelings with loved ones and friends, but as Emma did not welcome them into her home, this avenue was denied to him. As for consulting his doctor about his undoubted depression, there is no record that he ever went so far as to do this.

The fact that Hardy became more and more depressed during his marriage to Emma is reflected in his writings. Compare, for example, the happy scenes portrayed in *Under the Greenwood Tree* (written in 1871, three years prior to his marriage to Emma), with the harrowing and heart-rending scenes portrayed in *Jude the Obscure* (written in the seventeenth and eighteenth years of his married life). But was his physical health also affected adversely?

As his letters confirm, Hardy suffered continually with head colds and rheumatism, whether in London or in Dorset, and also with dyspepsia; though whether this was stress related cannot be said with certainty.

# 10

# Life Goes On

## *The Dynasts* Takes Shape

The reason why, at Max Gate, Hardy was never visited by his parents, siblings or other relatives, and only seldom by his friends, was evidently that Emma did not welcome them there. According to Hardy's acquaintance Sir Newman Flower, matters came to a head one day when Hardy, returning from a walk, discovered that a young relative – one of the very few who had managed to gain access to Max Gate and was staying there at Hardy's invitation – had been 'sent away' (by Emma) for no apparent reason. This, for Hardy, was the very last straw. He decided to spend his future home life in his study, and to this end he consulted a builder, with a view to having a stairway constructed which would lead directly to it from the garden. This would thus obviate the need for him to pass through the main part of the house. From now on: 'He would have all his meals in his room. He would live there.'[1]

On New Year's Eve 1901, Hardy made a profound statement in respect of how an individual should determine his own philosophy of life. '*Let every man make a philosophy for himself out of his own experience,*' was his advice. It was impossible, he admitted, for a person to avoid using the 'terms and phraseology' of earlier philosophers, but nonetheless, 'if he values his own mental life', then he should 'avoid adopting their theories'. Years of labour could be avoided by working out one's philosophy for oneself. Hardy's opinion, as far as he himself was concerned, was that it was best to adopt a pessimistic standpoint, for this was the only view of life in which one can never be disappointed. And, 'Having reckoned what to do in the worst possible circumstances, [then] when better arise, as they may, life becomes child's play'.[2]

In February 1902 Hardy lamented the fact that 'theological lumber' was still being allowed to discredit religion. If the Church were to replace 'the doctrines of the supernatural' by 'reverence & love for an ethical ideal', then the great majority of thinking people who hitherto had been 'excluded by the old teaching would be brought back into the fold, & our venerable old churches & cathedrals would become the centres of emotional life that they once were'.[3]

That April of 1902, Hardy wrote to Alderman Dr Elias Kerr, physician of Dorchester, to complain that visitors to the town were unable to find various streets and 'spots' on account of their names having been changed. Hardy put forward various suggestions as to how this matter could be rectified. They included the use of inscribed stone tablets to mark the former sites of The Old Theatre; the Gallows; the Romano-British burial ground; the Franciscan Friary and Dorchester Castle.[4]

In May, to celebrate the peace agreement signifying the end of the South African War, Hardy flew a flag (presumably the Union flag) in the garden of Max Gate.[5] Later that year he remarked on how 'motor-cars [were] rather a nuisance to humble roadsters like me, one never knowing whether the occupants are Hooligan-motorists or responsible drivers'.[6] (Hardy continued to rely on his bicycle and did not, as yet, possess a car.)

During the latter part of 1902, Hardy was working on Volume I of *The Dynasts*: a story which had been taking shape in his mind over a number of years. For this he moved location yet again, into a newly constructed study above a new kitchen. The extra space provided by the extension enabled Emma to commandeer the two attic rooms on the second floor, to which she withdrew for long periods, spending her time reading, sewing and painting.

At the beginning of 1903 Hardy remarked upon 'the decay of Parliamentary government' – a sentiment which might apply equally well today. The problem could be solved, he said, by 'electing a wise autocrat, & conceding to him unlimited sway [authority] for a fixed term'.[7] The following month he was advising caution in the restoration of an ancient building: in this case, the tower of Fordington church, which he described as a 'venerable monument' much admired by the famous architect Sir Gilbert Scott.[8] He also had an opinion on capital punishment, admitting that it was a deterrent, but questioning 'the moral right of a community to inflict that punishment'.[9] Meanwhile, Hardy was complaining of rheumatism, Emma was 'ailing', and both were suffering from lassitude.[10]

Emma, having gone to London with Hardy in June, was obliged to return to Dorset after she 'contracted a severe cough almost on the day of her arrival'. Hardy attributed this to the wet and cold weather. By July, because she had not recovered, he returned to Max Gate.[11]

Around this time Hardy was to voice his disapproval of vivisection, which, nevertheless, he felt was a small matter in comparison with 'the *general* cruelty of man to the "lower" animals'. Perhaps if, say, lions had won the upper hand instead of the human race, 'they wd [sic] have been less cruel by this time'.[12] Later, Hardy would say how he found it difficult, with his limited knowledge of the subject, to pronounce on which 'sport' was the most cruel. Those who derived pleasure from watching an animal struggling to 'escape the death-agony', which was deliberately inflicted on it by human beings, was to his mind 'one of the many convincing proofs that we have not yet emerged from barbarism'.[13]

In January 1904 the first volume of *The Dynasts* was published by Macmillan.

☙

In 1904 Hardy was introduced to a 25-year-old female schoolteacher, literary critic, published author of children's books, and long-standing admirer of his works. Her name was Florence Emily Dugdale, daughter of Edward Dugdale, headmaster of St Andrew's National School, Enfield, Middlesex, and his wife Emma Dugdale. One day, Florence would play a pivotal role in his life.

How this meeting came about is unclear, but as Florence Henniker was present at the time, it may be that the two Florences were friends. Not being in the best of health, Florence Dugdale was seeking an alternative and less arduous occupation to teaching. This Hardy was able to provide, by enlisting her support in helping him to research his books.

Hardy's mother Jemima died on 3 April 1904, which was Easter Sunday. She was buried at Stinsford in the same grave as her husband. Although 90 years of age, her memory and intellect had remained undimmed. 'It took me hours to be able to think & express what she had at the tip of her tongue,' said Hardy. The gap left by her departure was 'wide, & not to be filled'.[14] Mary, Katharine and Henry Hardy attended the funeral. Significantly, either from her own volition or on the instructions of her husband, Emma was absent.

The following month Hardy reported on the loss of his oldest friend in Dorchester, the historian, antiquarian and watercolour artist Henry Moule. His friendship with Moule, said Hardy, was a 'true friendship "which many waters cannot quench, nor the floods drown"'.[15]

Hardy's letter-writing continued unabated throughout the years. In July 1904 he was complaining to Alfred Pope, brewer and former Mayor of Dorchester, about odours emanating from the town's sewage system, which were so foul that he felt unable to invite friends to Max Gate[16] (though even if he had done so, it is debatable whether Emma would have allowed such visitors to venture beyond the threshold). In October he informed Edmund Gosse of the death of Emma's brother Walter, assistant manager of the general post office in Maida Vale, London, who had retired only six months previously. (Walter's wife, Charlotte, outlived him, dying in 1919.) With financial assistance from Hardy, Walter's son Gordon had trained to become an architect. Walter's daughter Lilian, however, had drifted from place to place, including Max Gate, where she spent prolonged periods of time.

In April 1905 Hardy steeled himself to make the long journey up to Aberdeen in Scotland, to receive from that city's university the honorary degree of Doctor of Laws. In London in May he attended a farewell banquet for the Lord Mayor, and visited the theatre to see plays by Ben Jonson and Bernard Shaw. In June he visited his old friend, the poet Swinburne.

A party of 200 members of the Institute of Journalists visited Hardy at Max Gate in September 1905, and were provided with tea served from a marquee 150ft long; the latter having been erected on the garden lawn especially for the purpose. It had been the members' own idea to visit Hardy, though he may not have shared their enthusiasm, having been the victim of no small amount of criticism from some of their number over the years.

In November, displaying his usual attention to detail, Hardy recorded the chronological order in which the trees were shedding their leaves that year: 'Chestnuts; Sycamores; Limes; Hornbeams; Elm; Birch; Beech.'[17]

February 1906 saw the publication of the second volume of *The Dynasts*. In London again that year, Hardy commented that he preferred 'late

Wagner', just as he also preferred 'late Turner'. As usual, time was spent at the British Museum Library verifying certain facts for the final volume (III) of *The Dynasts*.

Later that year, Hardy wrote to Captain G.L. Derriman, secretary of the Royal Society for the Prevention of Cruelty to Animals, stating that he feared that the rabbits, pigeons and other birds which featured in a conjuring performance at London's Alhambra Theatre, may possibly have been 'drugged or blinded to make them passive'.[18] Hardy was again ahead of his time in his concern for the animal kingdom.

In August 1906 Hardy and his brother, Henry, went on a cycling tour to visit the cathedrals of Lincoln, Ely and Canterbury; as well as the Cambridge colleges. Henry was then aged 55, whereas Hardy was eleven years his senior. This was no mean feat for a man of 66.

The following year, Emma went to London to join the suffragist procession. Hardy was himself in favour of women's suffrage, as he confirmed in a letter to the leader of its movement, Millicent Fawcett.[19] The couple went on to meet playwright George Bernard Shaw and his wife Charlotte, it is believed for the first time.[20]

In June 1906 they attended a garden party given by King Edward VII at Windsor Castle. Now Hardy had truly 'arrived' in society, whether he liked it or not. In November the Dorsetshire Regiment, then based in India, asked him to provide them with a marching tune – stipulating that it must have local affinities and be suitable for rendition with fifes and drums. He duly obliged with an old tune of his grandfather's called *The Dorchester Hornpipe*.

In March 1907 Hardy wrote to Florence Dugdale advising her, if she was 'not *quite* well', to refrain from carrying out searches (which she was doing on his behalf for *The Dynasts*) at the British Museum. He also suggested that she demand from her prospective publisher the sum of 21 guineas, rather than the £8 proposed, for a volume of children's stories which she was writing.[21] In April Hardy requested that 'Miss Dugdale' be permitted to be absent from school for a day, in order that she might join him in another search – this time at the South Kensington Museum.[22]

Hardy wrote an introductory letter to publisher Maurice Macmillan in July 1907, recommending Florence to the post of assistant in his firm, 'in the preparation of school books & supplementary readers'.[23] (Macmillan had previously published Hardy's *The Woodlanders* and *Wessex Tales*, and was currently engaged in publishing *The Dynasts*; the third and last volume of which appeared in February 1908.)

Copied from a photograph
M H.

1 Thomas Hardy Senior. Painting by Mary Hardy. Photo: Dorset County Museum.

2 Jemima Hardy. Painting by Mary Hardy. Photo: Dorset County Museum.

3  Hardy's birthplace. Photo: The National Trust.

4  Thomas Hardy aged 21. Photo: Dorset
County Museum.

5  Horace Moule. Photo: Dorset County
Museum.

*Above* 6 St Juliot, the Rectory. Photo: Sally and Chris Searle.

7 Church of St Juliot, Cornwall.

8 Emma Lavinia Hardy by an
unknown artist. Photo: Dorset
County Museum.

9 Lesnewth churchyard, Grave of Digory
Jose, in which his brother, Henry, is also
buried (though his details do not appear on
the tombstone). Photo: Valerie Gill, by kind
permission of the Revd Robert S. Thewsey.

14 Thomas Hardy in 1906, aged 66, by Griffin. Photo: Dorset County Museum.

15 Emma Hardy in later life. Photo: Dorset County Museum.

16 Claybury Asylum, Essex, *c.* 1895. Photo: Eric H. Pryor.

17 Warneford Asylum, Headington, Oxfordshire, 1901. Photo: Henry W. Taunt, courtesy of Images & Voices, Oxfordshire County Council.

18 Church of the Holy Trinity, Headington Quarry, and churchyard, where Richard Ireland Gifford is buried. Photo: Dr J.H. (Ian) Alexander.

19 Cornwall Lunatic Asylum, Bodmin, in the 1920s. Photo: Cornish Studies Library.

20 Cornwall Lunatic Asylum, Bodmin. Staff of the Carew block for private patients, early 1900s. Note the large bunches of keys, asylums were secure establishments. Photo: Bodmin Town Museum.

21 Parish church of St Clether, Cornwall. Photo: Vanda Inman.

22 St Clether, the Rectory. Photo: Vanda Inman.

23 St Clether, grave of William
Henry Serjeant. Photo: Vanda Inman.

24 St Clether, grave of William Henry Serjeant,
tombstone plinth. Photo: Vanda Inman.

25 St Clether parish church, the saint depicted in stained glass. Photo: Vanda Inman.

26 Florence Emily Hardy by R.G. Eves. Photo: Dorset County Museum.

27 Hardy and Florence at Max Gate. Photo: Dorset County Museum.

28  Sisters Gertrude and Norrie Bugler.

## The Dynasts: Time's Laughingstocks

At Max Gate, where Hardy spent a great deal of time alone in his study, the unresolved question of why his marriage had not worked travelled round and round in his head as he searched for an explanation. Now, in *The Dynasts: A Drama of the Napoleonic Wars, in Three Parts, Nineteen Acts, and Thirty Scenes,* and possibly again with his failed marriage in mind, he would address the question of whether supernatural forces have an influence on events taking place on earth.

*The Dynasts* is the longest dramatic composition in English literature. It is an historical narrative, written mainly in blank verse, but also in other metres and in prose, featuring France's Emperor Napoleon Bonaparte. It begins, in 1805, with Napoleon's threat to invade England; covers the Battle of Trafalgar; the war in the Spanish Peninsula; Napoleon's Russian Campaign, and finally, the Battle of Waterloo where the great French commander is defeated by the Duke of Wellington. Although *The Dynasts* was a play, said Hardy, it was 'intended simply for mental performance, rather than for production on the stage of a theatre'. There are many informative scenes: a debate in the House of Commons; Napoleon's coronation; Napoleon's divorce of his wife, Josephine, and his marriage to Marie Louise of Austria, and so forth. It features many characters: among them Lord Nelson and William Pitt. It may be argued that of even greater importance are the 'Spirits', which Hardy describes as 'supernatural spectators of the terrestrial action'. They include the 'Spirit of the Years', of the 'Pities', of 'Rumour', and the spirits 'Sinister' and 'Ironic'. The 'Shade of the Earth' and the 'Angels' provide the chorus.

In his Preface, Hardy describes *The Dynasts* as 'the Great Historical Calamity, or clash of Peoples, artificially brought about some hundred years ago'. No doubt Napoleon would have regarded the conclusion of the Napoleonic Wars as a 'calamity', though the victorious Duke of Wellington would have begged to differ. But Hardy had in mind a broader context, pertaining to the human race in general.

His 'Spirits' appear to reflect the various viewpoints of a 'normal' onlooker to what is happening on the Earth below, rather than having any religious connotation. The doctrines of the Spirits, however, 'are but tentative', and not intended to offer the reader a 'systematized philosophy' by which the mystery of 'this unintelligible world' might be explained.[24] Was it possible, from a study of Napoleon, to draw some general conclusions about life on Earth, and to shed light on the great unanswered questions of the 'Why' and the 'Wherefore'?

In *The Dynasts*, where Hardy postulates the existence of an 'Immanent (all-pervading, universal) Will', the words 'This Tale of Will, And life's impulsion by Incognizance' sum up the situation succinctly. The peoples of the Earth are being continually pushed hither and thither by some great force which he calls the 'Urging Immanence',[25] of which they are completely unaware; and hence, Hardy's comment that the Napoleonic Wars were brought about 'artificially'.

Despite his protestations to the contrary, Hardy has provided an explanation for how life on Earth progresses: that human beings, without their knowledge, are being manipulated by an external force. The corollary to this is that everything they experience is predetermined. What motivates this 'Will', what its values are, if any, and where it has its origins, is not explained, except to say that it 'reasonest not' and is both 'Loveless' and 'Hateless' at the same time.[26] The fact that it drove Napoleon to fight Wellington, together with the Prussians and the Russians, and vice-versa, suggests that it may even have a malicious, destructive component. *The Dynasts*, nevertheless, ends on a note of hope:

> ... the rages
> Of the ages
> Shall be cancelled.

And the Chorus sings out, 'deliverance' will be 'offered from the darts that were ...', so that finally, 'Consciousness the Will informing' will finally 'fashion all things fair'. In other words, the 'Will' will make sure that everything comes right in the end. (For Hardy, alleged to be an inveterate pessimist, this is a surprising conclusion for him to have come to.) He appears to be saying that until the universal 'Will' makes itself known to us, it is not possible for us to understand why things happen. Until then, human beings will continue to act, in his words, like 'puppets', like 'the mindless minions of the spell',[27] and will continue to become enmeshed in events not of their choosing, such as war.

⁂

In 1908 Hardy was as active as ever: receiving a visit from Lady St Helier; dining at the Royal Academy; attending a performance of some scenes from *The Dynasts* enacted by a Dorchester dramatic society; visiting Cambridge, and attending the Mansion House for a dinner commemorating the poet

John Milton. However, because Emma felt 'too weak to undertake house-keeping up there', the Hardys did not take lodgings in London that year, as was their usual practice.[28]

In September Hardy wrote at length about 'Marky', a favourite cat. In the process of making a bed for her forthcoming kittens, Marky had visited the bedroom of Jane, one of Max Gate's servants, and 'torn her Sunday hat in rents, so that she cannot wear it anymore'. The hat cost 4s 2d, said Hardy, who gave her 5s to buy another; whereupon, she was 'quite content'. When Marky duly gave birth to her kittens, Hardy stated that all but one were to be drowned the following morning. This may at first seem out of character for a professed animal lover such as himself. Nevertheless, it reflects the practicalities of country living.[29] Having been comforted by her feline companion, 'Daisy', until she got over the loss of her kittens, Marky recovered from her grief and excelled herself a month later by catching a leveret, which the Hardys cooked and ate.

In January 1909 Hardy admitted that while writing *The Dynasts*, he had experienced 'periodic frights, lest I should never live to finish the book'. In consequence, 'alas', he had 'rattled along too hurriedly [with the writing of it]'.[30] (This sentiment will ring a bell with any author over the age of about 65.) That year, Hardy was appointed governor of Dorchester Grammar School.

When his friend, the poet Algernon Swinburne, died, Hardy's rheumatism prevented him from attending the funeral, which took place on 15 April 1909. He deplored the attitude of the nation to Swinburne's death, describing it as 'ignoring and almost contemptuous'. That autumn he visited more cathedral cities: this time Chichester, York, Edinburgh and Durham.

In late April 1909 Hardy was to be found advising the Stinsford Church Restoration Committee. 'The only legitimate principle for guidance,' he said, was 'to limit all renewals to *repairs for preservation*, and never to indulge in alterations.' This was 'an interesting building, and one very easy to injure beyond remedy'. He gave detailed instructions to the committee, and included a sketch to illustrate how the replacement guttering should be applied. He could not help commenting, however, on how the erection, in about 1870, of the 'imitation Early English nave roof … in place of the good old sixteenth century waggon roof with bosses, which had become decayed', had irrevocably altered the relation of tower to nave. Not only that, but the 'Cholmondeley monument' (to Marcia Cholmondeley, a member of the Pitt family) had been destroyed to create a corbel.[31]

In May 1909 Hardy spoke of the good that he believed would come if women were given the vote. They would help abolish the 'slaughter-house inhumanities' of blood sports and the 'present blackguard treatment of animals generally'. Also, men would then feel free to knock down or rationalise 'all superstitious institutions' such as 'theologies, marriage, wealth-worship, labour-worship' and 'hypocritical optimism'.[32]

In a letter to Florence Henniker later that year, Hardy confessed to being 'not in the brightest of spirits [but] who can expect to be at my age, with no children to be interested in?'[33]

*Time's Laughingstocks*, a collection of poems by Hardy, some dating back to the mid-1860s, was published by Macmillan in December 1909. Titles include *The Fiddler*, *The Dead Quire* (in memory of those who used to sing and play in Stinsford church), and *Former Beauties* (remembering the 'young things … we loved in years agone'). But, as always with Hardy, it is the personal poems which hold the greatest fascination. In *To Carrey Clavel* (yet another of the numerous pseudonyms that he used for Emma), Hardy complains:

> You turn your back, you turn your back,
>> And never your face to me,
> Alone you take your homeward track,
>> And scorn my company.

*The Division*, meanwhile, speaks of 'our severance':

> … that thwart thing betwixt us twain,
> Which nothing cleaves or clears …

In *Bereft* he talks of 'my lone bed'. Whilst in *He Abjures Love* Hardy enquires:

> … after love what comes?
>> A scene that lours,
> A few sad vacant hours,
>> And then, the Curtain.

*The Dead Man Walking* begins:

They hail me as one living
    But don't they know
That I have died of late years,
    Untombed although?

These poems, which speak for themselves, are yet another terrible indict-
ment of Hardy's marriage.

# 11

# From Emma's Standpoint

## What Others Thought of Emma

The portrait painted of Emma has thus far relied largely on the testimony of her husband. But what of her own thoughts and feelings? How did she view him? Although Hardy destroyed Emma's manuscript entitled *What I Think of My Husband*, some of her letters have survived, together with her *Recollections* and a portion of her *Diaries*. So we may let her speak for herself in her own words.

Emma described the home in Plymouth where she was brought up as 'a most intellectual one and not only so but one of exquisite home-training and refinement – alas the difference the loss of these amenities and gentilities has made to me'.[1] She went on to describe her dancing lessons and the pretty dresses which she wore to parties, where 'the military and navy [were] usually present'.[2] She made her disdain for Hardy quite clear; for example, she told Edward Clodd that 'A man who had humble relations shouldn't live in the place where he was brought up'.[3] And subsequently, with his relatives in mind, she referred scathingly to 'the peasant class'.[4] (Here, it will be recalled that Hardy wrote his first novel, *The Poor Man and the Lady*, in the year 1867, whereas he first met Emma in 1870. Therefore, he was preoccupied with feelings of inadequacy in regard to his social status well before he first met her, and she merely reinforced these feelings in him.) In November 1894 she complained that Hardy's interest in the cause of women's suffrage was 'nil': 'He understands only the women he *invents* – the others not at all.'[5]

In a letter to Mary Hardy (currently headmistress of Bell Street Junior School for Girls in Dorchester), dated February 1896, Emma launched a diatribe of invective against her sister-in-law:

> I dare you, or anyone to spread evil reports of me – such as that I have been unkind to your brother, (which you actually said to my face,) or that I have 'errors' in my mind (which you have also said to me), and I hear that you repeat to others.
>
> Your brother has been outrageously unkind to me – which is *entirely your* fault: ever since I have been his wife you have done all you can to make division between us; also, you have set your family against me, though neither you nor they can truly say that I have ever been anything but just, considerate, & kind towards you all, notwithstanding frequent low insults.
>
> As you are in the habit of saying of people whom you dislike that they are 'mad' you should, & may well, fear, least (lest) the same be said of you ... it is a wicked, spiteful & most malicious habit of yours.
>
> You have ever been my causeless enemy – causeless, except that I stand in the way of your evil ambition to be on the same level with your brother by trampling upon me ... doubtless you are elated that you have spoiled my life as you love power of any kind, but you have spoiled your brother's & your own punishment must inevitably follow – for God's promises are true for ever.
>
> You are a witch-like creature and quite equal to any amount of evil-wishing & speaking – I can imagine you, & your mother & sister on your native heath raising a storm on a Walpurgis night [the eve of 1 May when witches convene and hold revels with the devil].[6]

This letter may have had a basis of truth, insofar as Mary may, in her exasperation at the situation which pertained at Max Gate, have been critical of Emma and expressed this criticism to her face. However, its extreme language, and the fact that it relates not only to Mary but to her sister Katharine and her mother Jemima – all thoroughly respectable people – is perhaps more a reflection of Emma's paranoid mental state than of the real situation on the ground. More will be said about this shortly.

Emma subsequently elaborated further, on the subject of witches:

> Well you know they always live on *Heaths*, or Moors or desolate plains or Mountains – but have no mediaval [sic] ways or any broom-sticks etc, but are *modern evil-wishers* as the name means ... [and] they can throw the odium of their

evil doings & wishings on the innocent. There are, as a matter of fact, many malicious defamers *here* in, ah even, in 'Casterbridge' [Hardy's name for Dorchester].[7]

Another of Emma's fears – a more rational one – was that the French would invade England and enforce the Catholic faith. For this reason, she always kept a suitcase filled with provisions to hand, so that should the necessity arise, she could take flight.[8]

By February 1897, Emma's comments about Hardy were becoming increasingly acidulated. Said she: 'One thing I abhor in Authors … is their blank materialism … I get irritated at their pride of intellect.'[9] In August 1899, in another thinly veiled criticism of her husband, she said: 'I can scarcely think that love proper, and enduring, is in the nature of men. There is ever a desire to give but little in return for our devotion, & affection.'

She spoke of her 'years of devotion' to Hardy, but warned: 'Interference from others is greatly to be feared – members of either family too often are the cause of estrangement.'[10]

In November 1902 Emma, in another reference to Hardy, declared:

I fear I am prejudiced against authors – living ones! – they too often wear out other's lives with their dyspeptic moanings if unsuccessful – and if they become eminent they throw their aider over their parapets to enemies below, & revenge themselves for any objections to this treatment by stabbings with their pen![11]

This comment by Emma leaves no doubt that she was aware Hardy was making, what she considered to be, disparaging allusions to her in his writings. Meanwhile, her criticisms of him continued unabated. In April 1910, for example, she stated:

I have my private opinions of men in general & of him in particular – grand brains – much 'power' – but too often, lacking in judgment of ordinary matters – opposed to *un*selfishness – as regards them*selves*! – utterly useless & dangerous as magistrates! [which Hardy was] & such offices – & to be put up with until a new order of the universe *arrives*, (IT WILL).[12]

As far as Christianity was concerned, it must have been a source of great regret to Emma, who had been brought up in a church-going family, and whose mother 'read the Bible with exceeding diligence', that her husband did not share her beliefs. Nevertheless, her faith was undimmed, for in

January 1911 she commented that 'an Unseen Power of great benevolence directs my ways; I have some philosophy and mysticism, and an ardent belief in Christianity and the life beyond this present one. Outward circumstances are of less importance if Christ is our highest ideal.'[13]

Emma donated money to various Christian charitable institutions, including the Salvation Army and the Evangelical Alliance. Also, it was her habit to have pamphlets printed, which she left in local shops or at the homes of people she visited. The purpose of these 'beautiful little booklets', as she described them (in her own, somewhat ungrammatical language), was to 'help to make the clear atmosphere of pure Protestantism in the land to revive us again – in the *truth* – as I believe it to be'.[14] As might be guessed, Emma was fervently anti-Catholic.

It would be easy to dismiss Hardy's diagnosis of Emma's condition as 'madness' simply as sour grapes on his part. She refused to have a sexual relationship with him; he would therefore revenge himself by denigrating her character. But Hardy was not the only person to realise that there was something fundamentally awry with his wife's make up. For example, Hardy's fellow author, Mabel Robinson, writing of Emma in the spring of 1891, said that her 'thoughts hopped off like a bird on a bough'.[15]

Christine Wood Homer of Athelhampton Hall, a friend of the Hardys, described how one day, when she (Christine) was a girl, Emma arrived at her house and asked if she might see her pet rabbits, guinea pigs and birds. Instead of looking at any of the animals, Emma 'spent the whole time watching the flies on the window panes' and expressing 'enthusiastic delight at the sweet way in which they washed their little faces and stroked their pretty wings'. When Christine was aged 16, Emma invited her to accompany her by train on a visit to Parkstone, to see a friend who had 'an aviary of foreign birds' in her garden. They arrived at the friend's house and viewed the birds together. Then Emma, ignoring Christine altogether, withdrew to the drawing room, where she and her friend read poetry to one another. When it was time to catch the train home, Emma travelled first class and left Christine to travel third class.

If a visitor arrived at Max Gate, said Christine, and Emma suspected that the person had 'no interest in or friendship for her, but had come only to see Mr Hardy and worship at his shrine', she would not inform her husband of the presence of that visitor, who would go away 'without seeing his hero'.

Emma 'would have liked to have received the admiration of the world for talents she believed she possessed'. But, according to Christine, the poems Emma wrote were 'indifferent', and as for her talents, they were 'not discernable to anybody else'. Christine states that Emma 'had the fixed idea that she was the superior of her husband in birth, education, talents, and manners. She could not, and never did, recognize his greatness.' (In other words, Christine believed Emma suffered from delusions in respect of her abilities. This possibility will be discussed shortly.)

In summary, Christine described Emma as 'a peculiar woman, and in many ways like a little child'; but whereas at first 'she had only been childish, with advancing age [she] became very queer and talked curiously'. Finally, said Christine, it had been 'a burdensome grief' to Hardy that Emma 'had not cared for any of his family'.[16]

It was not only friends, acquaintances and employees who remarked on Emma's bizarre behaviour, but also her own relatives. For example, 'Leonie' (Leonora Randolph) Gifford, Emma's second cousin, visited Emma in 1910 on an occasion when a visitor of some importance was expected for tea. The visitor failed to arrive, but despite this, Leonie was offered no tea herself.[17]

Lorna Heenan was the daughter of Dr Frederick B. Fisher, who (until he retired in 1910) was Hardy's medical adviser. Lorna states that Emma's 'mental condition progressively deteriorated, with a consequential increased strain on her husband. [Also, her] "heretical" outbursts in the local papers caused her husband great embarrassment.'[18]

As for Dr Fisher, he was of the opinion that Emma was 'the cause of much of the great man's pessimism and depression'.[19]

Evelyn Evans was the daughter of Mr Alfred H. Evans: by day a chemist, but by night a producer of Hardy's plays for the Dorchester Debating, Literary and Dramatic Society. Evelyn, who from an early age had been taught to 'reverence' Hardy, described the 'mauve, satin ribbons' that used to wave from Emma Hardy's bonnet as she bicycled around the town. 'She was considered very odd by the townspeople [of Dorchester],' said Evelyn, who would 'touch their foreheads significantly as she went by, free-wheeling ... with her feet off the pedals'.[20] According to Evelyn, during Emma's latter years:

> her delusions of grandeur grew more marked. Never forgetting [that] she was an archdeacon's niece who had married beneath her [a reference to Emma's uncle, the Revd Edwin Hamilton Gifford, Archdeacon of London, who had

conducted her marriage ceremony], she was heard to say in front of guests, 'Try to remember, Thomas Hardy, that you married a lady.' She persuaded embarrassed editors to publish her worthless poems, and intimated that she was the guiding spirit of all Hardy's work.[21]

Edward Clodd described the 'absurd' way in which Emma dressed as reminiscent of some nymph in a picture by Botticelli. (Clodd's assertion is amply borne out by contemporary photographs taken of Emma.)

Florence Dugdale described witnessing a heated quarrel which occurred between Hardy and Emma one Christmas Day. Hardy wished to take Florence with him to Bockhampton to visit Mary and Katharine. Emma resisted the idea on the grounds that Hardy's sisters would poison Florence's mind against her.[22]

Sir Newman Flower declared that Emma became 'eccentric', and 'would leave an open copy of the Bible [permanently] on the dressing-tables of the guests' bedrooms', even though the page might be 'thick with dust before the next visitors arrived'.[23] In her behaviour, she exhibited 'a mild form of religious mania'.

The writer A.C. Benson and Edmund Gosse visited Max Gate together in September 1912. Benson, who had not met Emma before, described her as:

> A small, pretty, rather mincing elderly lady with hair curiously puffed & padded [and] rather fantastically dressed. It was hard to talk to Mrs H. who rambled along in a very inconsequential way, with a bird-like sort of wit, looking sideways & treating my remarks as amiable interruptions.

As Emma showed him, 'in a curious peering way', the drawing room at Max Gate, she talked 'in a hurried voice, as if she was thinking aloud and not regarding me at all'. In the garden, Emma became obsessed with pinching the pods of the plant *noli-me-tangere* (yellow balsam) in order to make them eject their seeds. 'Mrs Hardy got entirely absorbed in this & went on doing it with little jumps and elfin shrieks of pleasure.'

The visit to Max Gate, said Benson, left him with:

> a melancholy impression. It gave me a sense of something intolerable the thought of his [Hardy's] having to live day & night with the absurd, inconsequent, huffy, rambling old lady. They don't get on together at all. The marriage was thought a misalliance for her, when he was poor & undistinguished, and she continues to resent it.

As for Hardy, said Benson: 'He is not agreeable to her either, but his patience must be incredibly tried. She is so queer, & yet has to be treated as rational, while she is full, I imagine, of suspicions & jealousies & affronts which must be half insane.'[24]

In July 1913 Edward Clodd visited Max Gate, where he was introduced to Hardy's brother Henry, whom he described as 'a well-set, sensible man', and his two sisters, whom he described as 'ladylike, refined' and 'well-informed'. However, Clodd remonstrated with Hardy for allowing his 'half-mad wife' to deny his family – 'these well-bred folk as well as his mother [Jemima]' – access to Max Gate.[25]

On 25 November 1914 Emma's cousin, Kate Gifford, wrote to Hardy thus: 'Emma and I met at my Brother's at Blackheath not long before her death & I was so glad to see her again. It must have been very sad for you that her mind became so unbalanced latterly.'[26]

The conclusion is, therefore, that Emma had a significant mental health problem, which, as members of her own family acknowledged, became progressively worse as the years wore on.

## Emma's Mental State: An Explanation

In addition to the sexual problems experienced by Hardy during his marriage to Emma, there are signs that in other respects all was not well. This was apparent to Hardy himself, for time and again in his writings he alludes to the fact that Emma is, in his view, suffering from some kind of mental disorder. For example, on 17 December 1912, when he wrote to Florence Henniker, he referred to 'certain painful delusions' which Emma 'suffered from at times'.[27]

In April 1913, after Hardy had visited him at his home in Aldeburgh, Suffolk, Edward Clodd recorded in his diary: 'Met Hardy … [He] talked about his wife. She had illusions that she was being followed by some man, that people were conspiring against her: all showing the mad strain in the family blood.'[28] In other words, Hardy was aware that not only Emma, but some other members of her 'Gifford' family, had mental health problems. The full extent of these problems will be revealed shortly.

Clodd also recorded that he had been told by Hardy of 'the illusion nursed [by Emma] that she had written his novels because he got her to copy his MSS [manuscripts]'.[29] In both of these instances, Hardy was describing not 'illusions' (misapprehensions of the true state of affairs), but 'delusions' (false beliefs) in his wife Emma.

In March 1914 (by which time Emma had been dead for sixteen months), Hardy wrote again to Florence Henniker to tell her that Emma's mind 'during her latter years ... [was] a little unhinged at times, & she showed unreasonable dislikes'.[30] In November he sent Emma's cousin, Kate Gifford, a copy of his newly published collection of poems, *Satires of Circumstance: Lyrics and Reveries*, 'not because I think you will care for a large number of them, but because it contains some that relate to Emma'. And he went on to tell Kate:

> In later years an unfortunate mental aberration for which she was not responsible altered her much, & made her cold in her correspondence with friends & relatives, but this was contrary to her real nature, & I myself quite disregard it in thinking of her.[31]

Hardy absolved Emma of all blame in regard to her condition. Given the fact that Hardy and others had made such observations about Emma, the question is, how can her condition be explained (given the fact that she did not seek medical help and therefore no professional diagnosis was made at the time)?

Modern-day psychiatrists divide such so-called 'personality disorders' into various categories:

**Paranoid** – Commencing by early adulthood, sufferers exhibit 'a pervasive distrust and suspiciousness of others such that their motives are interpreted as malevolent.'[32]

**Histrionic** – Commencing by early adulthood, sufferers exhibit 'a pervasive pattern of excessive emotionality and attention seeking'. They are 'uncomfortable in situations in which he or she is not the center of attention'.[33]

**Narcissistic** (otherwise known as 'egomania') – Commencing by early adulthood, sufferers exhibit 'a pervasive pattern of grandiosity, need for admiration, and lack of empathy'. They have 'a grandiose sense of self-importance', are 'preoccupied with fantasies of unlimited success, power, brilliance, beauty, or ideal love', believe themselves to be 'special and unique' and that they 'can only be understood by, or should associate with, other special or high-status people'. He or she requires 'excessive admiration; lacks empathy; is unwilling to recognize or identify with the feelings and needs of others; is often envious of others or believes that others are envious of him or her'. Such a person may display 'arrogant, haughty behaviour or attitudes'.[34]

**Schizoid** – Commencing by early adulthood, sufferers exhibit 'a pervasive pattern of detachment from social relationships and a restricted range of expression of emotions in interpersonal settings'. He or she 'neither desires nor enjoys close relationships, including being part of a family; almost always chooses solitary activities; has little, if any, interest in having sexual experiences with another person; takes pleasure in few, if any, activities; lacks close friends or confidants other than first-degree relatives'.[35]

**Schizotypal** – Commencing by early adulthood, sufferers exhibit 'a pervasive pattern of social and interpersonal deficits marked by acute discomfort with, and reduced capacity for, close relationships'. He or she may exhibit 'ideas of reference [a mistaken belief that external events, such as newspaper articles, voices heard on the radio, people talking, etc., relate specifically to themselves]; odd beliefs or magical thinking that influence behavior … (e.g. superstitiousness, belief in clairvoyance, telepathy, or "sixth sense"); odd thinking and speech; suspiciousness or paranoid ideation; inappropriate or constricted affect [mood]; behavior or appearance that is odd, eccentric, or peculiar'.[36]

The epithets 'childlike' and 'trusting' were often applied to Emma by those close to her and this may reflect the fact that she was emotionally immature. Such people will 'spend a large proportion of their lives creating situations in which they become the centre of attention' (as in Histrionic Personality Disorder – see above) in order, it is believed, to counter their own 'low levels of self-esteem and self-confidence'. However, 'the relief is temporary' because 'the underlying problem remains unaddressed'.[37]

Clearly, Emma's symptoms are not confined to just one of the above sub-groups, which is by no means unusual. After all, human beings are infinite in their variety, and such categorisation was originally created perhaps more for the benefit of the doctor than for the patient.

But what of Emma's delusions – a delusion being a false, personal belief which cannot be altered by reasoned argument? An individual may experience one or more of the following types of delusion, which are recognised by modern-day psychiatrists:

**Grandiose** – 'The central theme of the delusion is the conviction of having some great (but unrecognized) talent or insight or having made some important discovery. Grandiose delusions may have a religious content.'

**Persecutory** – The person believes that 'he or she is being conspired against, cheated, spied on, followed, poisoned or drugged, maliciously maligned, harassed, or obstructed in the pursuit of long-term goals'.

**Erotomanic** – A person believes that another person is in love with him or her. 'The delusion often concerns idealized romantic love and spiritual union rather than sexual attraction. The person about whom this conviction is held is usually of higher status.'[38]

Emma evidently experienced both grandiose and persecutory delusions. As to whether she experienced erotomanic delusions, more will be said about this shortly.

Finally, because there is evidence that many, if not all, of the above types of personality disorder and delusion have a familial basis, it is pertinent to enquire as to whether any of Emma's relatives also exhibited signs of these conditions.

# 12

# The Troubled Lives of the Giffords

Not one, but several members of Emma's 'Gifford' family had mental health problems. For example, on 25 July 1919 an 'Order for Reception of a Pauper Lunatic' was made by a London magistrate in respect of Emma's niece, Lilian Gifford, who was to be sent for admission to the London County Council's Claybury Asylum at Woodford Bridge, Essex. Lilian was described as aged 39, single, formerly a children's governess employed at 50 Gayton Road (Harrow, north-west London), but most recently a resident of the Holborn Union Institution (or workhouse). The likelihood is, therefore, that Lilian's mental illness caused her to lose her job. Whereupon, left with no means of support, she was admitted to the workhouse from where she was transferred to Claybury.

Dr E. Claude Taylor, who examined Lilian, described her symptoms, which had become more acute during the last two to three months, as follows:

> Patient said she had been very worried lately, chiefly because of a gang of thieves she believed to be about, and against whom she had barred her doors, but she saw them about and could hear their voices which said they were using a microphone and were going to gas her; she showed me her leg which she said showed signs of dropsy (it did not) and said she would rather die than go through such an illness.[1]

This record, made by Dr Taylor, indicates that Lilian was experiencing a combination of visual and auditory hallucinations, and persecutory delusions (paranoia).

Claybury was a vast complex of buildings set in 269 acres of land; a state-of-the-art asylum, designed by architect George T. Hine of Nottingham, it opened in May 1893. At the time of Lilian's admission, it housed in excess of 2,400 patients and contained a department dedicated to research into mental illnesses. Staff included a medical superintendent, several assistant medical officers, a matron, and both male and female medical nursing attendants. Claybury's first medical superintendent, Dr Robert Jones (later Sir Robert Armstrong Jones), was a great advocate of the benefits of hydrotherapy, and from 1910 a Turkish bath was available for the use of the patients.[2] (By the time of Lilian's admission, Jones had been succeeded by Dr Guy Foster Barham.)

Private patients from London were charged 30s per week, and those from elsewhere £2 per week. Lilian, however, was admitted as a 'pauper lunatic'[3] because the money required for her maintenance came in whole or in part from public funds.[4]

Those who were able were expected to contribute to their upkeep by working either on the asylum's farm and in the gardens, or in the workshops; the female patients worked mainly in the laundry or needle room, or on the wards. Apart from this 'occupational therapy', the importance of recreational and diversional activities were 'fully recognized [and] dances, concerts, magic-lantern shows, country walks and outings formed part of everyday life'.[5]

The patients had their own library and newspapers were provided. As far as was possible, a homely atmosphere prevailed. Each ward was provided with its own birdcage, complete with canary, and pictures hung on the walls. Lilian, however, was far from happy to be a patient in such an institution, as will shortly be seen. An accompanying document to the 'Order for Reception' indicates that she was probably discharged from Claybury on 16 January 1920.

As for other members of the Gifford family, Emma's brother, William Davie Gifford, who according to Emma was proficient at music, 'emigrated after leading an irregular life'.[6] Emma's uncle, Philip Henry Gifford, died at the age of 20 'after a steep decline'.[7] 'Family papers' elaborated on this 'vague non-medical phrase by adding the words *non compos mentis* [not in right mind]'.[8] This does not necessarily mean that Philip was mentally ill, though the possibility cannot be ruled out. Emma's second cousin, Leonie Gifford, in a letter to Hardy dated 28 October 1913, stated that her father, Charles Edwin Gifford, then aged 70, was suffering from 'a kind of nervous breakdown' and was 'very wretched'.[9] And as for Leonie herself, she was reported to have had 'a series of nervous breakdowns' from her forties onwards.[10]

The most well documented case is that of Emma's eldest brother, Richard Ireland Gifford. On 31 January 1888 Richard, then aged 53, single, and a civil engineer by profession, was examined by two surgeons, one of whom, William Joseph Square FRCS, stated as follows:

> His aspect is sullen but excited. Says he has got himself into a deplorable, miserable state, that he must be destroyed, that he can live no longer, that his clothes are rotting about him, that he has not had his clothes off or washed himself for many weeks, that he has not been out of doors since late summer, that he can not meet people, and does not deny that he has attempted to destroy himself.

Said the other surgeon, J.H. Square May MRCS:

> He stated to me that he could not go on; he was in such a filthy state, both inside and out, & that he must destroy himself, that he had tried to knock his brains out against the wall. He states that he is covered with vermin; this & his other statements are not the case.

Richard was suffering from delusions. Richard's sister, Helen, confirmed to Square that the former had attempted to strangle himself with a rope, and had looked for a knife with which 'to destroy himself'.

The following day, 1 February 1888, Richard was admitted as a private patient to Cornwall County Asylum, Bodmin. He was sent there by his father, John Attersoll Gifford, who the previous day had signed the 'Reception Order', in which he had stated that Richard was a 'person of unsound mind' who was suffering from 'melancholia' because of a 'disappointment in marriage' (meaning in his hopes of marriage, for Richard never married). Richard also had a 'strong suicidal tendency', his symptoms having been present for 'about three weeks'.

Nine months later, on 5 November 1888, Richard was transferred, 'uncured', to Bethlem Royal Hospital, London, where it was again noted that he was 'melancholic' and also 'suspicious':

> He is restless and much confused. Says his clothes are not his own, and believes he is ruined. During examination of his chest, he appeared suspicious of harm being done to him. He is generally [to be seen] walking up and down the gallery by himself, muttering a few unintelligible words. Seems in dread of something. Says he is only a boy of 25. Bites his nails and behaves like one.

On 6 February 1889 Richard was discharged, again 'uncured'. His stay at home was, however, to be a short one, for on 15 March he was admitted to the Warneford Asylum, Headington, Oxford, where the records state as follows:

> Patient was articled as a civil engineer but showed little aptitude, and his life has been dull and aimless, spent at home and without occupation. The first definite symptoms of insanity appeared in January 1888 and were attributed to some foolish love affair. He became violent and threatened to cut his throat.
>
> Confused and emotionally depressed. Is not sure where he came from today. Speaks in a low and indistinct voice. Movements sluggish. Dress untidy. Paranoid. Converses with attendants and other patients in rational and playful manner. But to the medical officers he is obstinately silent and watches them during the visits in a furtive and suspicious way.
>
> Whether Suicidal. Yes (attempts/threats by various means prior to admission).

It was also noted that Richard 'plays on the piano occasionally and with considerable skill'.[11]

The Warneford Lunatic Asylum, 'for the accommodation of lunatics selected from the higher classes of society', was originally founded in 1826 as the Radcliffe Asylum, but renamed in 1843 after its greatest benefactor, the Revd Samuel Wilson Warneford (1763–1855).[12] The asylum was run on humane lines, the patients (the preferred term to 'inmates', even from the early nineteenth century) being provided with books, magazines, card games and a pianoforte. In summer, they played croquet or shuttlecock and battledore on the lawn, and had supervised holidays in rented accommodation on the Hampshire coast at Southsea, and at Shanklin on the Isle of Wight. Male and female patients were strictly segregated, even when they attended chapel.

Relatives were not keen to advertise the fact that a member of their family was a 'lunatic'. However, had anyone cared to consult the censuses (taken on the first year of each new decade), they would have found their names there. For example, on the 1891 census Richard's details appear as follows: 'RI Gifford, Patient, single, civil engineer, born: Clifton, Bristol, Gloucestershire, Lunatic.'[13]

Richard's condition did not improve, as indicated by the asylum's records:

> Dec 1st 1898. Mental state childish. Most of the time is occupied with his great religious poem which requires a considerable amount of writing.

Amuses himself by playing the piano. [It was also noted that the poem was 'of interminable length on a Biblical subject'.]

Mar 1st 1899. Always busy with his poems … Some short ones are to be published first to get his name up, previous to the launching of his chef-d'oeuvre, the religious poem.

Dec 1st 1899. Still believes strongly in his poetic talent and is usually absorbed in his pursuit of the muse. He has an inordinate conceit both as to his looks and general attainments. He has a tremendous appetite.

Mar 1st 1900. At present engaged on a poem describing the Battle of Waterloo … Has great faith in the success which will attend the publication of his various works and is arranging for his discharge in order to attend to the details of publication. Enormous appetite and conceit of his personal appearance. [It was also noted that Richard was over 14 stone in weight and unwilling to participate in any activity such as gardening.]

Feb 26th 1901. Mind seems full of delusions e.g. that no one dies a natural death, that they are all strangled, that his food is filth and that his body is filth. That he has set the place on fire.

One cannot help but notice the similarity between Richard's symptoms – those of a deluded person, childlike in nature, paranoid, and with a tendency to talk to himself – and those demonstrated by his sister, Emma. And was it a coincidence that Richard chose the Battle of Waterloo as the subject for the epic poem which he commenced in the year 1900? Had Richard heard, through one of the Gifford relations, that Hardy was currently working on his epic Napoleonic drama, *The Dynasts* (which he had 'outlined and commenced the composition' of three years earlier in 1897), and if so, was Richard deluded enough to believe that he could compete with his famous brother-in-law, and even outdo him?[14]

After fifteen years spent at the Warneford Asylum, Richard died there on 5 November 1904, aged 69; the cause of death being given as 'Chronic Bright's disease' (or 'glomerulonephritis' – inflammation of the kidneys).[15] The symptoms of chronic glomerulonephritis, in its latter stages, are fatigue, headache, generalised itching, drowsiness, confusion, delirium and seizures. There is no way, therefore, that this disease could have accounted for Richard's symptoms of mental illness, as described above.

In death, as in life, the existence of 'lunatics' was not acknowledged, and Richard was no exception. As with his fellow patients, his body was buried in the cemetery of Holy Trinity church, Headington Quarry: the parish in which the Warneford Asylum was situated. Some tombstones of former

Warneford patients survive from this period, but not Richard's. It is possible that a wooden cross, which has since decayed, originally marked the place of his burial.[16]

~

It is sobering to reflect that, but for her marriage to Hardy, Emma might well, like her brother Richard, have spent her latter years in a mental asylum such as Warneford.

From the above, it is clear that mental health problems were present not only in first-degree relatives of Emma, but in more distant relatives of hers. Yet not all members of the Gifford family suffered from mental illness. In fact, many led perfectly normal lives and distinguished themselves in their careers. For example, Emma's grandfather, Richard Ireland Gifford, was a schoolmaster; her brother, Walter Edwin Gifford, became an employee of London's Post Office Savings Bank; her uncle, Edwin Hamilton Gifford, became Archdeacon of London; another uncle, Charles Frederick Gifford, became a doctor of medicine; a cousin, William George Gifford, was a British army royal engineer, and another cousin, Charles Edwin Gifford, was paymaster-in-chief of the Royal Navy.

## The Troubled Life of John Attersoll Gifford

Emma's father, John Attersoll Gifford's, offensive and inaccurate description of Hardy as 'a low-born churl who has presumed to marry into my family', indicates that he too suffered from delusions (chiefly of grandeur, in respect of the Gifford family name). Was he ever admitted to an asylum? It can be revealed for the first time that the answer is yes.

On 18 July 1859, when Gifford was aged 51 and living at 9 Bedford Terrace, Plymouth, he was admitted as a 'second class' private patient (at a fee of 16s per week) to the Cornwall Lunatic Asylum at Bodmin, as 'a person of unsound mind'. The reason for his admission was stated as 'Intemperance', for a period of three months, but it was also recorded that his first 'attack' of this type had occurred when he was aged 27, and that he had previously been seen and treated by Dr Duck of Bristol (1834), and by Dr Richard Langworthy, surgeon and proprietor of the Lunatic Asylum, Plympton House, Plympton, Devon (1844, 1846, 1847, 1853, 1857, 1858).

Dr Thomas Anthony Stewart, of the Dispensary, 19 Princess Square, Plymouth, who signed the medical certificate, noted of Gifford:

> Occasional great excitement and restlessness – uncontrollable desire for intoxicating drinks – which when indulged in leads him to commit acts of violence to others and [to display] great eccentricity of manner.
>
> Yesterday he rang violently at my door and the servant found him very noisy and in a state of great excitement, without hat, coat or vest – surrounded by a mob … Knowing the patient well, I am sure he would not be guilty of such conduct if of sound mind. He also threatened to kill two of his sons.

The other doctor who examined Gifford, Dr Charles Hingston of Plymouth, stated of his patient: 'I was informed by his Mother and Wife that he was extremely violent without any sufficient motive and that they were afraid of personal injury unless he were placed under restraint.'[17] (Although chains, fetters and the straitjacket were still used at this time to restrain violent patients, isolation in a 'padded cell' – one lined with coconut-matting – was increasingly becoming the treatment of choice.)[18]

The duration of Gifford's stay in the Cornwall Lunatic Asylum – which had its own farm, gardens and workshops, and which provided a wide range of periodicals for the benefit of its patients – is not known, but on 23 May of the following year, 1860, he was readmitted; the cause this time being given as 'excitement at his mother's death combined with drink'.

On this occasion, Dr Stewart reported as follows:

> Manner irritable and violent, conversation incoherent and natural disposition and habits totally perverted. Of these I can speak with the utmost confidence as Mr. G has been well known to me [for] many years and has frequently suffered from similar attacks of maniacal excitement requiring restraint.

And Dr John Nicholls Stevens, surgeon to the Parochial Infirmary, Princess Place, Plymouth, stated:

> Manner irritable, demeanour restless, frequently gives utterance to perverted ideas, has broken the windows of his home, injured the furniture, is very excitable and requires restraint.[19]

The medical records relating to these two admissions might lead to the conclusion that Gifford's violent and irrational behaviour was occasioned by excessive drinking. However, medical notes relating to a third admission to the Cornwall Lunatic Asylum, on 24 October 1871, reveal that his problems were of a more fundamental nature. (Four years earlier, in 1867, the 'Carew Building' for private patients, named after the Right Honourable Reginald Pole Carew and his son William Henry Pole Carew – leading lights in the establishment and management of the asylum – had been opened on the same site. From 1873 the asylum held a total of 760 patients, of whom 50 were private.)

Now aged 64, and residing with his wife at Kirland House, Bodmin,[20] it was noted that the 'pre-disposing' cause of Gifford's present 'attack' was 'intemperance', and that he had suffered 'five of six' similar such 'attacks' in the past.

This time, Gifford was examined first by Dr Bartholomew G. Derry of Bodmin, who noted as follows: 'Says he hears voices as of a man and woman disputing together – says he hears a voice speaking to him telling [him] he is the Lord Jesus Christ.' And Dr Thomas Q. Couch of Bodmin, who noted in Gifford: 'Great incoherency of speech; and great restlessness of manners. Says he cannot be mad, as he is only so in particular states of the wind! Has many delusions.'[21]

Finally, and most significant, is Gifford's answer to the following question, asked of him by the two doctors who examined him: 'Have any ... relatives of the Patient been the subject of Insanity, or other, and cerebral disease?' To which Gifford replied: 'Father.'

The conclusion is that Gifford suffered from auditory hallucinations and delusions, and that this, rather than drink, was the root of his problems. It may also be concluded that his father before him, Richard Ireland Gifford, experienced similar mental health problems. And it seems likely that it was on the advice – or possibly on the orders – of his doctor, that Gifford made the decision to relocate to Bodmin from Plymouth in 1860, because here he could be attended by the doctors and nurses of the town's Cornwall Lunatic Asylum, who were skilled in the care of the insane.

Insanity, as has been demonstrated, played havoc with the lives of at least four generations of the Gifford family. How much insight each sufferer had into his or her individual illness is not known. However, the thoughts of the 80-year-old John Attersoll Gifford in January 1888, as he signed the document committing his son, Richard Ireland Gifford, to the Cornwall Lunatic Asylum – where he himself had so often been incarcerated as a patient – may be imagined.

The conclusion is, therefore, that some members of the Gifford family were genetically predisposed to mental illness, and that Emma was no exception. And as for those Giffords mentioned above who experienced mental illness, there is no question that their disordered lives impinged greatly and deleteriously upon those closest to them – Thomas Hardy being a case in point. No wonder Hardy's acrimonious meeting with Emma's father, John Attersoll Gifford, in the summer of 1872 had come as such a shock to the young man.

One day, in the not too distant future, the genetic basis for what are regarded as mental disorders, such as paranoia and delusions, and the mechanism by which they are transmitted from one generation to another, will be elucidated in more detail. And this, in turn, may lead to a cure for these conditions.

# 13

# The Death of Emma:
# An Outpouring of Poetry

In March 1910 Hardy visited the grave of his friend, the poet Swinburne, on the Isle of Wight, and composed a poem entitled *A Singer Asleep* in his memory. In May, when he and Emma were in London as usual – staying in a rented flat – there came the announcement that King Edward VII had died.

Now aged 69, Hardy was as active as ever. Advising Lady Grove about her writing, he confessed modestly 'that I am no authority'. He had, he said, 'written heaps of ungrammatical sentences', and had learnt his grammar by 'general reasoning, rather than by rules'. To Sidney Trist, editor of the publication *Animals' Guardian*, he explained how difficult it was to extend 'the principle of equal justice to all the animal kingdom', when nature herself was 'absolutely indifferent to justice'.[1]

His name having appeared in the Birthday Honours List in June 1910, Hardy went to Marlborough House the following month to be invested with the Order of Merit by the new king, George V. When Emma returned to Max Gate without him, Hardy wrote to her saying how depressing it was to come home late in the evening to a 'dark, silent flat' which was 'full of the ghosts of all those who have visited us there'.[2] On the subject of suffrage, he held that a woman had as much right to vote as a man, but wondered 'if she may not do mischief with her vote'. What the nature of this mischief might be, he did not specify.[3]

In August Hardy was complaining to the superintendent of the Dorchester police about some boys whom the servants had caught stealing apples from the garden at Max Gate. He wished the superintendent to enquire into the matter, and 'at least caution the boys' – whose names were known to him. However, he did not wish them 'to be punished further than that' (which presumably would have meant the birch).[4]

That November, Hardy was honoured by being given the Freedom of Dorchester (his native county town). In December he described as 'such a loss' the death of 'Kitsey' the 'study cat', who was accustomed to sleeping 'on any clean sheets of paper' and 'to be much with me'.⁵ By this time, Florence Dugdale had become a permanent feature of the Hardy household.

The year 1911 saw Hardy energetically continuing with his programme of visits to all the English cathedrals. In April he was at Lichfield, Worcester and Hereford. In June, together with his brother, Henry, he was at Carlisle. This latter visit to the Lake District gave him the opportunity to see the grave of the poet Wordsworth at Grasmere church, and to take in Chester Cathedral on the return journey. In July, this time in company with his sister, Katharine, he visited Devon, where yet another cathedral was ticked off the list; that of Exeter. In November the Dorchester Debating and Dramatic Society staged performances of plays derived from his *Wessex* novels.

The sinking of the steamship *Titanic*, off the Grand Banks of Newfoundland in April 1912, occasioned Hardy to write a poem, *The Convergence of the Twain*, in aid of a fund for the victims. This season, instead of renting a flat in London, he and Emma stayed in a hotel.

On Hardy's 72nd birthday he was visited at Max Gate by the poets Henry Newbolt and W.B. Yeats, who had been asked by the Royal Society of Literature to present him with that society's Gold Medal in celebration of the occasion. Newbolt, in setting the scene, cannot disguise his discomfiture:

The dinner lives on in my memory as beyond all others unusual and anxious. Mr. and Mrs. Hardy faced one another the longer way of the table: Yeats and I sat rather too well spaced at the two sides: we could hold no private communication with each other ... Hardy, an exquisitely remote figure, with the air of a nervous stranger, asked me a hundred questions about my impressions of the architecture of Rome and Venice, from which cities I had just returned. Through this conversation I could hear and see Mrs. Hardy giving Yeats much curious information about two very fine cats, who sat to right and left of her plate on the table itself. In this situation Yeats looked like an Eastern Magician overpowered by a Northern Witch – and I too felt myself spellbound by the famous pair of Blue Eyes, which surpassed all that I have ever seen.

At last Hardy rose from his seat and looked toward his wife: she made no movement, and he walked to the door. She was still silent and unmoved: he invited her to leave us for a few minutes, for a ceremony which in accordance with his wish was to be performed without witnesses. She at once remonstrated, and Yeats and I begged that she should not be asked to leave us. But Hardy insisted and she made no further appeal but gathered up her cats and her train with perfect tranquillity and left the room.

From his summary, it is clear that Newbolt had no doubt that Emma was the subject of Hardy's novel *A Pair of Blue Eyes*. He also indicates that Hardy's wife was more concerned with her cats than with the presentation of the medal to Hardy. The implication is, therefore, that Hardy asked Emma to leave the room out of fear that she would disrupt the ceremony.[6]

In July 1912 Emma gave what was to be her last garden party, and in August she went on what would be her last visit to the theatre. On 22 November Emma felt unwell and was obliged to remain upstairs in her bedroom. On the 26th, the doctor called and pronounced that the illness was not of a serious nature. With this news, and with the assent of Emma, Hardy fulfilled a longstanding engagement that evening by attending the rehearsal of a play by local players in Dorchester. By the time he returned home at 11 p.m. Emma was asleep. The following morning, the maid informed Hardy that Emma had seemed brighter, but was now worse. Hardy immediately went to her and found her lying unconscious. By the time the doctor arrived, she was dead.

A few days before her death, Emma had been involved in a violent quarrel with Hardy, she having ventured into the study into which he had retreated. Hardy believed that this quarrel had contributed to her death and forever thereafter blamed himself.[7] Emma was buried in Stinsford churchyard on 30 November 1912; her tomb having been designed by Hardy himself. Rebekah Owen, Hardy's acquaintance from New York, who attended the funeral, commented on 'the exceeding pathos' of the event.[8]

Soon after Emma's funeral, Hardy discovered in Emma's room two 'book-length' manuscripts which she had written: one entitled *The Pleasures of Heaven and the Pains of Hell*, and the other, *What I Think of My Husband*. Having read them he tore out the pages, one by one, and burnt them in the fire.[9] Hardy also destroyed some 'useless old MSS, entries in notebooks, and marks [footnotes] in printed books'.[10]

That same year, 1912, Hardy's siblings, Henry, Katharine and Mary Hardy, left the family home at Higher Bockhampton (which now reverted to the Kingston Maurward Estate). They moved into a large house, Talbothays Lodge – designed by Hardy in 1893 and built by Henry – situated a mile or so to the east of Max Gate.

## Satires of Circumstance, Lyrics and Reveries

Hardy now embarked on poetry writing on a grand scale. In March 1913 he made a nostalgic visit to Cornwall, to St Juliot and other favourite places which he had known with Emma. Calling at Plymouth on the return journey, he arranged for a memorial tablet, designed by himself, to be placed in the church where she had played the organ as a young woman. Here in the city, Hardy was particularly anxious to keep in contact with Emma's 'Gifford' cousins. Subsequently, Professor (Charles) Henry Gifford (1913– 2003), Emma's third cousin, declared: 'There was something he wanted to put right, and her family must see that he had cared for her more deeply than they knew.'[11] June found him in Cambridge receiving the honorary degree of Doctor of Letters (Litt.D.). In July, in London, he met Prime Minister Herbert Asquith and his wife Margot.

On 10 February 1914, at St Andrew's church, Enfield, Hardy married the 35-year-old Florence Emily Dugdale; the only others in attendance, apart from the vicar and an official, were Florence's father and sister, and Hardy's brother, Henry. After the ceremony the couple did not have a honeymoon, but returned to Max Gate. Despite the fact of having remarried, Hardy admitted that 'the romance of S. Juliot abides none the less, & will if I live to be a hundred'. He derived consolation, however, from the fact that Florence had been 'a great friend of my late wife', and therefore there would be no 'rupture of continuity' in his life; something which he so disliked. His ghost, he said, would haunt St Juliot 'by reason of the experiences I was there blest with before my first marriage, long before the sadness came that was a result of the slight mental aberration which occasionally afflicted my wife's latter years.'[12]

Hardy again refrained from blaming Emma for her mental condition. (Nevertheless, either Hardy was in denial about Emma's condition or he prefered to cover up for it, because his writings make it quite obvious that he was aware of these 'aberrations' in Emma almost from the very start of his relationship with her.)

Hardy evidently regarded Florence as a kindred spirit, and hoped that 'the union of [their] two rather melancholy temperaments may result in cheerfulness'.[13] It transpired that flower-gardening was a hobby of hers, at which Hardy said she worked 'rather too hard'. Later, he was to describe her as a 'tender companion' who was 'quite satisfied with the quietude of life here [at Max Gate]'. Theirs was probably not a physical relationship, because as parlour-maid Ellen Titterington states, the couple 'occupied separate bedrooms with a common dressing-room between'.[14]

In the spring of 1914 Hardy and Florence dined at the Royal Academy and met with friends, before leaving for Cambridge to be entertained by various 'worthy Heads & Fellows' of its university. One of these people was Charles Moule (son of the late Revd Henry Moule, vicar of Fordington), former tutor of Corpus Christi whom Hardy had known since his youth.[15]

In early summer 1914 the couple motored down to the West Country; Hardy having progressed (if that is the correct word) from bicycle to car. In fact, the car, a 'Benz', was not owned by Hardy (who never learned to drive), but by Tilley's Garage in Dorchester, which also provided the chauffeur, Harold Voss.[16] While in Plymouth, Hardy took the opportunity to answer questions about the Gifford family vault; an attempt to clear up what he considered to be some loose ends from the past concerning his former wife's ancestors. In June 1914 he was again in London, at a dinner of the Royal Institute of British Architects with which he had kept in touch throughout the years.

At Max Gate Hardy enjoyed the company of 'Wessex', Florence's wire-haired terrier, whom he described as 'spoilt', but nonetheless was 'thriving' and 'fond of other dogs'. Yes, he said, it would be in order for her to bring her other dog, 'Milner', to Max Gate also.[17] Florence, however, worried in case Wessex's barking, and her playing of the pianola, disturbed Hardy in his writings. As ever, Emma was always in his thoughts and in a letter to Florence Henniker in July 1914, he confessed to feeling 'miserable, lest I had not treated her considerately in her latter life'.

Having returned from Stourhead in Wiltshire – where he and Florence had been guests of Sir Henry and Lady Hoare – Hardy wrote in his diary: 'August 4, 11 P.M. War declared with Germany.' Hardy had previously managed to convince himself of 'the gradual bettering of human nature'. This news, therefore, came as a tremendous shock, and he was astonished, disillusioned and depressed at the German invasion of Belgium, which had precipitated hostilities. Dorchester would soon be 'teeming with soldiers, mostly drunk', he said.[18]

In November 1914, *Satires of Circumstance, Lyrics and Reveries* was published by Macmillan. Included in this volume was *Channel Firing*, a tirade against those who make war in the name of Christ:

> All nations striving strong to make
> Red war yet redder. Mad as hatters
> They do no more for Christés sake
> Than you do who are helpless in such matters.

In *God's Funeral* Hardy indicates his absolute loss of faith. 'Mangled', he says, is 'the Monarch of our fashioning [God], Who quavered, sank; and now has ceased to be'. And yet for Hardy there is no joy to be found in the loss of God, only sadness; for 'who or what shall fill his place?' he asks. However, the words 'I … long had prized' what was now 'mourned for' implies that he did, at one time, have a faith.

Other poems in the *Satires of Circumstance* collection relate to Emma, who despite her death was forever in his thoughts. For example, *When I Set Out For Lyonnesse* – a poem of hope, wonder and expectation – recalls his first journey to St Juliot in 1870. In *The Torn Letter* he tells of how, despite everything, his longing for Emma never ceased:

> That ache for you, born long ago,
> Throbs on: I never could outgrow it.

Professor C. Henry Gifford once declared that as far as Hardy was concerned, all was 'delightful' in Emma, 'The free generous impulse, the daring [person] that had once clambered over the rocks and galloped down steep hills, and the zest for living – came back to possess his mind'.[19]

In *The Voice* Hardy imagines that the late Emma is calling to him, to say that she has reverted to that delightful creature which he had originally perceived her to be:

> Woman much missed, how you call to me, call to me,
> Saying that now you are not as you were
> When you had changed from the one who was all to me,
> But as at first, when our day was fair.

In *Had You Wept* he regrets her lack of emotional warmth:

> Had you wept; had you but neared me with a hazed uncertain ray,
> Dewy as the face of the dawn, in your large and luminous eye,
> Then would have come back all the joys the tidings had slain
>     that day,
> And a new beginning, a fresh fair heaven, have smoothed the
>     things awry.
> But you were less feebly human, and no passionate need for
>     clinging
> Possessed you soul to overthrow reserve when I came near;
> Ay, though you suffer as much as I from storms the hours are
>     bringing
> Upon your heart and mind, I never see you shed a tear.

And the poem ends: 'And hence our deep division, and our dark undying pain.'

In *The Going* he describes what a shock the suddenness of her death was to him:

> Why did you give no hint that night
> That quickly after the morrow's dawn,
> And calmly, as if indifferent quite,
> You would close your term here, up and be gone.

Referring to the separate lives which they had led in their latter years at Max Gate, he asks himself why this had been so:

> Why, then, latterly did we not speak,
> Did we not think of those days long dead,
> And ere your vanishing strive to seek
> That time's renewal? We might have said,
>     'In this bright spring weather
>     We'll visit together
> Those places that once we visited.'

It has to be said that Hardy would in no way have wished to cut himself off from Emma — in fact, quite the reverse — but in the circumstances he was obliged to make the preservation of his own sanity an essential part of the equation. He ends the poem:

… O you could not know
   That such swift fleeing
   No soul forseeing –
Not even I – would undo me so!

A host of other such poems, including *Rain on the Grave, Lament, A Dream or No, Beeny Cliff*, and *St Launce's Revisited*, all reveal the abject misery and remorse of the desolate Thomas Hardy. Today, these poems would be interpreted as a 'cry for help' on Hardy's part.

Finally, *The Wistful Lady* features 'A plaintive lady pale and passionless', and *The Re-Enactment* describes how 'in the [bed] chamber':

So came it that our fervours
   Did quite fail
Of future consummation –

Which gives yet another indication that Hardy's marriage to Emma was never physically consummated.

In December 1914 Hardy reported that Wessex had 'developed a tendency to fight other dogs, quite to our surprise. We fancy he will get a nip from a big dog who lives near here, which will make him less bumptious!'[20]

In 1915 Hardy decided not to have his customary 'season' in London, 'owing to the war & other circumstances'.[21] In September he learned that a relative of his, a Lieutenant Frank George, had been killed at Gallipoli, bringing the tragedy of war home to him in even sharper relief. The following month, in a letter to Charles Edwin Gifford, his late wife Emma's first cousin, Hardy appealed for help in trying to piece together Emma's full, genealogical family tree.

Hardy's elder sister, Mary, died on 24 November 1915; she died at their brother Henry's house at Talbothays. A school teacher by profession, her hobbies had been portrait painting and playing the organ at local churches, where she was much in demand. Hardy described her as 'almost my only companion in childhood'.[22] She was buried in Stinsford churchyard.

In June 1916 Hardy fulfilled his duty as grand juror at the Assizes, and attended rehearsals of scenes from *The Dynasts* by Dorchester's Hardy Players. In the same month he made a nostalgic visit to Sturminster Newton, where he had written *The Return of the Native*. That September saw Hardy and Florence at St Juliot, revisiting the sites of his youthful romance with his late wife Emma. Florence appears to have taken this in good part; at any rate disguising any feelings of jealousy or annoyance which she may have had. By autumn, according to Hardy, the number of German prisoners of war at Dorchester had risen to 5,000. He went to see them and also visited wounded English servicemen in the local hospital.

In February 1917 the commandant of the local prisoner-of-war camp sent some prisoners to Max Gate to root up some trees so that the kitchen garden could be enlarged. 'Nothing has made me feel more sad about the war than the sight of these amiable young Germans, in such a position through the machinations of some vile war-gang or other,' said Hardy.[23] In March Hardy could not contain his indignation at the 'Good-God' theory, which 'after some thousands of years of trial, [had] produced the present infamous and disgraceful state of Europe … that most Christian Continent!' As for the 'fifty meanings [which] attach to the word "God",' he said, the only reasonable one was the '*Cause of Things*, whatever that cause may be'. His own theory of God as both 'Goodless-and-Badless' (as portrayed by him in *The Dynasts*), might, he said, 'perhaps be given a trial with advantage'.[24]

In May 1917 Hardy confessed that (owing to poor eyesight, possibly occasioned by the presence of cataracts) he was 'compelled to write by machinery nowadays' – a reference to the typewriter.[25] In October Hardy and Florence visited Plymouth, doubtless with the object of exploring the late Emma's former haunts.

# 14

# Hidden Meanings

One of the most intriguing poems in Hardy's *Satires of Circumstance* collection is entitled *The Face at the Casement*, which begins:

If ever joy leave
An abiding sting of sorrow,
So befell it on the morrow
    Of that May eve …

The travelled sun dropped
To the north-west, low and lower,
The pony's trot grew slower,
    Until we stopped.

'This cosy house just by
I must call at for a minute,
A sick man lies within it
    Who soon will die.

'He wished – to marry me,
So I am bound, when I drive near him,
To inquire, if but to cheer him,
    How he may be.'

A message was sent in,
And wordlessly we waited,

Till some one came and stated
　　The bulletin.

And that the sufferer said,
For her call no words could thank her;
As his angel he must rank her
　　Till life's spark fled.

Slowly we drove away,
When I turned my head, although not
Called to: why I turned I know not
　　Even to this day:

And lo, there in my view
Pressed against an upper lattice
Was a white face, gazing at us
　　As we withdrew.

And well I did divine
It to be the man's there dying,
Who but lately had been sighing
　　For her pledged mine.

At this, the author of the poem (Hardy) puts his arm around his 'plighted love' (Emma) in order to make their position clear to the person at the window. In effect, he is saying: 'She is mine, and not yours.' However, for this action he afterwards confesses, in the poem, that he feels ashamed.

Who was this man who had wished to marry Emma but had fallen ill? A clue is given in the penultimate verse of the poem:

Long long years has he lain
In thy garth, O Sad Saint Cleather …

By 'garth' Hardy means 'churchyard', and 'Saint Cleather' is a reference to Cornwall's small village of St Clether (sic), which, as already mentioned, is situated only 7 miles from St Juliot.[1] Also, the 'May eve' must refer to 1871 (which was the year after Hardy had first met Emma), when he paid another visit to her at St Juliot.

In order to identify the person to whom Hardy is referring in this poem, it is necessary to peruse the burial register of the parish of St Clether for a period of, say, four years, from May 1871[2] (the assumption being that a dying man is unlikely to have survived for longer than this period). In doing this, if all the males older or younger than Emma by a period of ten years are eliminated, then this leaves only one possible candidate, namely William Henry Serjeant.[3]

William, a draper by trade, was the elder son of the Revd Henry Matthias Atwood Serjeant, curate of St Clether from 1869–79[4] (where his uncle, the Revd James Serjeant, had been curate before him, from 1840–53). The Revd Henry's wife was Betsy (*née* Clemens of St Keyne, Cornwall), whom he married in 1847. (St Clether's rector (1837–80), the Revd Henry Morshead, lived elsewhere.)

Born in 1849, William was at least eight years Emma's junior. An unmarried man, he died aged 23 at the vicarage, St Clether, on 20 January 1872, 'after a long and painful illness'.[5] He was buried in the churchyard six days later. Whereas his father, the Revd Henry, normally conducted St Clether's burial services, on this occasion the service was conducted by a colleague, the Revd John King Lethbridge. William's death certificate gives his occupation as 'draper' and the cause of his death as 'phthisis pulmonalis – 18 months'.[6] ('Phthisis' means 'wasting disease' – the most likely cause in this case being pulmonary tuberculosis.) The certificate also records that in attendance on William at his death was Hugh Pearse of Higher Bassils, aged 58, who had a 400-acre farm at North Petherwin, 5 miles to the north-east of St Clether. This suggests that when he died, William was visiting Pearse, either at his home or at his farm.[7]

How did Emma and William come to meet one another? The Revd Henry Serjeant of St Clether, and Emma's brother-in-law, the Revd Cadell Holder of St Juliot, were both Anglican clergymen whose parishes lay within the diocese of Truro, separated by only a handful of miles. Undoubtedly, therefore, soon after the Serjeants arrived at St Clether in November 1868,[8] the two men and their families, Emma included, would have become acquainted. It is likely that by the time Hardy first arrived on the scene in March 1870, Emma had known William for a year or even longer.[9] (In fact, Emma may have known the Serjeant family from the time when she and her parents were living at Kirland House, Bodmin. This is because Emma's friend, Captain Charles Eldon Serjeant of St Benet's Abbey, Lanivet, near Bodmin, and the Revd Henry M.A. Serjeant were first cousins.)[10]

It may, therefore, be assumed that the Serjeants' home – the seventeenth-century rectory at St Clether – was the place at which Emma asked Hardy to stop at sunset on that 'May eve'; this being situated, as already mentioned, a mere 7 miles from St Juliot, and well within range for Emma's pony and trap. It may also be assumed that it was from one of the casement windows of the rectory that the dying man's face could be seen looking out.

So why did Emma not marry William Serjeant, a draper from a respectable family, of whom her father could scarcely have disapproved? Was it because of William's serious chest complaint which (according to his death certificate) had commenced in July 1870, four months after Hardy's first meeting with her at St Juliot? Or was there another reason altogether?

From the poem, it is clear that Hardy was convinced that Emma was in love with William Serjeant and he with her, but was this really the case? In 1921 French psychiatrist Gaëtan de Clérambault published a paper entitled 'Les Psychoses Passionelles', in which he described a condition which now bears his name. De Clérambault's syndrome (or 'erotomania') is a type of delusion (which can co-exist with other delusions) in which a person believes that another person, and sometimes a number of other people, are in love with himself or herself. The disorder is almost entirely confined to single women, who believe that their 'supposed lover' is more in love with them than they are with him.[11] Also, this 'supposed lover' is 'usually inaccessible', perhaps because he is a person of exalted position.

This description fits with that of Emma and William; he being out of reach by virtue of the disparity in their ages, and also, more latterly, by virtue of his terminal illness. However, William could hardly claim to be an 'exalted' person. His paternal grandfather, John Serjeant, had been a lieutenant in the Royal Marines with a large family to support both from his first and his second marriages.[12] His father, the Revd Henry Serjeant, who as yet was only a curate,[13] had commenced his studies at Queens' College, Cambridge (to which he was admitted for the Michaelmas term, 1943), as a 'sizar' – a poor student who acted as a servant in return for free tuition;[14] his mother Betsy (*née* Blake) was the daughter of a farmer from St Keyne, near Liskeard.[15] But in order to gain entry to such a prestigious institution as Cambridge University, the Revd Henry must have had influential connections.

Whether Emma's delusion was of the 'de Clérambault' type or not is open to question. But what seems likely is that her love affair with William Serjeant was the product of her deluded mind rather than a reality. Additionally, it will not go unnoticed that the description of the deluded woman which de Clérambault describes is reminiscent of Sue Bridehead in

*Jude the Obscure* (in reality, Emma), who derives pleasure from the fact that her lover is more in love with her than she is with him.

## The Telegram

Hardy's poem *The Telegram* (also to be found in the *Satires of Circumstance, Lyrics and Reveries* collection), also relates to a sick man who was evidently loved by Emma:

'O he's suffering – maybe dying – and I not there to aid,
And smooth his bed and whisper to him! Can I nohow go?
Only the nurse's brief twelve words thus hurriedly conveyed,
    As by stealth, to let me know.

'He was the best and brightest! – candour shone upon his brow,
And I shall never meet again a soldier such as he,
And I loved him ere I knew it, and perhaps he's sinking now,
    Far, far removed from me!'

The yachts ride mute at anchor and the fulling moon is fair,
And the giddy folk are strutting up and down the smooth parade,
And in her wild distraction she seems not to be aware
    That she lives no more a maid.

But has vowed and wived herself to one who blessed the ground she trod
To and from his scene of ministry, and thought her history known
In its last particular to him – aye, almost as to God,
    And believed her quite his own.

So rapt her mind's far off regard she droops as in a swoon,
And a movement of aversion mars her recent spousal grace,
And in silence we two sit here in our waning honeymoon
    At this idle watering-place ...

What now I see before me is a long lane overhung
With lovelessness, and stretching from the present to the grave.
And would I were away from this, with friends I knew when young,
    Ere a woman held me slave.

One might assume that *The Telegram* relates to a real-life telegram, which apparently arrived when Hardy was on his 'waning honeymoon' with Emma at an 'idle watering-place' (Brighton, where he and Emma spent Sunday 20 September and Monday 21 September 1874, the couple having married on 17 September). One might also assume that Emma had left word with her former lover's nurse, that if the sick man's condition were to deteriorate further, then she wished to be kept informed, but 'by stealth' in order to conceal the matter from Hardy. And his condition did deteriorate, hence the arrival of the telegram. On learning that her former lover was now desperately ill, Emma is distraught, knowing that she cannot be 'there to aid' the man whom she loved and who is now dying.

It is surely too much of a coincidence to believe that Emma had such profoundly loving feelings for *two* dying men – the one referred to in *The Face at the Casement* and the other referred to in *The Telegram*. The conclusion must be that the two poems refer to one and the same person – William Henry Serjeant. And yet William died in January 1872, two years and eight months *prior* to Hardy's honeymoon. So how can the discrepancy in chronology be explained?

The answer is that the time frame alluded to in *The Telegram* (in contrast with that alluded to in *The Face at the Casement*) should not be taken too literally. What seems certain is that sometime shortly prior to William's death in January 1872, Emma received news (either by telegram or by some other means) that he was desperately ill, and was overcome with remorse. Hardy's honeymoon was such a disaster that he altered the sequence of events to make it appear that it was then that Emma heard the news of William's grave illness. In fact, it is possible that thoughts of Serjeant *were* in Emma's mind during her honeymoon, and that she *did* forget, temporarily, that she was married and 'no more a maid'. (Hardy may also have moved the telegram episode forward to coincide with his honeymoon in order to give the poem greater dramatic effect.)

Finally, how can the words 'a soldier such as he' from the poem be explained, when it is known for a fact that William was, by trade, a draper? The most likely explanation is that Hardy, in attempting to disguise the true identity of Serjeant, used a play on words: he exchanged the 'j' in his name for a 'g', and called him a soldier.

Hardy's honeymoon should, particularly after all the long years of waiting, have been a blissfully happy time, for, as the poem suggests, he believed that he knew everything about his new wife and was under the impression that her heart belonged entirely to him. Instead, he was in for a rude awakening, for instead of responding to his loving gestures, her 'spousal grace' is marred by her 'aversion' to him. (The word aversion has resonances with *Jude the Obscure* and Sue Bridehead's aversion to Phillotson.)

Perhaps the most chilling fact of all to be revealed in *The Telegram* is that Hardy, even at the very beginning of married life to Emma, had evidently resigned himself to the fact that his marriage would be a loveless one, and would continue to be so until the end of his days.

⌒

Surely it was no coincidence that in Hardy's novel *A Pair of Blue Eyes*, first published in late 1872 and early 1873, in which Elfride Swancourt's admirer, Stephen Smith, interrogates her about possible past lovers, the following passage occurs:

> Smith: 'And had you really never any sweetheart at all?'
> Elfride: 'None that was ever recognized by me as such.'
> Smith: 'But did nobody ever love you?'
> Elfride: 'Yes – a man did once; very much, he said.'

The person referred to by Elfride is Felix Jethway, whose mother was a widow but is now deceased.

Later in the novel, it is Henry Knight, her other suitor, who interrogates Elfride. 'Have you ever had a lover? I am almost sure you have not; but, have you?' he asks her. Eventually, she admits that she did once have a lover, to whom she was engaged to be married, 'but not formally' engaged. When Knight realises that Elfride has been less than frank with him, he declares: 'What a poor mortal I am to play second fiddle in everything and be deluded by fibs!'

Surely Hardy, through the characters of Smith and Knight, is voicing his own insecurities in regard to Emma ('Elfride'). He is aware that Emma is a rare beauty who was undoubtedly the talk of north Cornwall as she rode out on the moors on her pony, her beautiful auburn hair, in her words, 'floating on the wind'.[16] During his courting days, when he was away from her in London, he may have imagined her with other men. After all, he was aware of at least two of her previous amorous attachments: to Henry Jose, the farmer's son–cum–churchwarden, and of course to William Serjeant of St Clether.

The following scenario may be imagined. It is September 1874 and Hardy is on his honeymoon, when he expects, quite reasonably, that he and Emma will enjoy sexual intercourse. In fact, smitten as he is with her beauty, and particularly after so long a courtship, this is something which he longs for. However, it is not to be. Emma previously believed herself to be in love with William Henry Serjeant, and he with her, and this may possibly have been the case. On the other hand, it may have been a delusion – of the previously discussed 'erotomanic' type – which persisted in her mind even after William's death in January 1872. One can almost hear Emma's voice as she says to Hardy, whom she has just married, 'I loved William and he loved me. There will never be another in my life'; and when Hardy suggests that they make love, her reaction is 'No, for this would be to commit adultery'. Hardy, dazed and dejected by her reaction, expresses himself in the way that he knows best: he composes a poem, *The Telegram*. And because this delusion in regard to William Serjeant remains fixed in her mind – as delusions do – this explains why, all through her married life, she refuses to make love to her husband, or indeed to show him any demonstrable affection. It also explains why the couple's relationship was doomed, from the very beginning, to failure.

# 15

# Florence Emily Hardy

Florence Emily Hardy was, in many ways, the complete antithesis of Emma, and in consequence, the changes which she brought about to Hardy's life were truly remarkable. Unlike Emma, Florence was a modest person, as her letter of 24 October 1915 to Rebekah Owen illustrates. 'I am not tall enough for it or graceful enough,' she says, of a hat which she has purchased in London's Regent Street, and which she therefore offers to Rebekah. 'The brim is lined with shell pink which does not suit my sallow complexion.' And referring to some photographs of herself, which she had had taken, she tells Rebekah: 'After considering them long and earnestly I am bound to confess that I have no claims at all to anything approaching good looks.'[1]

While Emma was alive, Florence's relationship with her was outwardly cordial. For example, when she wrote to Emma in July 1910 from her home at Enfield, Middlesex, Florence said: 'I am truly grieved to learn how sadly you have been [with a cough]. I trust that you are recovering strength in the country air. I cannot find words to thank you sufficiently for all your goodness to me.'[2]

However, to Edward Clodd, in whom she confided, Florence, in November 1910, was able to voice her true feelings:

Mrs Hardy seems to be queerer than ever. She has just asked me whether I have noticed how extremely like *Crippen* Mr TH. [Hardy] is, in personal appearance. She added darkly, that she would not be surprised to find herself in the cellar one morning. All this in deadly seriousness.[3]

This was a reference by Emma to American physician Hawley Harvey Crippen, who had allegedly murdered his wife in the January of that year.

To Hardy's siblings, Florence was equally cordial. 'I wish I was back in Dorset. Hope I shall soon see you again,' she wrote on a postcard to Katharine Hardy on 20 October 1910.[4] To Mary Hardy, in August 1911, Florence sent a postcard from the seaside resort of Worthing, to say: 'I hope you're well. I have had a delightful fortnight here bathing once & sometimes twice a day. This card shows the house where I have been staying, & the road I cross daily in bathing dress!!'[5]

In December 1911 Florence informed Clodd that 'Mr T.H., his sister & I [but evidently not Emma] had a pleasant little trip last week to Bath, Gloucester & Bristol. He is very well, & seemed quite gay.'[6]

Florence, in her letters, reveals just how important pets were in Hardy's life. For example, she described to Clodd how Hardy had been 'in the depths of despair at the death of a pet cat', something which he described as 'an entirely gratuitous & unlooked for blow'. The cat would be buried in the pet cemetery at Max Gate, and Hardy '[is] finding a melancholy pleasure in writing an appropriate inscription for "Kitsey's" headstone,' said Florence.[7] True to form, Hardy commemorated Kitsey in a poem entitled *The Roman Gravemounds*, but when Florence read the line 'But my little white cat was my only friend!', from the penultimate verse of the poem, she was highly indignant. 'I tell him that it is *monstrous* ingratitude on his part,' she told Clodd.[8] Why did his pets mean so much to Hardy? Simply because, in the absence of a wife (at least, in any meaningful sense of the word) and children, they gave him the love and companionship which he craved. In other words, Hardy's cats and dogs were his surrogate family.

On 16 January 1913, the month after Emma's death, Florence, in a lengthy epistle to Clodd, wrote of Hardy as follows:

His life here is *lonely* beyond words, & he spends his evenings in reading & re-reading voluminous diaries that Mrs H. has kept from the time of their marriage. Nothing could be worse for him. He reads the comments upon himself – bitter denunciations, beginning about 1891 & continuing until within a day or two of her death – & I think he will end by *believing* them.

Despite this, however, Florence did all in her power to make Hardy's life bearable. Said she: 'I read aloud to him every evening after dinner, until eleven o'clock & take as much care of him as I possibly can.' And in a postscript to her letter to Clodd, she added: 'Of course nothing could be more lonely than the life he used to lead – long evenings spent alone in his study, insult & abuse his only enlivenment. It sounds cruel to write like that, & in atrocious taste, but truth is truth, after all.'⁹

On 30 January 1913 Florence, writing from Enfield, told Clodd that she had received a letter that day from Hardy, who had informed her that he was 'getting through E's papers', and speaking of her abuse of him, Hardy declared: 'It was, of course, sheer hallucination in her, poor thing, & not wilfulness.' Yet again, Hardy is protective towards Emma; but his opinion was certainly not shared by Florence. In fact, so exasperated did she become that she told Clodd:'I feel as if I can hardly keep back my true opinion much longer.'¹⁰

Florence was able to report to Clodd, on 7 March 1913, that Hardy 'has been extremely well in health, & quite cheerful'. However, she was clearly exasperated by the fact that Hardy was still in denial about his disastrous marriage to Emma. Said she: 'Today he goes to Cornwall, to St Juliot's Rectory, where he first met his "late, espousèd saint", forty-three years ago this very week.'¹¹ Florence, in fact, accompanied him on this visit.

Referring to Emma's 'diabolical diaries', which she had hoped had been destroyed, Florence told Clodd:

> … only the other night he [Hardy] produced one from his pocket & read me a passage – written about six weeks before her death – in which she [Emma] says that her father & *Mr Putman* were right in their estimate of TH's charac-ter: he is … [various oft-repeated adjectives of abuse], & '*utterly worthless*'. Of course Mr Putnam, if she means the publisher, could *never* have belittled Mr Hardy to her. It is in this sort of way that the diaries are so poisonous. [This is a reference to George Haven Putnam, American publisher and author, who visited Max Gate in June 1911.]¹²

Four days later, after she and Hardy had returned home to Max Gate, Florence described their visit to Cornwall: '[It] has been a very painful one to me, & I have said a dozen times I wish I had not come – What possessed me to do it!'¹³

Writing to Clodd again in April, Florence described how Hardy's doctor (Edward W. Mann) had declared: 'the state of things here, before Mrs Hardy's death – was quite alarming, so far as T.H. was concerned. [Mann] said that the lack of attention & general discomfort must have had a serious effect sooner or later. He told this to the sisters & brother [of Hardy].'¹⁴

On 21 August 1913 Florence was able to report to Clodd that Hardy was 'in good health, & *wonderfully cheerful*. He has had no fit of depression for quite a long time.'¹⁵

Florence was at the end of her tether by December, on account of the presence at Max Gate of Emma's niece, Lilian Gifford, whose manner she found to be obnoxious, and whose presence she found to be intolerable. Said she:

> We had an awful scene. I have only seen a similar one when Mrs Hardy was alive. My poor sister [Florence's younger sister Constance] could hardly keep from bursting into tears. This woman [Lilian] insulted her, in fact, behaved like a mad-woman. Of course, her [Lilian's] brother is an imbecile – one of them at least – and an uncle died in an asylum, and her grandfather was mad at times, so I ought to be profoundly sorry for her – but *I can't* be that.

The 'brother' to whom Florence refers in the above letter could only have been Emma's nephew, Warren Randolph Gifford (about whom little is known – Warren evidently preferred to use his middle name, Randolph; his youngest brother Randolph Gifford having died in infancy). The 'uncle' was Emma's brother, Richard Ireland Gifford, and the 'grandfather' was Emma's father, John Attersoll Gifford. (In this, some have accused Florence of exaggeration, or have even gone so far as to imply that she was not telling the truth.[16] In fact, Florence was a thoroughly reliable witness in this respect, as has already been demonstrated.) Continued Florence, dryly: 'Mr Hardy had more than 20 years of insults, and apparently enjoyed them very much – according to what he says now. I don't enjoy them [from Lilian] now.'[17]

On 1 January 1914 Florence told Clodd that she had given Hardy an ultimatum, that 'if the niece is to remain here *permanently*, as one of the family ... [I will] return to my own home, & *remain* there'.[18]

Florence wrote to Lady Hoare in July to say: 'I am so delighted & proud to know that you are fond of him [Hardy]. I think he really needs affection & tenderness more than anyone I know – life has dealt him some cruel blows. I am sure my husband's sisters would be *very very* delighted to see you.' In other words, Florence, unlike Hardy's late wife Emma, was more than willing to welcome her husband's relatives and friends to Max Gate.[19]

On the first day of December 1914, Florence confided to Rebekah Owen: 'You would hardly believe – but sometimes I, too, feel that awful loneliness – the feeling that there is no one much in the world who cares whether I be happy or sad. It is of all feelings the worst.'[20] A few days later Florence told Rebekah, having read Hardy's poem *Wessex Heights* (from his *Satires of Circumstance* collection): 'It wrung my heart. It made me miserable to think that he had ever suffered so much. It was written in '96, before I knew him.' And, referring to Hardy's poems in general, Florence declared:

> He tells me that he has written *no* despondent poem for the last eighteen months, & yet I cannot get rid of the feeling that the man who wrote some of those poems is utterly weary of life – & cares for nothing in this world. If I had been a different sort of woman, & better fitted to be his wife – would he, I wonder, have published that volume? [*Satires of Circumstance*, published in the previous month of November].[21]

In late 1914 Lady Hoare evidently wrote to Florence, singling out two of Hardy's poems –*The Death of Regret* and *Wessex Heights* (both from the *Satires of Circumstance* collection) – which she used to illustrate her argument that, in Florence's words, 'one must not make the man responsible for what the poet writes'.[22] In other words, Lady Hoare was making a distinction between Hardy 'the man' and Hardy 'the poet'. Lady Hoare was undoubtedly hoping that her words would comfort and reassure Florence, which they did. However, in her analysis of the situation she was mistaken, for in this case, Hardy the man and Hardy the poet were one and the same.

Florence had already indicated to Lady Hoare, in a previous letter dated 6 December 1914, that in the poem *Wessex Heights*, the four women referred to by Hardy were all 'actual women', though only three were still alive in 1896 when the poem was written. And, of course, one of these women was Emma.

The sixth and seventh (final) verses of *Wessex Heights* read as follows:

> As for one rare fair woman, I am now but a thought of hers,
> I enter her mind and another thought succeeds me that she prefers;
> Yet my love for her in its fullness she herself even did not know;
> Well, time cures hearts of tenderness, and now I can let her go.
> So I am found on Ingpen Beacon, or on Wylls-Neck to the west,
> Or else on homely Bulbarrow, or little Pilsdon Crest,
> Where men have never cared to haunt, nor women have walked with me,
> And ghosts then keep their distance; and I know some liberty.

Much as Hardy would have liked to believe the sentiments expressed by him in these two verses, the reality was that he *never* succeeded in 'letting Emma go', even after her death; nor did he ever manage to rid himself entirely of the ghosts that haunted him in respect of her. Likewise, although in *The Death of Regret* Hardy is ostensibly writing about a person who has lost a male comrade, it is difficult to escape the conclusion that this poem is also about Emma; and in its final verse Hardy is again trying to convince himself that he can live contentedly without her:

And ah, seldom now do I ponder
At the window as heretofore
On the long valued one who died yonder,
And wastes by the sycamore.

To Lady Hoare, Florence expressed her feelings of tenderness for Hardy. She sometimes felt towards her husband, she said, 'as a mother towards a child with whom things have somehow gone wrong – a child who needs comforting – to be treated gently & with all the love possible'.[23]

On 3 December 1915 Florence told Rebekah Owen that, to her 'great dismay', Hardy had reverted to his former self. 'Tom ... says he feels that he never wants to go anywhere or see anyone again. He wants to live on here [at Max Gate], quite quietly, shut up in his study.'[24] In January 1916 Florence, again in a letter to Rebekah Owen, referred to 'the *awful* diary the first Mrs T.H. kept (which he burned) full of venom, hatred & abuse of him & his family'.[25]

On 9 December 1916 Florence described a visit to St Juliot rectory, where she and Hardy 'had tea ... with the very nice Rector [the Revd John H. Dickinson] & his sister'. She also described exploring King Arthur's castle where the couple 'lay for an hour or so, on the grass, in the sunshine, with sheep nibbling around us, & no other living thing – while cliffs & greenyblue sea & white surf seemed hundreds of feet below'. In other words, unlike on the first occasion, Florence appears to have enjoyed her visit to Cornwall this time.[26]

# 16

# Explaining the Poems

### *Moments of Vision*

*Moments of Vision and Miscellaneous Verses* was published by Macmillan in November 1917. Of this collection, *Logs on the Hearth* and *In the Garden* were poems written by Hardy in memory of his sister Mary. In other poems, such as *Joys of Memory* and *To My Father's Violin*, he looks back nostalgically at the past, which to him always seems preferable to the present. Similarly, in *Great Things*, where Hardy admits to a love for 'sweet cider', 'the dance' and 'love' itself, he uses the past tense, as he ends with the words 'Will always have been great things'.

The theme of *Moments of Vision and Miscellaneous Verses*, said Hardy, was to 'mortify the human sense of self-importance by showing or suggesting, that human beings are of no matter or appreciable value in this nonchalant universe'.[1] This, as will be seen, was only part of the story, for there are many poems in the collection which relate, inevitably and vicariously, as always, to Emma. Had she been alive, she would undoubtedly have been just as offended by them as she had been with *Jude the Obscure*.

In 1920 publisher Vere H. Collins, during a series of discussions with Hardy at Max Gate, questioned the latter about one of his *Moments of Vision* poems, namely *The Interloper*, which he could not make sense of. It reads as follows:

> There are three folk driving in a quaint old chaise,
> And the cliff-side track looks green and fair;
> I view them talking in quiet glee
> As they drop down towards the puffins' lair

By the roughest of ways;
But another with the three rides on, I see,
    Whom I like not to be there!

No: it's not anybody you think of. Next
A dwelling appears by a slow sweet stream
Where two sit happily and half in the dark:
They read, helped out by a frail-wick'd gleam,
    Some rhythmic text;
But one sits with them whom they don't mark,
    One I'm wishing could not be there.

No: not whom you knew and name. And now
I discern gay diners in a mansion-place,
And the guests dropping wit – pert, prim, or choice,
And the hostess's tender and laughing face,
    And the host's bland brow;
But I cannot help hearing a hollow voice,
    And I'd fain not hear it there.

No: it's not from the stranger you once met. Ah,
Yet a goodlier scene than that succeeds;
People on a lawn – quite a crowd of them. Yes,
And they chatter and ramble as fancy leads;
    And they say, 'Hurrah!'
To a blithe speech made; save one, mirthless,
    Who ought not to be there.

Nay: it's not the pale Form your imagings raise,
That waits on us all at a destined time,
It is not the Fourth Figure the Furnace showed;[2]
O that it were such a shape sublime
    In these latter days!
It is that under which best lives corrode;
    Would, would it could not be there!

Clearly, the first verse of the poem relates to Hardy's early visits to St Juliot in the 1870s, the 'three folk' in the chaise being himself, Emma and probably Emma's sister, Helen, and the cliffs being probably those in the vicinity of nearby Boscastle. In the second verse, the 'dwelling' may in reality be 'Riverside Villa', Sturminster Newton, Dorset, and the 'stream', the adjacent River Stour. The third verse refers to a mansion, to which Hardy and Emma have been invited for dinner – presumably after he became famous. The 'lawn' referred to in the fourth verse may be the one at Max Gate. All the events described in the above-mentioned poem should, for Hardy, have been happy ones. Instead, because of the presence of the unwanted stranger, they are not. But who was this stranger?

Vere H. Collins asked Hardy to explain the penultimate line: 'What is "that under which best lives corrode"?' To which Hardy replied:

'Madness.'
Collins: 'In each case?'
Hardy: 'Yes. I knew the family.'[3]

When Collins suggested that Hardy give *The Interloper* a subtitle, in order to make its meaning clearer, Hardy responded (for the 1923 edition) with 'And I saw the figure and visage of Madness seeking for a home'. Said Collins: 'When Hardy uttered that word ['madness'] … there burst on me a revelation' – the subtitle was a *reference to Emma*. (Hardy, of course, whatever his thoughts, would never have used the word 'madness' openly had Emma still been alive.) Said Collins:

This was the clue. *The Blow, The Blot, The Wound* [references to other poems of Hardy's]; the spectre haunting that beautiful girl while she sang and played; the shadow darkening and chilling that passionate union; the lovers struck by an unexpected, unprovoked, undeserved foe; now at last I grasped what … had put an end to happiness in Hardy's marriage and life.[4]

And this is why Hardy 'had tended to concentrate his attention on the tragedies and ironies in love'.[5] But who was 'the interloper' – the 'one who ought not to be there' and who corrodes the lives of others? The only interpretation possible is that it was a representation of Emma's alter ego; this being seen by Hardy as a separate entity to Emma, the physical being.

From the first verse, the conclusion, extraordinary as it may seem, must be that Emma was displaying features of insanity even before Hardy married her. (He may only have recognised this with the benefit of hindsight.) And what is equally extraordinary is that he went ahead with the marriage, notwithstanding this fact. And from Hardy's words to Collins – 'Madness …

I knew the family' — it is clear that it was to Emma's family that the former was referring.

Another poem which Collins mentions above is *The Blow*, in which Hardy demands to know why someone had found it necessary 'To have hurled that stone Into the sunshine of our days!' — the days in question being, of course, those which he and Emma had shared together. The answer was that:

> No aimful author's was the blow
>> That swept us prone,
> But the Immanent Doer's That doth not know,
>
> Which in some age unguessed of us
> May lift Its blinding incubus,
>> And see, and own:
> 'It grieves me I did thus and thus!'

(This, of course, was an echo of the 'Immanent Will' of *The Dynasts*.)

Collins also mentions Hardy's poem *The Wound*, a reference not to any physical wound, but to an inner hurt which he had chosen to keep to himself:

> … that wound of mine
> Of which none knew,
> For I'd given no sign
> That it pierced me through.

And when Collins talks about a beautiful girl singing and playing, he is referring to Hardy's poem *At the Piano*:

> A Woman was playing,
>> A man looking on;
>> And the mould of her face,
>> And her neck, and her hair,
>> Which the rays fell upon
>> Of the two candles there,
> Sent him mentally straying
>> In some fancy-place
>> Where pain had no trace.
> A cowled Apparition
>> Came pushing between;

> And her notes seemed to sigh;
> And the lights to burn pale,
> As a spell numbed the scene.
> But the maid saw no bale,
> And the man no monition;
> And Time laughed awry,
> And the Phantom hid nigh.

This poem, of course, is again about Emma (who is known to have played the pianoforte). When Hardy is in her company he is happy, and imagines himself to be in a place where pain does not exist – and by implication, where there is only pleasure. However, a 'phantom' (ghost or spectre) appears and intervenes between them. Emma is unaware of the evil and woe ('bale') which the phantom's presence portends, and Hardy fails to recognise its presence as a warning ('monition') of things to come.

In the above three poems, as Collins so rightly guessed, the 'stone' in the first, the 'wound' in the second, and the 'cowled apparition' or 'phantom' in the third, were all metaphors for Emma's 'madness'. Collins might also have mentioned *The Man with a Past*, where Hardy alludes to the fact that neither he nor Emma saw the 'dart' which was winging its way towards them; another metaphor, undoubtedly, for Emma's insanity:

> There was merry-making
> When the first dart fell
> As a heralding, –
> Till grinned the fully bared thing,
> And froze like a spell.
> Like a spell.
>
> Innocent was she,
> Innocent was I,
> Too simple we!
> Before us we did not see,
> Nearing. Aught wry –
> Aught wry!

It is difficult to be precise about when exactly the penny first dropped and Hardy realised that Emma was insane (or 'mad', as he called it). This is because works of his which allude to Emma's insanity were written subsequent to the events which they describe, and therefore with the benefit of hindsight. Nevertheless, by the time he came to write *The Interloper*, which was published in late 1917, her 'madness' was a fact of which he was certain beyond all doubt.

Of other poems in *Moments of Vision*, *Honeymoon Time at an Inn* undoubtedly relates to Hardy's own honeymoon. The poem begins ominously:

> At the shiver of morning, a little before the false dawn,
> The moon was at the window-square,
> Deedily brooding in deformed decay ...

From whence, the atmosphere deteriorates even further:

> Her speechless eyeing reached across the chamber,
> Where lay two souls opprest,
> One a white lady sighing, 'Why am I sad!'
> To him who sighed back, 'Sad, my Love, am I!'

Suddenly, a 'pier-glass' (large, elongated mirror) comes crashing down from the 'mantel' and lies shattered on the floor. This, for the lady (Emma), was a portent of 'long years of sorrow' for herself and her new husband (Hardy).

*You Were the Sort that Men Forget* begins:

> You Were the Sort that Men Forget;
> Though I – not yet! –
> Perhaps not ever. Your slighted weakness
> Adds to the strength of my regret.
>
> You'd not the art – you never had
> For good or bad –
> To make men see how sweet your meaning,
> Which, visible, had charmed them glad.
> You would, by words inept let fall,
> Offend them all,
> Even if they saw your warm devotion
> Would hold your life's blood at their call.

In other words, although in Hardy's eyes Emma had some excellent qualities, she had a habit of offending everybody, because in his view, her finer
qualities were not discernible to them.

In *The Glimpse*, Hardy reveals how the memory of Emma continues to
haunt him, even after her death:

> She sped through the door
> And, following in haste,
> And stirred to the core,
> I entered hot-faced;
> But I could not find her,
> No sign was behind her.
> 'Where is she?' I said:
> "Who?" they asked that sat there;
> "Not a soul's come in sight."
> 'A maid with red hair.'
> "Ah." They paled. "She is dead.
> People see her at night,
> But you are the first
> On whom she has burst
> In the keen common light."
>
> It was ages ago,
> When I was quite strong:
> I have waited since, – O,
> I have waited so long!
> Yea, I set me to own
> The house, where now lone
> I dwell in void rooms
> Booming hollow as tombs!
> But I never come near her,
> Though nightly I hear her.
> And my cheek has grown thin
> And my hair has grown gray
> With this waiting therein;
> But she still keeps away!

There are more poems on the theme of lost love and bereavement, which
resound with words and phrases such as 'my own heart nigh broke', 'sorrow-

wrung' and 'mourn', and it requires but little discernment on the reader's part to realise that, as so often is the case, it is about Emma that Hardy is really writing.

In *Moments of Vision*, Hardy also reveals his morbid side with his references to 'death', 'mournful mould' (of one deceased), 'tombs' and 'vaults'. This brooding side of his nature cannot entirely be attributed to his failed marriage, for it will be remembered that on his honeymoon he insisted on paying a visit to the Paris morgue. The remainder of the poems deal with such subjects as war and patriotism.

It is now obvious why Hardy chose the title *Moments of Vision* for this collection of poems, for what the title really means is 'Now I see Emma more clearly for what she really was'. In other words, Hardy had now come to a full realisation of the true state of mind of his late wife Emma (which he may well have previously been in denial about), even though he lacked the medical knowledge and expertise to make the 'diagnosis'. Likewise, the title of the poem's predecessor, *Satires of Circumstance*, translates to 'Behold, here I have satirised my unhappy life with Emma', and *Time's Laughingstocks* translates to 'Time has made me a laughingstock'.

# Hardy Approaches 80

In January 1918 Hardy gave his opinion on the subject of pessimism – something of which he had often been accused. Said he: 'My motto is, first correctly [to] diagnose the complaint ... and ascertain the cause; then set about finding a remedy if one exists.'[6] As for the subject of poetry, its glory, he said, lay 'in its largeness, admitting among its creators men of infinite variety'.[7]

In February Florence wrote to Sydney Cockerell (director of the Fitzwilliam Museum, Cambridge) in respect of a biography of Hardy which she was currently working on:

> T.H. declares that he would never write an autobiography, the mere idea – or suggestion – annoys him. It would be a thousand pities if the MS were burned now. The safest plan is to say as little as possible about it until the thing is completed – as far as we are able to complete it.[8]

(The outcome was that *The Early Life of Thomas Hardy* and *The Later Years of Thomas Hardy*, both by Florence Emily Hardy, were published in 1928 and 1930 respectively by Macmillan.)

Hardy was now aged 77, and it is a measure of his fame and popularity that in the spring of 1918, such eminent people as Lady Ilchester and Lady Londonderry came to visit him at Max Gate. In June 1918, with the Great War still in progress, he gave a chilling view of what future wars would be like. This one was horrible enough, but would be 'merciful in comparison', bearing in mind that 'scientific munition-making is only in its infancy'.[9] The war ended at 11 a.m. on 11 November of that year.

Hardy signed a petition in February 1919 in support of 'the reconstitution of Palestine as a national home for the Jewish people'. In May he was 'destroying papers [presumably letters and diaries] of the last 30 or 40 years' which, he said, 'raise ghosts'.[10]

On his birthday, 2 June, he took Florence and his sister Katharine by car to visit one of his favourite places, Salisbury. Soon afterwards, Siegfried Sassoon arrived at Max Gate with a birthday present: a volume of the poems of some fifty living poets, intended as a 'tribute'.[11] Hardy confessed to Florence Henniker that he would care more about his birthdays if with every succeeding one he could see 'any sign of real improvement in the world. All development [was] of a material & scientific kind', but despite this, 'scarcely any addition to our knowledge is applied to objects philanthropic or ameliorative'.[12]

On 10 August 1919 Florence wrote to Louise Yearsley (whose surgeon husband, Macleod, four years previously had performed an operation on her nose), to say:

> I have to go to Town [London] to see a Miss [Lilian] Gifford – niece of the
> first Mrs T.H. She has gone off her head, poor thing, & been put in an asylum,
> & I am going to see her as my husband is really not fit for the journey [in] this
> weather. He is rather attached to her as she lived here as a child for some years
> – & she has stayed with us from time to time since we were married. She was
> always a *most* difficult person to live with – but now I understand that the
> poor woman could not really help her trying ways & temper.[13]

[The institution mentioned is the London County Council's Claybury Asylum, to which, as previously mentioned, Lilian had been committed.]

It is to Florence's credit that she was prepared, in all the circumstances, to make this visit to 'poor Lilian', as she now described Emma's niece. Florence wrote to Sydney Cockerell to tell him about her visit. Said Florence: 'I did not perceive any particular symptom of insanity [this statement being a measure of Florence's fair-minded attitude towards Lilian], but the doctor and the medical superintendent assured me that she *was* insane.' And she went on to tell Cockerell how, when she was at Claybury, she had met Lilian's brother Gordon, who 'told me that he and his wife [Violet] had had a dreadful time with her [during] the last few years'. Gordon told Florence that Lilian had regarded his wife Violet, a mere dressmaker, as someone 'not fit to associate' with her; that there had been 'continual scenes and unkindness ... and that absurd obsession about the grandeur of the Gifford family'.

Finally, the medical superintendent had told Florence that 'from what he knew of the case, she [Lilian] can never have been quite sane'. (It is likely, of course, that had the doctor examined Emma, he would have reached the same conclusion.) Lilian was evidently very unhappy at Claybury, for she begged Florence to 'take her out'. However, this Florence was unable to do without the consent of the authorities.[14]

In September 1919 Florence complained to Sydney Cockerell that Hardy 'has just paid £10 for altering the tomb of the first Mrs T.H. and yet he will not buy himself a thread of clothing and he upsets himself about trifles of household expenditure involving only a few pence'.[15]

Hardy continued to demonstrate his endless fascination with the legal system by attending (with Florence) the Dorchester Assizes. On 18 November, the birthday of Thomas Hardy II, he visited his late father's grave. In December he opened the Bockhampton Reading Room and Club, which would be that village's memorial to the fallen. In his speech on that occasion, he reminisced about the 'poor-houses', where parish paupers were accommodated before the workhouses were built.

A letter sent by Hardy to Emma's cousin, Charles Edwin Gifford, in early November 1919, shows that the author's old sparkle had returned, after lying dormant for so many decades. Gifford had apparently sent Hardy congratulations for his 80th birthday – prematurely as it transpired, for this date would not be reached until 2 June 1920. Replied Hardy:

> Many thanks for your congratulation. But it is rather amusing that, though I have been 80 in America for several years, & am now called 80 in England, I shall not really be 80 till the middle of next year, when people will doubtless begin to say: 'How many more times is that Hardy going to be fourscore!'[16]

On 27 December 1919 Florence stated that she and Hardy had visited Talbothays (the home of Hardy's siblings) two days previously on the afternoon of Christmas Day.[17] In May 1920 she said that 'on Sundays we nearly always go to see his [Hardy's] brother & sister'.[18] That December, following a visit to Max Gate by the mummers, Florence declared that 'Miss Bugler looked prettier than ever in her mumming dress. T.H. has lost his heart to her entirely, but as she is soon getting married I don't let that cast me down *too* much.'[19] (This was a reference to Gertrude Adelia Bugler, born in 1897, amateur actress of Dorchester.)

On 30 December Florence informed Louise Yearsley that 'we have had a rather lively Christmas in one way & another – so many people having desired to pay their "respex" to T.H. I estimate that between 50 and 60 people have been in this house since Christmas Day.' What a contrast this was to the era of Emma.[20]

In April 1921 Florence generously acknowledged how Emma, in her lifetime, had helped Hardy with his work: 'Emma did indeed frequently copy for him any pages that had many alterations. She liked doing it.'[21]

Accolades now followed, thick and fast. In February 1920 Hardy was in Oxford to receive an honorary degree of Doctor of Letters, and also to see a performance of *The Dynasts* by the university players. In March he was elected Honorary Fellow of the Royal Institute of British Architects. April saw Hardy visiting London for the last time, when he and Florence attended Harold Macmillan's wedding to Lady Dorothy Cavendish at St Margaret's, Westminster. Macmillan's grandfather, Daniel (with brother Alexander), had founded the publishing firm of that name (which had published a number of Hardy's works), and his father, Frederick, was its chairman. The month of May saw Hardy at Exeter with Florence and Katharine, attending a service at the cathedral and calling on friends. In a letter to author and critic Harold Child, he admitted to being 'most averse to anything like an "interview", and have been for many years'.[22]

On 2 June 1920, the occasion of Hardy's 80th birthday, he received a deputation from the Society of Authors, which organisation included John Galsworthy, whose works Hardy greatly admired. Those who sent congratulatory messages included the king, the prime minister, the vice-chancellor of Cambridge University and the Lord Mayor of London.[23]

By November Hardy was expressing a view with which many will identify: that the name 'English', as the name of this country's people, should be insisted upon, and not 'the vague, unhistoric, and pinchbeck title of "British"'.[24] In December he modestly described his philosophy merely as 'a confused heap of impressions, like those of a bewildered child at a conjuring show'.[25]

That Christmas, the carol singers came to Max Gate, as was the tradition; the mummers also visited, and gave a performance of the *Play of Saint George*. The fact that Hardy 'sat up' to see the New Year in may perhaps indicate a more contented, if not happier, frame of mind.

⁓

The death of Charles Moule occurred on 11 May 1921, the last of the Revd Henry Moule's seven sons. In June Hardy and Florence travelled to Sturminster Newton for a performance of *The Mellstock Quire* in the castle ruins. In July a company arrived in Dorchester preparing to make a film of *The Mayor of Casterbridge*. That same month Hardy attended morning service at Dorchester's church of St Peter, and he opened a bazaar in aid of the Dorset County Hospital.

Hardy may have exchanged his bicycle for a motor car, but in other respects he displayed great energy. For example, he remained a prodigious letter-writer. Those with whom he corresponded included friends, eminent authors, poets, members of the Macmillan family, distinguished university academics, members of the Gifford family, plus inquisitive media correspondents anxious for him to explain aspects of the behaviour of his characters, and to reveal the locations where his novels were set.

## Late Lyrics and Earlier

*Late Lyrics and Earlier* was published by Macmillan in May 1922. However, some of the poems in this collection – as the title implies – had been written several years prior to this date. In Hardy's words:

> Owing to lack of time, through the necessity of novel-writing for magazines, many of the poems [in this and in other collections] were temporarily jotted down to the extent of a stanza or two when the ideas occurred, and put aside till time should serve for finishing them – often not till years later … This makes it difficult to date those not dated in the volumes.[26]

In the Preface to *Late Lyrics and Earlier*, Hardy expressed his disappointment that the proposed revisions to the Church of England's Book of Common Prayer had not been 'in a rationalistic direction'; according to his wife, Florence, from that time onward 'he lost all expectation of seeing the Church [as] representative of modern thinking minds'.[27] (In the event, the revisions to which he referred were rejected by the House of Commons in 1927, and again in 1928.)

The fact that the poems included in this volume, unlike many of their predecessors, are less morbid, and display less nostalgia for years past, indicates that Hardy had now become somewhat less dissatisfied with life. Some of them, in fact, are quite jolly; for example, *Weathers*:

> This is the weather the cuckoo likes,
> And so do I …

Hardy's new lease of life is entirely attributable to the presence of Florence. Nonetheless, the past and Emma were never far from his thoughts. In *Faintheart in a Railway Train* Hardy speaks of a lost opportunity to introduce himself to a 'radiant stranger' – female, of course – encountered on a station platform. In *The West-of-Wessex Girl* he regrets that the subject of the poem was 'never … squired' by him. Judging by the mention Emma's home town, and that the two never had a romantic relationship, the subject is almost certainly Emma.

The very title of *If It's Ever Spring Again* indicates that for Hardy, those early, happy times in which he spent courting Emma will not come again. In *Two Serenades*, written, poignantly, one Christmas Eve, he complains that Emma is indifferent to his overtures of love:

> But she would not heed
> What I melodied
> In my soul's sore need –
> She would not heed.

So that finally:

> Sick I withdrew
> At love's grim hue …

In *The Rift*, Hardy refers to 'those true tones – of span so brief!' – in other words, to what he remembers as the true Emma, before her 'old gamut [musical note 'G'] changed its chime'. After this:

> So sank I from my high sublime!
> We faced but chancewise after that,
> And never I knew or guessed my crime …

Hardy could not understand why Emma had changed, and wondered if he was to blame for that change; but if so, in what way?

In a poem entitled, ironically, *Side by Side*, the terrible consequences of Hardy's and Emma's union become apparent when the 'estranged two' meet one day, by chance, at church, and find themselves sharing the same pew:

Thus side by side
Blindly alighted,
They seemed united
As groom and bride,
Who's not communed
For many years –
Lives from twain spheres
With hearts distuned.

In *Read by Moonlight* he (Hardy) reads the last letter which Emma had written to him, the last of many such 'missives of pain and pine'. In *A Gentleman's Epitaph on Himself and a Lady, Who were Buried Together*, Hardy appears to anticipate his own death and burial next to his late wife Emma. In the poem, Hardy discloses that although the 'Lady' was and would be his companion forever, she was also a person whom he did not really know:

Not a word passed of love all our lifetime,
    Between us, nor thrill;
We'd never a husband-and-wife time,
    For good or for ill.

Nevertheless, the fact that he loved Emma is borne out by the poem *The Woman I Met*, where he declares:

Well; your very simplicity made me love you
    Mid such town dross
Till I set not Heaven itself above you,
    Who grew my Cross.

And yet:

… despite how I sighed for you;
So you tortured me, who fain would have died for you!

Finally, in *Fetching Her*, he is in total and absolute despair, as he agonises with himself over whether it might have been better had he not:

> … pulled this flower
> From the craggy nook it knew,
> And set it in an alien bower;
>    But left it where it grew!

What of Hardy's relationship with the household staff at Max Gate? Opinions are mixed. His chauffeur, Harold Voss, says that he never saw Hardy in a temper. He was a 'real gentleman' who was 'never flurried' but always calm. On the other hand, Hardy's gardener, Bertie Stephens, who managed the 1-acre garden, conservatory, greenhouse and paddock single-handed, says: 'At no time did Hardy express any appreciation or give any praise for anything that was done.' Hardy could also 'get into a bit of a mood' and be 'irritable'. Hardy's barber, W.G. Mills of Dorchester, states that his client never gave a tip, or a Christmas present, but instead was always 'very close with his money'. His cook, Mrs A. Stanley, describes Hardy's trousers as being so worn that they had 'fringes' at their bottoms. 'He was too mean to buy himself a decent pair.' When, on Boxing Day, she generously gave the postman 2*s* 6*d* on behalf of the family, Hardy refused to reimburse her the money on the grounds that 'Dorchester people never give tips'.

Hardy's cleaner, Margaret Male, says that Hardy would never acknowledge people who worked for him if he passed them in the street. She attributed this to his shyness. Hardy's parlour maid, Miss Ellen E. Titterington, says that although Hardy gave the maids at Max Gate 'quiet little smiles as he passed them on the stairs, he never passed the time of day with them, unless it was to talk about the weather'. If she put too much coal on the fire, he would take it off again. Nevertheless, she was prepared to give him the benefit of the doubt. 'The memory of his early days when he was poor,' she said, 'must have remained with him and influenced his behaviour.'[28]

# 17

# Declining Years

In May 1922 Hardy visited his old home at Higher Bockhampton and was distressed to see that both house and garden had become shabby through lack of care. July brought visits from Florence Henniker, Siegfried Sassoon, Edmund Blunden and E.M. Forster. In August he cycled with Florence to visit his brother, Henry, and sister, Katharine, at Talbothays Lodge.

In August 1922 Florence reported: 'T.H. is really wonderfully well. Yesterday he cycled to Talbothays and did it well, not even feeling tired afterwards.'[1]

In November Florence, who was now answering Hardy's letters on his behalf, wrote to Lady Josephine Sackville, who had requested that Hardy autograph some books for her. The answer was that yes, Mr Hardy was prepared to do so, but only on payment of the fee of half a guinea for each one; the sum of which would be forwarded to the Dorset County Hospital.[2]

The tenth anniversary of Emma's death fell on 27 November 1922, and he and Florence marked the occasion by placing flowers on her tomb and on the tombs of other members of the Hardy family.

On 4 April 1923 Florence Henniker died, bringing to an end her thirty-year friendship with Hardy. In May Hardy was visited by the poet Walter de la Mare and Max Beerbohm (the caricaturist and author) and his wife Florence. In June the Hardys visited Oxford and stayed two nights at Queen's College (which made him an Honorary Fellow), calling on the way at Fawley in Berkshire, where his maternal grandmother had lived the first thirteen years of her life as an orphan. In July Hardy was invited to Dorchester to meet the Prince of Wales (later King Edward VIII), who was there to open a new drill hall for the Dorset Territorial Army, after which the prince was entertained to luncheon by the Hardys at Max Gate. The following month Hardy explained why he objected to 'anything like an interview for press purposes'. It was because he had been the victim of 'so much fabrication and misrepresentation in the past'.[3]

In September 1923 Florence said that Hardy had told her 'he would have welcomed a child when we married first, ten years ago, but now it would kill him with anxiety to have to father one'.[4]

*The Famous Tragedy of the Queen of Cornwall*, a poetic, one-act play for mummers, was published by Macmillan on 15 November 1923. Swinburne had already written a romance in couplets on the subject in 1882, but now Hardy himself had brought back to life the legendary tale of Tristram, who falls in love with Queen Iseult of Ireland, but actually marries her namesake, Iseult of Brittany.

☞

At the end of December in 1923, dramatist George Bernard Shaw and his wife, Charlotte, visited the Hardys; as well as Colonel T.E. Lawrence (of Arabia), who had enlisted earlier that year as a private soldier in the Tank Training School at Bovington under the assumed name of 'T.E. Shaw'. Lawrence lived in a remote cottage called Clouds Hill, which lay 7 miles from Max Gate.

Anniversaries were very important to Hardy, who on 3 April 1924 recorded in his diary: 'Mother died twenty years ago today.' On 21 April he wrote to General John H. Morgan (lawyer and author, who had been involved in the implementation of the disarmament provisions of the Treaty of Versailles, which marked the end of the Great War). In his letter, Hardy expressed the hope that the League of Nations (which had been inaugurated in January 1920) would offer 'a real hope' that 'principalities & powers will discern more & more clearly that each personality in them stands himself to lose by war'. He thought it wrong to blame the English, either entirely, or mainly, for the current poverty in Ireland, which he believed was caused by 'the temperament' of that country's people – whom he considered romantic and generous nonetheless.[5]

In July 1924 players from Balliol College, Oxford, arrived to perform the Greek tragedy *Oresteia* in the garden of Max Gate. On 31 December Hardy 'sat up' and heard the chimes of Big Ben on the wireless, heralding the New Year.

A deputation arrived from the University of Bristol on 15 July 1925, to confer on Hardy the honorary degree of Doctor of Literature. This was the fifth university to honour him in this way. In December players from London's Garrick Theatre gave a performance of Hardy's *Tess of the D'Urbervilles* in Max Gate's drawing room.

It was clear that Hardy was enjoying a social life at Max Gate such as he had never experienced with Emma. 'Would you care to spend Wednesday or Thursday night here?' Florence asked Sydney Cockerell. Prior to that, said she: 'We have promised to lunch with Dr & Mrs Head at Lyme Regis on Thursday next, & go on to tea with Lady Pinney at Racedown [House, in Dorset].'[6]

Hardy's *Human Shows, Far Phantasies, Songs, and Trifles* was published on 20 November 1925 by Macmillan. The poems contain a medley of favourite themes: *The Turnip Hoer, The Monument Maker, A Sheep Fair, The Graveyard of Dead Creeds*, and so forth; the majority of them revealing Hardy in a lighter mood than heretofore. However, Emma is never far from his mind, as for instance in *Last Love-Word*, which ends with the couplet:

When that first look and touch,
Love, doomed us two.

In *A Second Attempt* he describes how:

Thirty years after
I began again
An old-time passion:
And it seemed as fresh as when
The first day ventured on:
When mutely I would waft her
In Love's past fashion
Dreams much dwelt upon
Dreams I wished she knew.

But he realises that his 'hot hopes' that the relationship will progress to 'consummation' are only a dream, for 'Twice-over cannot be!' (This poem was written, according to the original manuscript, in 'about 1900' – four years before he first met Florence Dugdale. So did Hardy actually make another attempt to woo Emma, who he had first met thirty years previously in

March 1870, or was the wooing simply a figment of his imagination? The latter proposition would seem to be the more likely.

In his poem *A Poor Man and a Lady*, Hardy's feelings of inferiority surface once again, when, after a period of 'timorous secret bliss', the couple become divided: '... never a kiss Of mine could touch you', says Hardy, whose marriage to 'a comely woman of noble kith' was therefore 'not a valid thing' (because it was loveless on her part). Other poems, such as *Known Had I*, *Her Haunting-Ground* and *Days to Recollect*, also reflect his remorse and regret for lost or absent love.

On 23 December 1925 Hardy remembered the tenth anniversary of his beloved sister Mary's death in his diary: 'She came into the world ... and went out ... and the world is just the same ... not a ripple on the surface left.'[7] This was not strictly true, for apart from anything else, Mary left for posterity some fine portraits which she had painted in oils of members of her family, without which our knowledge of them would have been that much the poorer.

On 25 December Florence recalled a previous Christmas Day, that of 1910:

> when I sat here [at Max Gate] alone, & vowed that no power on earth would ever induce me to ever spend another Christmas Day at Max Gate. T.H. had gone off to Bockhampton to see his sisters, after a violent quarrel with the first Mrs T.H. because he wanted me to go to see the sisters too, and she said I shouldn't because they would poison my mind against her.[8]

In January 1926 Hardy relinquished his governorship of the Dorchester Grammar School. Sitting on committees, which 'controlled or ordained the activities of others', had never been his favourite pastime. Instead, he preferred to be 'the man with the watching eye' (in other words, simply an observer of events).[9]

Hardy's letter-writing continued unabated, albeit with the help of Florence, upon whom he was increasingly reliant in this respect due to his failing eyesight. Among those with whom he corresponded in 1926 were J.B. Priestley, H.G. Wells, John Galsworthy and Gustav Holst. He also wrote to Marie Stopes (the Scottish birth-control campaigner); in fact, it was characteristic of him to associate with avant-garde women. February found him entering into correspondence regarding the condition of the bells of Stinsford church, which had fallen into a sad state of disrepair.[10]

In March 1926 Hardy's sister, Katharine, accompanied Florence to a matinee performance by the *Tess* touring company at Bournemouth. However, Hardy himself 'did not feel equal' to the outing.[11]

In his poem *He Never Expected Much*, Hardy reflects on his 86th birthday, which he had celebrated on 2 June 1926. The poem begins:

> Well, World, you have kept faith with me,
>> Kept faith with me;
> Upon the whole you have proved to be
>> Much as you said you were.
> Since as a child I used to lie
> Upon the leaze and watch the sky,
> Never, I own, expected I
>> That life would all be fair.

The second verse of the poem contains a clear reference to Emma, showing that even now, thirteen years after her death, her treatment of him still rankled:

> Many have loved me desperately,
> Many with smooth serenity,
> While some have shown contempt of me
>> Till they dropped underground.

And the poem ends with a voice speaking to Hardy which is reminiscent of that of his mother, Jemima, when she warned him about the 'figure [which] stands in our path with arm uplifted, to knock us back from any pleasant prospect we indulge in':

> 'I do not promise overmuch,
>> Child; overmuch;
> Just neutral-tinted haps and such,'
>> You said to minds like mine.
> Wise warning for your credit's sake!
> Which I for one failed not to take,
> And hence could stem such strain and ache
>> As each year might assign.

In July 1926 Hardy confessed, in a letter to his old friend, the author Edward Clodd, his fear that 'rational religion does not make much [head] way at present'. In fact, the 'movement of thought' appeared to have 'entered a back current in the opposite direction', which was however 'not uncommon in human history'.[12]

Two months later he received an ovation at the William Barnes Theatre in Weymouth, where he was attending a dramatisation of *The Mayor of Casterbridge*. In November he and Florence made what was to be his last visit to the old family home at Higher Bockhampton. That same month T.E. Lawrence, of whom Hardy was immensely fond, set out for a new RAF posting in India.

Carol singers arrived at Max Gate at Christmas 1926, as was traditional, this time from St Peter's church, Dorchester. On the 27th, the 'devoted and masterful' dog Wessex died. He was buried in the garden, under the trees. Wessex's headstone, designed by Hardy himself, was inscribed with the words:

The Famous Dog
**WESSEX**
August 1913 – 27 Dec. 1926
Faithful. Unflinching.

Hardy also commemorated his canine friend and companion for thirteen years with a poem, in which Wessex, in his after life, is searching in vain for his master. That New Year's Eve Hardy did not 'sit up' to see the New Year in.

On 2 June 1927 Hardy celebrated his 87th birthday not at home, but in Devonshire in the company of his friends, Harley Granville Barker (the actor, producer, dramatist and critic) and his wife Helen. On 21 July he laid the foundation stone of the new Dorchester Grammar School – an event which would have given one such as he, who cherished education and learning, great pleasure. In August, in company with the composer Gustav Holst, Hardy travelled to 'Egdon Heath' and visited Puddletown church, where his ancestors had played in the choir ('quire'). This month and the following one brought visits to Bath, Ilminster and Yeovil, Lulworth Castle and Charborough Park.

At the end of October 1927 Hardy and Florence took a short stroll from Max Gate across the fields. However, from now on he would depend on being driven around by chauffeur in a hired car; for example, to Stinsford (to put flowers on the family graves) and to Talbothays (to see his siblings, Henry and Katharine).

On Armistice Day, 11 November 1927, the ninth anniversary of the end of the Great War, Hardy and Florence listened to the Service of Thanksgiving broadcast on the wireless from Canterbury Cathedral.[13] Thursday 24 November and Sunday 27 November marked the anniversaries of the deaths of his sister Mary and Emma respectively. On the latter occasion, Hardy wore a black hat and carried Emma's black walking stick as tokens of his mourning.

Over the years it had been Hardy's habit to sit at his writing-table every morning at 10 a.m. If the spirit moved him, he would write; if it did not, he would find something else to do. This was a ritual which he always observed. On 11 December 1927, however, he was unable to work. On Christmas Day he wrote to (now 'Sir') Edmund Gosse: 'I am in bed on my back, living on butter-broth & beef tea, the servants being much concerned at my not being able to eat any Christmas pudding.'

Hardy was attended by his doctor, Edward Weller Mann, and also by his friend, the distinguished neurologist Sir Henry Head – who could discover no specific reason for his patient's weakness. J.M. Barrie (Scottish playwright and novelist), a friend of longstanding, also arrived from London with offers of help.[14]

This was a severe winter and snow lay deep on the ground. As the evening of 11 January 1928 fell, Hardy asked Florence to read him a verse from the *Rubaiyat* of Omar Khayyam:

Oh, Thou, who Man of baser Earth did'st make,
And who with Eden did'st devise the Snake;
For at the Sin wherewith the Face of Man
Is blacken'd, Man's forgiveness give – and take!

In this, Hardy demonstrated that his relationship with the 'Creator' must of necessity be a two-way process; his Creator must forgive Hardy his sins, in which case Hardy would oblige by doing likewise for his Creator. Thomas Hardy died shortly after 9 p.m.

# 18

# Aftermath

Hardy's ashes were interred in Westminster Abbey in Poets' Corner at 2 p.m. on Monday 16 January 1928; a spadeful of his beloved Dorset soil being sprinkled on the casket. The last novelist to be buried there prior to this was Charles Dickens in 1870. Hardy had never been introduced to Dickens, a fellow champion of the poor and underprivileged, although he had attended some of his readings at the Hanover Square Rooms in London in the 1860s.

Present at the funeral were: Conservative prime minister, Stanley Baldwin; leader of the opposition, Ramsay MacDonald; and the heads of Magdalene College, Cambridge, and Queen's College, Oxford. Sir James Barrie, John Galsworthy, Sir Edmund Gosse, A.E. Housman, Rudyard Kipling and George Bernard Shaw – all eminent literary figures of the day – acted as pallbearers. Members of the Macmillan publishing house, who also attended, organised the event.

Florence and Katharine were in attendance, but not so Henry, who was in poor health. In fact, Henry was at Stinsford church where, at the same time as the Westminster service, Hardy's heart (which had been previously removed from his body) was being buried in the tomb of Emma, his first wife. (According to his cousin Teresa, Hardy in life had expressed the wish to be buried at Stinsford, 'to lie with his own folk in the churchyard'. But it was not to be.)[1] On the one side of Hardy and Emma's tomb was that of his sister Mary, and on the other that of his parents, Thomas II and Jemima. Beyond that were buried his grandfather, Thomas I; his grandmother, Mary; his uncle, James, and finally, his aunt, Jane, and cousin, Theresa.

Also simultaneously with the Westminster ceremony, a memorial service to Hardy was held in Dorchester, in the presence of the mayor and corporation and many distinguished dignitaries.

⁀

Florence now set about ensuring that the memory of Hardy was preserved for posterity. In February 1928 she told Sir Edmund Gosse that: 'With regard to the biography of my husband I have for many years been collecting material which has been put somewhat roughly into shape. T.H. allowed me to take a great many extracts from his diaries & notebooks, & supplied all the information that I required.'[2]

On 5 March 1928 Florence wrote to T.E. Lawrence, thanking him for his kind letters to her and saying:

> besides my loneliness which will never be less, I have to suffer remorse, almost beyond expression, because I know I failed him at every turn. Time will not help me for I know my own nature, and I shall miss him more and more. The thought of years that may have to be lived through without him fills me with terror. There was really nothing in my life except T.H. nor will there ever be.[3]

⁀

Published by Macmillan in October 1928, nine months after Hardy's death, the collection of poems entitled *Winter Words* contain yet more thinly disguised sentiments about Emma. In *To Louisa in the Lane*, Hardy declares, 'Wait, I must, till with flung off flesh I follow you', but in *Song to Aurore* he issues a caveat:

> We'll not begin again to love
> It only leads to pain ...

And in *The Destined Pair* he ponders on whether 'Fate' would have been 'kinder ... Had he failed to find her' (had he never met Emma in the first place).

An outsider, who was unfamiliar with the personal circumstances of Hardy's marriage to Emma, might miss altogether the possible relevance of another poem in his *Winter Words* collection:

**Henley Regatta**
She looks from the window: still it pours down direly,
And the avenue drips. She cannot go, she fears;
And the Regatta will be spoilt entirely;

And she sheds half-crazed tears.
Regatta Day and rain come on together
Again, years after. Gutters trickle loud;
But Nancy cares not. She knows nought of weather,
　　Or of the Henley crowd:

She's a Regatta, quite her own. Inanely
She laughs in the asylum as she floats
Within a water-tub, which she calls 'Henley',
　　Her little paper boats.

Imagine for a moment that Hardy and Emma are in London for the season, and that they have decided to attend the Henley Royal Regatta – traditionally held at Henley-on-Thames, Oxfordshire. It is raining, and Emma ('Nancy') therefore declines to go. Years later, at the time when the regatta is being held, Emma behaves childishly and makes some paper boats. By this time she has become so deluded that she believes the Henley Regatta is taking place in her bath, in which she is floating her home-made boats. In other words, she has created her own 'asylum'.

(Some might argue that this poem applies not to Emma, but to someone else. However, circumstantial evidence makes this an unlikely proposition.)

⁀

Following the death of Hardy's brother, Henry, on 9 December 1928, Gordon Gifford expressed the desire to attend the funeral. Said Florence: '*That* will not suit Katie [Hardy's sister, Katharine], I fear, though a more harmless & well-meaning man [than Gifford] could not exist.'[4]

On 11 July 1929 Florence wrote to Siegfried Sassoon to say: 'I do not think I shall take a house in London, or make any change in my life. I feel that I belong to Max Gate where I can visit Stinsford & go to see my husband's sister [Katharine] every few days.'[5]

That September Florence paid a visit to St Juliot, 'to the great pleasure of the solitary little clergyman who lives there' (the Revd David Rhys Morris). However, despite the 'atmosphere of romance', Florence found the experience 'all very sad'.[6]

On 10 January 1931 Florence declared: 'With regard to the letters written by T.H. to E.L.G. – afterwards E.L.H. [Emma] – it was *she* who burnt his letters, & he told me he much regretted that at the time, & since. She asked him for her letters to him which he had carefully preserved, & she burnt those too.'[7]

Florence continued to live at Max Gate until her death there on 15 October 1937, after a long illness. She is buried in Stinsford churchyard in the tomb of Hardy and his first wife, Emma. In her will she directed that Max Gate and its contents be sold at auction. In the event, Hardy's sister Katharine purchased the property (even though she continued to live at Talbothays), and when she herself died in October 1940, the property was left to the National Trust. (Hardy's boyhood home at Higher Bockhampton also now belongs to the National Trust.)

# Epilogue

The genius of Thomas Hardy is multi-faceted; each facet reflecting his brilliance as a diamond reflects the light. His literary and classical allusions are drawn from his immense mental 'data-base' of knowledge, laid down in his mind after years of sustained and devoted study. Stories collected by him on his journey through life, from personal observation, newspaper articles and conversations with others – whether amusing or macabre – were stored away, to be woven (sometimes years later) into the tapestry of his novels, and retold with all the rustic wit and wisdom of the true countryman. His prose is exquisite. His empathy with underprivileged people is universally recognised, and millions identify with the struggles of the characters in his novels.

During the lifetime of Thomas Hardy, publisher Vere H. Collins was one of the very few people to suspect, and have the fact confirmed by Hardy himself, that some of Hardy's writings – notably his poem *The Interloper* – contained coded messages which revealed insights into his personal life. Nevertheless, neither Collins nor those who have studied the life of Hardy since his death have realised the full extent to which this is true.

The challenge has been to discover the hidden meanings contained in the works of this shy and secretive man. One may imagine him sitting in his study at Max Gate after the great schism when he decided to live a separate life from Emma, albeit under the same roof. By now, all his romantic dreams have been irrevocably shattered, and he is experiencing all the symptoms of a bereaved person: denial, numbness and unreality, followed by extreme sadness, anxiety and loneliness.[1]

However, because of his shyness he tends to keep his thoughts to himself, rather than to confide in others. But he must have some outlet for his emotions, so he chooses to express himself in the best way that he knows

– on paper, where he simply cannot resist alluding to his increasingly problematical relationship with Emma. This is a catharsis for him. And not only that, it provides him with a motivation to portray scenes in which his characters experience and wrestle with the same problems as he does.

Hardy's writings reveal the immense torment and grief which attends one whose life is a living hell, on account of the fact that his spouse is mentally deranged. And this, of course, explains why his latter novels and poems are so sad and introspective, while his early writings are full of joy, humour and romance.

In his writings, Hardy reveals how Emma's delusions manifested themselves. They also reveal how he himself was largely in denial about Emma (although he did go so far as to admit that she suffered from delusions); he preferred stubbornly to cling to the original image which he had formed in his mind of her, instead of recognising the reality of the situation. Hardy's works show that he wrestled with his problems in vain, and failed to find an answer as to why Emma, this beautiful woman whom he once adored, failed to reciprocate his feelings, and, in particular, why she refused to consummate the sexual side of their relationship (even though, at least in the early years of their marriage, she was prepared to be a friend to him).

After a bereavement, the surviving partner may, as Hardy did after Emma's death, experience 'overwhelming waves of yearning for the dead person [and] feel guilt that they failed to do enough for the deceased' during his or her lifetime. Finally, however, these symptoms subside, and he or she is able to recall 'the good times shared with the deceased in the past'.[2] Not so for Hardy, for even after Emma's death in November 1912, his grief continued unabated. Although Emma now rested in peace in Stinsford churchyard, for him there would be no closure. He became obsessed with his late wife; she occupied almost his every wakeful moment, and anguished, grief-stricken poems about her – in one disguise or another – continued to issue forth from him for another eighteen years; right up until the time of his own death in January 1928.

In the face of Emma's increasing mental dysfunction, Hardy displayed loyalty and forbearance, steadfastness and stoicism, to an almost superhuman degree, and it is truly amazing that he remained on cordial terms with his wife for as long as he did. But suppose for a moment that he had married a jovial, loving, caring, well-adjusted and outward-looking person. Would a contented Hardy have been equally inspired to produce works as profound as *Tess of the D'Urbervilles*, *Jude the Obscure*, *The Dynasts*, and a host of love poems? Probably not, for it is likely that his particular brand of creative genius had, of necessity, to be born out of pain. Therefore, perhaps posterity has something to thank Emma for after all. (In this, Hardy was not alone, for the same might be said of John Keats, Charlotte Brontë and her sisters, Charles Dickens, Edward Thomas and the Great War poets, and Aleksandr Solzhenitsyn, to name but a few. It may also be said of painters, such as Vincent van Gogh and Henri de Toulouse-Lautrec, and of musicians such as Ludwig van Beethoven, Pyotr Tchaikovsky and Frédéric Chopin.)

In 1994, in an editorial in the *American Journal of Psychiatry*, American psychiatrist Joseph J. Schildkraut, and his colleagues, attempted to shed more light on the relationship between mood (or what psychiatrists call 'affect') and creativity.[3] In their study of a small cohort (fifteen in all) of mid-twentieth-century painters of the New York School, they noted that: 'Over 50% of the 15 artists in this group had had some form of psychopathology, predominantly mood disorders and preoccupation with death.' And they concluded with these words:

By bringing the artist into direct and lonely confrontation with the ultimate existential question, whether to live or to die, depression may have put them in touch with the inexplicable mystery that lies at the very heart of the 'tragic and timeless' art that they aspired to produce.[4]

How, it may be asked, does this apply to Hardy? There is no doubt that for the greater part of his marriage to Emma, Hardy suffered from depression; also, that he had a preoccupation with the subject of death – whether that of a relative, a friend, a family pet, or even a complete stranger, such as those whom he encountered in the various mortuaries which he visited. Additionally, he was an explorer of questions of existentialism in the broadest sense, such as why are we here, what is our purpose, what is the meaning of life, how can life's tragedies be explained? This begs the question, was it Hardy's depression which led him to address the 'ultimate existential question', as Schildkraut implies is the case with other artists (again, to use the word in its broadest sense)?

The editorial referred to above draws attention to a question posed by psychiatrist N.J.C. Andreasen, who wondered whether, if American poet Sylvia Plath had taken anti-depressants, would the 'confessional power' of her *Arid* poems have been lessened in any way?[5] And Schildkraut, et al., affirm that the existence of 'powerful treatments now available for depression [pose] serious questions for both the clinician and the artist'. For Hardy the implication is, therefore, that had modern-type anti-depressants been administered to him for his depression, then this would have led to the instant extinguishing of his creative spirit.

⌢

Hardy was the chronicler, par excellence, of a way of life which has now largely disappeared. As the lives of his heroes and heroines are played out, beneath the surface lurk the great questions and conundrums with which he, and countless others before and since, have wrestled during their life-times: religion; the class system; the law; man's place in the universe, and the paradoxical contrast between the loyalty and steadfastness of human beings on the one hand, and their fickleness on the other. But most of all he deals with the subject of love, and the death of love – no person being better qualified to write about this subject than he.

The characters portrayed both in Hardy's novels and in his poems are as fresh and colourful today as they were when he first sketched them. To us they are living creatures, as they were to him. However, his works can only be fully appreciated by recognising that in so many ways, their struggle was also his struggle – that of Hardy, the man behind the mask. So much that he wrote has an inner meaning, and deciphering it has been akin to solving a cryptic crossword. Doubtless, many more clues remain to be discovered.

# Notes

Note: All material from Michael Millgate (ed.), *Letters of Emma and Florence Hardy*, and from Michael Millgate (ed.), *The Collected Letters of Thomas Hardy*, Volumes 1–7, is reproduced by kind permission of Oxford University Press.

## Foreword

1. Florence Hardy to Howard Bliss, 10 January 1931, in Michael Millgate (ed.), *Letters of Emma and Florence Hardy*, p. 312.
2. Before destroying Emma's diaries after her death, Hardy first read them aloud to his second wife, Florence.
3. Bertie Stevens, gardener at the Hardys' Dorchester home, Max Gate, describes how 'Mrs [Florence] Hardy herself burnt … baskets full of the letters and private papers that I had carried down from the study. It was a devil of a clear out. I never knew so much stuff come out of a room or such a burn up. My impression was she did not want any of the letters or papers to be seen by anyone and she was very careful to destroy every one of them.' In Martin Seymour-Smith's *Hardy*, p. 834.
4. Florence Henniker, for example.
5. Millgate (ed.), *Letters of Emma and Florence Hardy*, Foreword, p. xi.
6. Millgate (ed.), *The Collected Letters of Thomas Hardy*, Vol. 2, p. 54.

## 1. Early Life: Influences

1. Florence Emily Hardy, *The Life of Thomas Hardy*, pp. 14–15.
2. Michael Millgate (ed.), *The Collected Letters of Thomas Hardy*, Vol. 3, p. 235.
3. Florence Emily Hardy, op. cit., p. 8.
4. J. Stevens Cox, *Thomas Hardy: Materials for a Study of his Life, Times and Works*, No 14.
5. Florence Emily Hardy, op. cit., p. 3.
6. Thomas Hardy, *Under the Greenwood Tree*, Notes, 6, p. 43.

7. Evelyn Hardy, *Thomas Hardy: A Critical Biography*, p. 17.
8. Florence Emily Hardy, op. cit., p. 21.
9. Evelyn Hardy, op. cit., p. 15.
10. Ibid., p. 13.
11. Florence Emily Hardy, op. cit., pp. 8–9.
12. Ibid., p. 12.
13. Ibid., pp. 13–14.
14. Ibid., p. 11.
15. Evelyn Hardy, op. cit., p. 13.
16. Florence Emily Hardy, op. cit., p. 15.
17. Thomas Hardy, *Under the Greenwood Tree*, Preface.
18. Florence Emily Hardy, op. cit., p. 7.
19. Mr King remains unidentified.
20. Evelyn Hardy, op. cit., p. 19.
21. Ibid., p. 28.
22. Florence Emily Hardy, op. cit., p. 19.
23. Ibid., p. 16.
24. Evelyn Hardy, op. cit., p. 19.
25. Florence Emily Hardy, op. cit., p. 16.
26. Evelyn Hardy, op. cit., p. 35.
27. Ibid., p. 39. George Payne Rainsford James was a novelist and historian.
28. Florence Emily Hardy, op. cit., p. 5. (Florence Hardy states, in the Prefatory Note to her biography of her husband, that Hardy himself had agreed that 'the facts of his career should be set down'; so clearly Florence's account of his life was sanctioned by him.)
29. 'Efts' means eels.

# 2. Religion: Love: Crime: Punishment

1. Evelyn Hardy, *Thomas Hardy: A Critical Biography*, p. 39.
2. Florence Emily Hardy, *The Life of Thomas Hardy*, p. 25.
3. Sir Newman Flower, *Just as it Happened*, pp. 91–2.
4. Evelyn Hardy, op. cit., p. 41.
5. Ibid.
6. Michael Millgate (ed.), *The Collected Letters of Thomas Hardy*, Vol. 7, p. 5.
7. Thomas Hardy, *Notebook*, I, p. 32.
8. Timothy Hands, *Thomas Hardy and Stinsford Church*, p. 6.
9. Desmond MacCarthy, *Memories*, pp. 108–9.
10. Millgate (ed.), *The Collected Letters of Thomas Hardy*, Vol. 1, pp. 1–2.
11. J. Stevens Cox, *Thomas Hardy: Materials for a Study of his Life, Times and Works*, No 11.
12. Millgate, op. cit., Vol. 1, p. 3.
13. Ibid., p. 6.
14. Desmond Hawkins, *Hardy, Novelist and Poet*, p. 24.
15. Millgate, op. cit., Vol. 1, p. 7.
16. Florence Emily Hardy, op. cit., p. 153.
17. Millgate, op. cit., Vol. 1, p. 8.
18. Florence Emily Hardy, op. cit., p. 58.
19. Ibid., pp. 61–2.

20. Ibid., p. 63.
21. Ibid., p. 65.

# 3. Emma: A Successful Author

1. Emma Hardy, *Some Recollections*, p. 4.
2. Ibid., p. 6.
3. Ibid., p. 14.
4. Census, Cornwall, 1861. John Attersoll Gifford's name does not appear on the Law List – the Directory of Courts and Offices, Barristers, Solicitors, Magistrates, Coroners, etc. – after the year 1851, indicating that from that year onwards he was no longer practising his profession. Information kindly supplied by the Solicitors Regulation Authority.
5. Emma Hardy, op. cit., p. 30.
6. Memorial tablet in memory of Emma Gifford, designed by Hardy for the church of St Juliot and erected in 1913.
7. Kenneth Phelps, 'Thomas Hardy and St Juliot Church', *Thomas Hardy Year Book*, No 5 (St Peter Port, Guernsey: Toucan Press, 1976), pp. 31–2.
8. Emma Hardy, op. cit., p. 33.
9. Ibid.
10. Ibid., p. 34.
11. Ibid., p. 31.
12. *Desperate Remedies*, Chapter 8.
13. Robert Gittings, *Young Thomas Hardy*, Chapter 21.
14. Florence Emily Hardy, *The Life of Thomas Hardy*, p. 76.
15. Emma Hardy, op. cit., p. 34.
16. Ibid., p. 35.
17. Ibid., p. 37.
18. Ibid.
19. 'Re-opening of St Juliot Church near Camelford', in Kenneth Phelps, 'Thomas Hardy and St Juliot Church', *Thomas Hardy Year Book*, p. 31.
20. Ibid., p. 33.
21. *Royal Cornwall Gazette*, Saturday 27 April 1872, p. 6.
22. Vere H. Collins visited Hardy at Max Gate in December 1920.
23. Vere H. Collins, *Talks with Thomas Hardy at Max Gate*, p. 26.
24. Emma Hardy, op. cit., p. 10.
25. Florence Dugdale to Edward Clodd, 3 July 1913, Brotherton Library Collection, University of Leeds.
26. William Charles Eldon Serjeant of the 5th Battalion, the Rifle Brigade, who was elected Fellow of the Royal Geographical Society in 1892.
27. Thomas Hardy to Harold Child, 11 February 1919, in Millgate (ed.), *The Collected Letters of Thomas Hardy*, Vol. 5, p. 295.
28. Evelyn Hardy & F.B. Pinion, *One Rare Fair Woman: Thomas Hardy's Letters to Florence Henniker, 1893–1922*, p. 179.
29. Thomas Hardy to Edmund Gosse, 28 January 1918, in Millgate (ed.), *The Collected Letters of Thomas Hardy*, p. 246.
30. Florence Hardy to Rebekah Owen, 24 October 1915. By kind permission of Colby Special Collections, Miller Library, Waterville, Maine, USA.

# 4. Emma Inspires a Novel

1. Michael Millgate (ed.), *The Collected Letters of Thomas Hardy*, Vol. 2, pp. 131–3.
2. Ibid., p. 54.
3. Florence Emily Hardy, *The Life of Thomas Hardy*, p. 96.
4. Desmond MacCarthy, *Memories*, p. 111.
5. Sir Newman Flower, *Just as it Happened*, p. 94.
6. Florence Emily Hardy, op. cit., p. 93.
7. Ibid., p. 96.

# 5. Marriage

1. Michael Millgate (ed.), *The Collected Letters of Thomas Hardy*, Vol. 1, p. 31.
2. Millgate, *Letters of Emma and Florence Hardy*, p. 46.
3. Emma Hardy, *Diaries*, 1874–76 (Dorset County Museum), p. 12.
4. Ibid., p. 32.
5. Sir Newman Flower, *Just as it Happened*, p. 91.
6. Millgate (ed.), *The Collected Letters of Thomas Hardy*, Vol. 1, p. 33.
7. Emma Hardy, op. cit., p. 56.
8. Margaret Newbolt (ed.), *The Life and Letters of Sir Henry Newbolt*, pp. 121–2.
9. Millgate (ed.), *The Collected Letters of Thomas Hardy*, Vol. 1, p. 37.
10. *The Hand of Ethelberta*, Preface.
11. Florence Emily Hardy, *The Life of Thomas Hardy*, p. 106.
12. Emma Hardy, op. cit., pp. 65–6.
13. *The Hand of Ethelberta*, Preface.
14. Carl J. Weber, *Hardy and the Lady from Madison Square*, p. 68.
15. Emma Hardy, op. cit.
16. *The Return of the Native*, 4:7.

# 6. A Plethora of Novels

1. *The Trumpet Major*, Chapter 16.
2. Evelyn Hardy, *Thomas Hardy: A Critical Biography*, p. 176.
3. Michael Millgate, *Thomas Hardy: A Biography*, p. 215.
4. Thomas Hardy, *Notebook*, I, p. 61.
5. The Bible, Book of Revelation, 3:14.
6. 'They [Emma Gifford's family] had nearly secured a farmer [as a husband for Emma] when T.H. [Hardy] appeared.' Florence Emily Hardy to Rebekah Owen, 24 October 1915. By kind permission of Colby College, Miller Library, Waterville, Maine, USA.
7. Thomas Hardy's Prayer Book, Trustees of the Hardy estate, deposited in Dorset County Museum.
8. Cornwall Census, 1871.
9. Denys Kay-Robinson, *The First Mrs Thomas Hardy*, p. 19.
10. Emma Hardy, *Some Recollections*, p. 36.
11. Information kindly supplied by the Revd Robert Thewsey, priest-in-charge of the Boscastle group of churches.
12. Evelyn Hardy, *Thomas Hardy: A Critical Biography*, p. 178.

13. Florence Emily Hardy, *The Life of Thomas Hardy*, p. 154.
14. Ibid., p. 157.
15. Richard H. Taylor (ed.), *The Personal Notebooks of Thomas Hardy*, p. 35.
16. *Longman's Magazine*, Vol. 2, 1883, pp. 252–67.
17. Florence Emily Hardy, *The Life of Thomas Hardy*, p. 312.

# 7. Dorchester: Max Gate

1. Florence Emily Hardy, *The Life of Thomas Hardy*, p. 169.
2. Ibid., p. 170.
3. Ibid., p. 171.
4. *The Mayor of Casterbridge*, Preface.
5. Florence Emily Hardy, op. cit., p. 196.
6. *The Mayor of Casterbridge*, Preface.
7. Ibid., Chapter 26.
8. Evelyn Hardy, *Thomas Hardy: A Critical Biography*, p. 197.
9. Ibid., p. 206.
10. Florence Emily Hardy, op. cit., p. 174.
11. Michael Millgate (ed.), *The Collected Letters of Thomas Hardy*, Vol. 1, p. 154.
12. Ibid., p. 158.
13. Florence Emily Hardy, op. cit., p. 153.
14. Ibid., p. 176.
15. Ibid., p. 185.
16. Emma Hardy, *Diaries*, 1874–76, pp. 113, 119, 138, 192–3.
17. Florence Emily Hardy, *The Life of Thomas Hardy*, p. 209.
18. Millgate (ed.), *The Collected Letters of Thomas Hardy*, Vol. 1, p. 190.
19. Florence Emily Hardy, op. cit., p. 224.
20. Thomas Hardy, op. cit., Vol. 1, p. 205.
21. Ibid., p. 239.
22. J.I.M. Stewart, *Thomas Hardy: A Critical Biography*, p. 150.
23. Florence Emily Hardy, op. cit., p. 237.
24. Ibid., p. 240.
25. Ibid., p. 246.

# 8. *Jude the Obscure*

1. George Egerton, *Keynotes* (annotated by Thomas Hardy and Florence Henniker, collection of Richard Little Purdy), pp. 29–30.
2. *Jude the Obscure*, Preface.
3. Michael Millgate (ed.), *The Collected Letters of Thomas Hardy*, Vol. 2, p. 94.
4. *Jude the Obscure*, Preface.
5. Ibid., Postscript, April 1912.
6. *Jude the Obscure*, Preface.
7. Florence Hardy to Rebekah Owen, 24 October 1915. By kind permission of Colby Special Collections, Miller Library, Waterville, Maine, USA.
8. *Jude the Obscure*, 4/2.
9. Florence Emily Hardy, *The Life of Thomas Hardy*, pp. 271–2.
10. Millgate (ed.), *The Collected Letters of Thomas Hardy*, Vol. 2, p. 99.

11. *New Review*, June 1894, p. 681, in Michael Millgate, *Thomas Hardy: A Biography*, p. 357.
12. Millgate, op. cit., p. 104.
13. Ibid., p. 109.
14. Ibid., p. 125.
15. Ibid., p. 124.
16. Florence Emily Hardy, op. cit., pp. 284–5.
17. Gordon Gifford, Letter to *The Times Literary Supplement*, 1 January 1944.

## 9. Hardy Reveals Himself in Novels & Poems

1. *The Well-Beloved,* Part 1, Chapter 2.
2. Ibid., Part 1, Chapter 9.
3. Some psychologists of today believe that every person's psyche contains both male and female elements, described as the 'animus' and the 'anima' respectively. This begs the question, had Pierston therefore fallen in love with the female part of his own psyche, his 'anima'?
4. Hardy's biographer, Evelyn Hardy, has pointed out that although Florence Henniker kept a substantial number of the letters which Hardy wrote to her, many (which may have shed more light on the subject) appear to be missing, the reason being that she 'probably burnt some of them'. Evelyn Hardy and F.B. Pinion, *One Rare Fair Woman: Thomas Hardy's Letters to Florence Henniker, 1893–1922*, p. xxvi.
5. Mrs Norrie Woodhall, conversation with the author, September 2007.
6. Michael Millgate (ed.), *The Collected Letters of Thomas Hardy*, Vol. 2, p. 143.
7. Ibid., p. 144.
8. Ibid., pp. 176, 178.
9. Ibid., p. 181.
10. Ibid., p. 188.
11. Ibid., pp. 186–7.
12. Ibid., p. 189.
13. Ibid., p. 193.
14. Ibid., p. 194.
15. Ibid., p. 202.
16. Ibid., p. 206.
17. Ibid., p. 208.
18. Ibid., p. 221.
19. Ibid., pp. 225, 232, 238.
20. Ibid., p. 248.
21. Ibid., p. 264.
22. Ibid., p. 269.
23. Ibid., pp. 282–3.
24. Florence Emily Hardy, *The Life of Thomas Hardy*, p. 309.
25. Millgate (ed.), *The Collected Letters of Thomas Hardy*, Vol. 2, p. 303.
26. Chris M. Wilson and Andrew J. Oswald, 'How Does Marriage Affect Physical and Psychological Health? A Survey of the Longitudinal Evidence', p. 3.
27. Ibid., p. 6.
28. Ibid., p. 19.

29. Ibid., p. 20.
30. Ibid., p. 15.
31. Ibid., p. 7.
32. Ibid., p. 11.
33. Ibid., p. 22.
34. Ibid., p. 23.

# 10. Life Goes On

1. Sir Newman Flower, *Just as it Happened*, p. 95.
2. Florence Emily Hardy, *The Life of Thomas Hardy*, pp. 310–1.
3. Michael Millgate (ed.), *The Collected Letters of Thomas Hardy*, Vol. 3, p. 5.
4. Ibid., pp. 17, 19.
5. Ibid., p. 23.
6. Ibid., p. 33.
7. Ibid., p. 46.
8. Ibid., p. 50.
9. Ibid., p. 58.
10. Ibid., p. 53.
11. Ibid., pp. 64, 68.
12. Ibid., p. 74. In his view of lions Hardy was mistaken; they are not 'cruel' in the sense that they indulge in gratuitous torture (like one of Hardy's favourite animals, the cat), or kill for the sake of killing (like the fox). As carnivores they are obliged to kill in order to survive.
13. Ibid., p. 110.
14. Ibid., p. 119.
15. Ibid., pp. 114–5.
16. Ibid., p. 130.
17. Florence Emily Hardy, op. cit., p. 327.
18. Millgate (ed.), *The Collected Letters of Thomas Hardy*, Vol. 3, p. 213.
19. Ibid., p. 238.
20. Florence Emily Hardy, op. cit., pp. 334.
21. Millgate (ed.), *The Collected Letters of Thomas Hardy*, Vol. 3, p. 249.
22. Ibid., p. 253.
23. Ibid., p. 261.
24. *The Dynasts*, Preface.
25. Ibid., Act 7, Scene 8.
26. Ibid., Volume 2, After-Scene.
27. Ibid., Act 1, Scene 5.
28. Millgate (ed.), *The Collected Letters of Thomas Hardy*, Vol. 3, p. 327.
29. Ibid., pp. 333, 335.
30. Ibid., Vol. 4, p. 5.
31. Ibid., pp. 18–19.
32. Ibid., p. 21.
33. Ibid., p. 61.

# 11. From Emma's Standpoint

1. Emma Hardy, *Some Recollections*, pp. 1–2.
2. Ibid., p. 6.
3. Edward Clodd, *Diary* (unpublished), 1 October 1895, quoted in Michael Millgate, *Thomas Hardy: A Biography Revisited*, p. 326.
4. D. MacCarthy: Professor Harold Hoffman (Miami University of Ohio) interview.
5. Michael Millgate (ed.), *Letters of Emma and Florence Hardy*, p. 6.
6. Ibid., pp. 7–8.
7. Ibid., pp. 34–5.
8. Henry Gifford, *Thomas Hardy and Emma*, p. 115.
9. Millgate (ed.), *Letters of Emma and Florence Hardy*, p. 10.
10. Ibid., p. 15.
11. Ibid., p. 26.
12. Ibid., p. 48.
13. Emma Hardy, op. cit., pp. 12, 37.
14. Millgate (ed.), *Letters of Emma and Florence Hardy*, p. 52.
15. Mabel Robinson to I. Cooper Willis, 17 December 1937, Dorset County Museum.
16. J. Stevens Cox, *Thomas Hardy: Materials for a Study of his Life, Times and Works*, Monogram No 18.
17. Professor C.H. Gifford, interview, 1975.
18. Stevens Cox, op. cit., Monogram No 14.
19. Dr F.B. Fisher to Lady Hoare, 25 January 1928, Wiltshire Record Office.
20. Stevens Cox, op. cit., Monogram No 16.
21. Ibid.
22. Florence Emily Hardy to Sydney Carlyle Cockerell, 25 December 1925.
23. Sir Newman Flower, *Just as it Happened*, p. 95.
24. A.C. Benson, *Diary*, 5 September 1912, Magdalene College, Cambridge.
25. Clodd, *Diary* (unpublished), 13 July 1913, quoted in Denys Kay-Robinson, *The First Mrs Thomas Hardy*, p. 257.
26. Kate Gifford to Thomas Hardy, 25 November 1914, Dorset County Museum.
27. Evelyn Hardy and F.B. Pinion, *One Rare Fair Woman: Thomas Hardy's Letters to Florence Henniker, 1893–1922*, p. 155.
28. Clodd, *Diary* (unpublished), quoted by Kay-Robinson, op. cit., p. 235.
29. Ibid., p. 60.
30. Millgate (ed.), *The Collected Letters of Thomas Hardy*, Vol. 5, p. 19.
31. Thomas Hardy to Kate Gifford, 23 November 1914, by kind permission of Bristol University Library.
32. American Psychiatric Association, DSM-IV-TR, 301.0, p. 694.
33. Ibid., 301.50, p. 714.
34. Ibid., 301.81, p. 717.
35. Ibid., 301.20, p. 697.
36. Ibid., 301.22, p. 701.
37. www.bullyonline.org, 19.07.03.
38. American Psychiatric Association, op. cit., p. 325.

## 12. The Troubled Lives of the Giffords

1. 'Order for Reception of a Pauper Lunatic' (Ethel Lilian Attersoll Gifford), signed 25 July 1919 to Claybury Asylum, Essex. The original copy of this order has been destroyed, but mercifully, Professor Michael Millgate previously obtained a copy of it, which he has most generously made available to the author.
2. Eric H. Pryor, *Claybury 1893–1993: A Century of Caring*, p. 56.
3. Michael Millgate, *Thomas Hardy: A Biography Revisited*, p. 486.
4. Pryor, op. cit., p. 47.
5. Ibid., pp. 54–5.
6. Emma Hardy, *Some Recollections*, p. 9.
7. *Felix Farley's Bristol Journal*, 1830, Bristol Central Library, quoted by Robert Gittings in *Young Thomas Hardy*, p. 187.
8. Robert Gittings, *Young Thomas Hardy*, p. 187.
9. Leonie Gifford to Thomas Hardy, 28 October 1913, Dorset County Museum.
10. 'Gifford Family Information', quoted by Robert Gittings in *Young Thomas Hardy*, p. 188.
11. Information kindly supplied by Warneford Hospital, Oxford. Case Books WV 154 vi–viii and Reception Papers WV 169i.
12. *Gardner's Directory*, 1852.
13. Census, 1891.
14. Richard Little Purdy, *Thomas Hardy; A Bibliographical Study*, p. 122.
15. Information kindly supplied by Warneford Hospital, Oxford.
16. Stephanie Jenkins, Oxford History home, 9 June 2008.
17. Reception Order for John Attersoll Gifford to the Cornwall Lunatic Asylum. Doc. HC/1/34/37. Cornwall Records Office.
18. C.T. Andrews, *The Dark Awakening: A History of St Lawrence's Hospital, Bodmin*, p. 68.
19. Reception Order, op. cit., Doc. HC/1/45/19. Cornwall Records Office.
20. Emma describes the difficulty which her parents encountered in finding a house suitably big enough to accommodate the family furniture, which was 'very large'. Eventually, the Giffords were approached by James Kempthorne, Esq., who agreed that they should take (presumably lease) a property which he owned: Kirland House. Emma Hardy, *Some Recollections*, pp. 21–2.
21. Reception Order, op. cit., Doc. HC/1/45/20. Cornwall Records Office.

## 13. The Death of Emma: An Outpouring of Poetry

1. Michael Millgate (ed.), *The Collected Letters of Thomas Hardy*, Vol. 4, p. 90.
2. Ibid., p. 105.
3. Ibid., p. 107.
4. Ibid., p. 113.
5. Ibid., p. 132.
6. Margaret Newbolt (ed.), *The Life and Letters of Sir Henry Newbolt*, pp. 166–7.
7. Sir Newman Flower, *Just as it Happened*, p. 96.
8. Carl J. Weber, *Hardy and the Lady from Madison Square*, p. 165.
9. Ibid.
10. Thomas Hardy, *Notebook*, p. 117.

11. Henry Gifford, *Thomas Hardy and Emma*, p. 116.
12. Millgate (ed.), *The Collected Letters of Thomas Hardy*, Vol. 5, pp. 15–16.
13. Ibid., p. 16.
14. J. Stevens Cox, *Thomas Hardy: Materials for a Study of his Life, Times and Works*, Monogram No 5.
15. Millgate, op. cit., Vol. 5, p. 27.
16. Stevens Cox, op. cit., Monogram No 7.
17. Millgate, op. cit., Vol. 5, p. 30.
18. Ibid., p. 42.
19. Henry Gifford, op. cit., pp. 120–1.
20. Millgate, op. cit., Vol. 5, p. 71.
21. Ibid., p. 91.
22. Ibid., p. 135.
23. Ibid., p. 203.
24. Florence Emily Hardy, *The Life of Thomas Hardy*, pp. 375–6.
25. Millgate, op. cit., Vol. 5, p. 212.

# 14. Hidden Meanings

1. The association between Hardy's 'St Cleather' and the real-life village of 'St Clether' was first made by author Denys Kay-Robinson in his 1975 article 'The Face at the Casement'.
2. Burials in the parish of St Clether. Courtesy of Cornwall Record Office.
3. In 1966 Thomas Hardy enthusiast Kenneth Phelps proposed Charles Raymond – instead of William Serjeant – as the subject of *The Face at the Casement*. Raymond was a master miller, first of Lewannick and subsequently of Tremeer, St Clether, who died on 30 November 1873 (the date 1874 is inscribed, incorrectly, on his tombstone) and is buried at St Clether. It is impossible, however, to see how this could be so, when at the time in question, May 1871, Raymond was a married man with an 8-year-old daughter, Susanna, three younger children and a wife Mary (*née* Jenkin), whom he had married in August 1864 (Cornwall, 1871 Census, Tremeer, St Clether. Marriage certificate for Charles Raymond and Mary Jenkin, 23 August 1864, courtesy of Plymouth Record Office). It was Denys Kay-Robinson who arrived at the correct conclusion – that William Henry Serjeant was the person in question – in his 1975 article 'The Face at the Casement'.
4. Prior to that, the Revd Henry M.A. Serjeant was curate of the Isles of Scilly from 1863–68.
5. Royal Cornwall Gazette, 27 January 1872, p. 8.
6. Copy of death certificate kindly supplied by Cornwall Council.
7. William Henry Serjeant's younger brother, John Benny Serjeant, died on 11 November 1879, and is buried at Tremeer, where his father was now vicar.
8. This date is deduced from the fact that the first burial performed by the Revd Henry M.A. Serjeant at St Clether was on 9 November 1868.
9. The fact that the Serjeants and the Holders were acquainted is borne out by the fact that Cadell Holder officiated at a baptism at the Revd Serjeant's church of St Clether in October 1870. Also, Serjeant was in attendance at a service held on 11 April 1872 at St Juliot to celebrate that church's reopening, and on the following Sunday he preached there 'in aid of the [church's] building fund'. Kenneth Phelps, 'Thomas Hardy and St Juliot Church', *Thomas Hardy Year Book*, No 5 (St Peter Port, Guernsey: Toucan Press, 1976), p. 33.

10. See Serjeant family tree. Information kindly supplied by the Devon Family History Society.
11. Gelder, Michael, et al., *Shorter Oxford Textbook of Psychiatry*, p. 316.
12. John Serjeant married (first) Mary Ann Peters Benny, on 26 November 1810, at Callington, Cornwall, and had seven children, the sixth of whom was Henry Matthias Attwood Serjeant. John married (second) Louise Carter in 1840, at Charles church, Plymouth, and had at least three more children. (Information kindly supplied by Cornwall Family History Society.)
13. The Revd Henry M.A. Serjeant was appointed vicar of Tresmere, Cornwall, when he left St Clether in 1879.
14. Information kindly supplied by the Keeper of the Records, Queens' College, Cambridge.
15. Betsy Serjeant (born 1826), daughter of Richard Clemens, farmer of St Keyne, Cornwall, and his wife Betsy Blake. Cornwall Census, 1841.
16. Emma Hardy, *Some Recollections*, p. 31.

# 15. Florence Emily Hardy

1. Florence Hardy to Rebekah Owen, 24 October 1915. By kind permission of Colby Special Collections, Miller Library, Waterville, Maine, USA.
2. Florence Dugdale to Emma Hardy, 15 July 1910(?), in Michael Millgate (ed.), *Letters of Emma and Florence Hardy*, p. 61.
3. Florence Dugdale to Edward Clodd, 19 November 1910, in Millgate, op. cit., p. 68.
4. Florence Dugdale to Katharine Hardy, 20 October 1910, in Millgate, p. 64.
5. Florence Dugdale to Mary Hardy, 9 August 1911, in Millgate, p. 72.
6. Florence Dugdale to Edward Clodd, 11 December 1911, in Millgate, p. 73.
7. Ibid., p. 65.
8. Ibid., p. 74.
9. Florence Dugdale to Edward Clodd, 16 January 1913, in Millgate, pp. 75–6.
10. Florence Dugdale to Edward Clodd, 30 January 1913, in Millgate, pp. 76–7.
11. A quotation from John Milton's Sonnet XXII.
12. Florence Dugdale to Edward Clodd, 7 March 1913, in Millgate, pp. 78–9.
13. Florence Dugdale to Edward Clodd, 11 March 1913, in Millgate, p. 80.
14. Florence Dugdale to Edward Clodd, 20 April 1913, in Millgate, p. 81.
15. Florence Dugdale to Edward Clodd, 21 August 1913, in Millgate, p. 83.
16. See Robert Gittings, *Young Thomas Hardy*, p. 187, where Gittings states, incorrectly, that 'Emma's father was not "in an asylum" or insane at the time of her marriage or at any other time; nor was he, as the second Mrs Hardy also said, a bankrupt'. Gittings was correct in stating that Gifford was not technically a bankrupt, but had it not been for the legacy left to him by his mother, he may well have been. See also Michael Millgate, *Letters of Emma and Florence Hardy*, p. 89, where Millgate, in his textual notes, states that 'FEH [Florence] refers – with some exaggeration – to ELH's [Emma's] … father John Attersoll Gifford'. This is in reference to Florence Hardy's letter to Edward Clodd of 3 December 1913, in which she describes John Attersoll Gifford as being 'mad at times'. In fact, this was no exaggeration on Florence's part, and mental illness among members of Emma's family was more widespread, and yet at the same time closer to home, than either Gittings or Millgate imagined.
17. Florence Dugdale to Edward Clodd, 3 December 1913, in Millgate, op. cit., pp. 87–9.

18. Florence Dugdale to Edward Clodd, 1 January 1914, in Millgate, pp. 91–2.
19. Florence Hardy to Lady Hoare, 22 July 1914, in Millgate, pp. 98–9.
20. Florence Hardy to Rebekah Owen, 1 December 1914, in Millgate, pp. 101–2.
21. Florence Hardy to Lady Hoare, 6 December 1914, in Millgate, pp. 103–4.
22. Florence Hardy to Lady Hoare, 9 December 1914, in Millgate, p. 105.
23. Florence Hardy to Lady Hoare, 9 December 1914, in Millgate, pp. 104–5.
24. Florence Hardy to Rebekah Owen, 3 December 1915, in Millgate, p. 111.
25. Florence Hardy to Rebekah Owen, 18 January 1916, in Millgate, p. 114.
26. Florence Hardy to Sydney Cockerell, 9 September 1916, in Millgate, p. 119.

# 16. Explaining the Poems

1. Florence Emily Hardy, *The Life of Thomas Hardy*, p. 378.
2. From the Book of Daniel in the Bible.
3. Vere H. Collins, *Talks with Thomas Hardy at Max Gate*, p. 25.
4. Evelyn Hardy, *Thomas Hardy: A Critical Biography*, p. 273.
5. Ibid., p. 273.
6. Florence Emily Hardy, op. cit., p. 383.
7. Ibid., p. 384.
8. Florence Hardy to Sydney Cockerell, 17 February 1918, in Michael Millgate (ed.), *Letters of Emma and Florence Hardy*, p. 139.
9. Florence Emily Hardy, op. cit., p. 387.
10. Michael Millgate (ed.), *The Collected Letters of Thomas Hardy*, Vol. 5, pp. 303–4.
11. Florence Emily Hardy, op. cit., p. 390.
12. Millgate (ed.), *The Collected Letters of Thomas Hardy*, Vol. 5, p. 309.
13. Florence Hardy to Louise Yearsley, 10 August 1919, in Millgate (ed.), *Letters of Emma and Florence Hardy*, pp. 159–60.
14. Florence Hardy to Sydney Cockerell, 19 August 1919, in ibid., p. 161.
15. Florence Hardy to Sydney Cockerell, 25 September 1919, in ibid., p. 163.
16. Hardy to Charles Edwin Gifford, 3 November 1919. Bristol University Library: Special Collections.
17. Millgate (ed.), *Letters of Emma and Florence Hardy*, p. 165.
18. Ibid., p. 166.
19. Ibid., p. 171. Gertrude Bugler married her cousin, Ernest F. Bugler, farmer of Woodbury House, Beaminster, Dorset.
20. Ibid., p. 172.
21. Ibid., p. 175.
22. Ibid., Vol. 6, p. 16.
23. Florence Emily Hardy, op. cit., p. 405.
24. Ibid., p. 407.
25. Millgate (ed.), *The Collected Letters of Thomas Hardy*, Vol. 6, p. 48.
26. Thomas Hardy to Edmund Gosse, 28 January 1918, in ibid., p. 246.
27. Florence Emily Hardy, op. cit., p. 415.
28. J. Stevens Cox, *Thomas Hardy: Materials for a Study of his Life, Times and Works*, Monogram Nos 5, 6, 7, 14.

# 17. Declining Years

1. Florence Hardy to Sydney Cockerell, 3 August 1922, in Michael Millgate (ed.), *Letters of Emma and Florence Hardy*, p. 186.
2. Michael Millgate (ed.), *The Collected Letters of Thomas Hardy*, Vol. 6, p. 169.
3. Ibid., p. 206.
4. Florence Hardy to Marie Stopes, 14 September 1923, in Millgate (ed.), *Letters of Emma and Florence Hardy*, p. 203.
5. Millgate (ed.), *The Collected Letters of Thomas Hardy*, Vol. 6, p. 247.
6. Florence Hardy to Sydney Cockerell, 8 August 1925, in Millgate (ed.), *Letters of Emma and Florence Hardy*, p. 226.
7. Florence Emily Hardy, *The Life of Thomas Hardy*, p. 430.
8. Florence Hardy to Sydney Cockerell, Christmas Day 1925, in Millgate (ed.), *Letters of Emma and Florence Hardy*, p. 234.
9. Florence Emily Hardy, op. cit., p. 431.
10. Millgate (ed.), *The Collected Letters of Thomas Hardy*, Vol. 7, p. 9.
11. Florence Hardy to Philip Ridgeway, 16 March 1926, in Millgate (ed.), *Letters of Emma and Florence Hardy*, pp. 238–9.
12. Millgate (ed.), *The Collected Letters of Thomas Hardy*, Vol. 7, p. 32.
13. Florence Emily Hardy, op. cit., p. 443.
14. Millgate (ed.), *The Collected Letters of Thomas Hardy*, Vol. 7, p. 89.

# 18. Aftermath

1. J. Stevens Cox, *Thomas Hardy: Materials for a Study of his Life, Times and Works*, Monogram No 12.
2. Florence Hardy to Edmund Gosse, 5 February 1928, in Michael Millgate (ed.), *Letters of Emma and Florence Hardy*, p. 267.
3. Florence Hardy to T.E. Lawrence, 5 March 1928, in ibid., pp. 274–5.
4. Florence Hardy to Sydney Cockerell, 10 December 1928, in ibid., p. 285.
5. Florence Hardy to Siegfried Sassoon, 11 July 1929, in ibid., pp. 296–7.
6. Florence Hardy to Howard Bliss, 29 September 1929, in ibid., p. 301.
7. Florence Hardy to Howard Bliss, 10 January 1931, in ibid., p. 312.

# Epilogue

1. Michael Gelder, Paul Harrison & Philip Cowen, *Shorter Oxford Textbook of Psychiatry*, p. 169.
2. Ibid.
3. Editorial, *American Journal of Psychiatry*, 151: 4 April 1994.
4. Joseph J. Schildkraut, Alissa J. Hirshfeld & Jane M. Murphy, 'Mind and Mood in Modern Art, II: Depressive Disorders, Spirituality, and Early Deaths in the Abstract Expressionist Artists of the New York School', *American Journal of Psychiatry*, 151: 1994, pp. 482–8.
5. N.J.C. Andreasen, 'Ariel's Flight: the Death of Sylvia Plath', *Journal of the American Medical Association*, 228: 1974, pp. 595–9.

# Bibliography

American Psychiatric Association. 2000. *Diagnostic and Statistical Manual of Mental Disorders* (DSM-IV-TR) Washington, DC: American Psychiatric Association

Andrews, Charles T. 1978. *The Dark Awakening: A History of St Lawrence's Hospital.* London: Cox & Wyman

Benson, A.C. 5 September 1912. *Diary* (Magdalene College, Cambridge)

Collins, Vere H. 1978. *Talks with Thomas Hardy at Max Gate.* London: Gerald Duckworth

Comer, Ronald J. 1999. *Fundamentals of Abnormal Psychology* (2nd edn). New York: Worth Publishers, Inc.

*Dictionary of National Biography.* Oxford University Press

Egerton, George. 1977. *Keynotes.* New York & London: Garland Publishing Inc. (reprint of the 1893 edn published by Roberts Bros, Boston, USA)

Flower, Sir Newman. 1950. *Just as it Happened.* London: Cassell & Company

Gelder, Michael, Harrison, Paul & Cowen, Philip. 2006. *Shorter Oxford Textbook of Psychiatry.* Oxford University Press

Gifford, Henry. 1966. *Thomas Hardy and Emma* in *Essays & Studies* (edited by R.M. Wilson). London: John Murray

Gittings, Robert. 1975. *Young Thomas Hardy.* London: Penguin Books

Gregory, Richard L. (ed.). 1987. *The Oxford Companion to the Mind.* Oxford University Press

Hands, Timothy. 1992. *Thomas Hardy and Stinsford Church.* Stinsford Parochial Church Council

Hardy, Emma. 1985. *Diaries* (edited by Richard H. Taylor). Manchester: Carcanet New Press and Mid-Northumberland Arts Group

——. 1979. *Some Recollections.* Oxford University Press

Hardy, Evelyn & F.B. Pinion. 1972. *One Rare Fair Woman: Thomas Hardy's Letters to Florence Henniker, 1893–1922.* London: Macmillan

Hardy, Evelyn. 1954. *Thomas Hardy: A Critical Biography.* London: The Hogarth Press

Hardy, Florence Emily. 1965. *The Life of Thomas Hardy.* London: Macmillan Publishers

Hardy, Thomas. 1976. *The Complete Poems* (edited by James Gibson). London: Macmillan

——. 1990. 'The New Wessex Edition' of his novels, including *Desperate Remedies, Far from the Madding Crowd, The Hand of Ethelberta, Jude the Obscure, A Laodicean,*

*The Mayor of Casterbridge, A Pair of Blue Eyes, The Return of the Native, Tess of the D'Urbervilles, The Trumpet Major, Two on a Tower, Under the Greenwood Tree, The Well-Beloved* and *The Woodlanders*. London: Macmillan

——. 1955. *Notebook* (edited with notes by Evelyn Hardy). London: Hogarth Press

——. 1978. *The Personal Notebooks of Thomas Hardy* (edited by Richard H. Taylor). London: Macmillan

Hawkins, Desmond. 1976. *Hardy, Novelist and Poet*. London: David & Charles

Kay-Robinson, Denys. 1979. *The First Mrs Thomas Hardy*. London: Macmillan

——. 1975. 'The Face at the Casement'. *Thomas Hardy Year Book No 5*, pp. 34–5

Lewer, David. 1990. *Hardy in Swanage*. Wincanton: Dorset Publishing Company

Lewis, Heulyn & Lewis, Ginny. 2003. *In the Footsteps of Thomas and Emma Hardy*. North Cornwall Coast and Countryside Service.

MacCarthy, Desmond. 1953. *Memories*. London: MacGibbon & Kee

Millgate, Michael & Little Purdy, Richard (eds). 1988. *The Collected Letters of Thomas Hardy*. Volumes 1–7. Oxford: Clarendon Press

Millgate, Michael. 1982. *Thomas Hardy: A Biography*. Oxford University Press

——. 1996. *Letters of Emma and Florence Hardy*. Oxford: Clarendon Press

Margaret Newbolt (ed.). 1942. *The Life and Letters of Sir Henry Newbolt*. London: Faber & Faber

Phelps, Kenneth. 1966. *Annotation by Thomas Hardy in his Bibles and Prayer-Book* in *Thomas Hardy: Materials for a Study of his Life, Times and Works* (edited by J. Stevens Cox), No 32.

——. 1975. *The Wormwood Cup*. Cornwall: Lodenek Press

Pitfield, F.R. 1992. *Hardy's Wessex Locations*. Tiverton: Halsgrove

Pryor, Eric H. 1993. *Claybury 1893–1993: A Century of Caring*. Published by the Mental Health Care Group and Forest Health Care Trust

Purdy, Richard Little. 1954. *Thomas Hardy; A Bibliographical Study*. Oxford: Clarendon Press

Stevens Cox, J. 1968. *Thomas Hardy: Materials for a Study of his Life, Times and Works*. Monograph Nos 1–35. Guernsey: Toucan Press

Stewart, J.I.M. 1971. *Thomas Hardy: A Critical Biography*. London: Longman Group

*Story of the Tolpuddle Martyrs, The*. 1991. London: Trades Union Congress

Seymour-Smith, Martin. 1994. *Hardy*. London: Bloomsbury

Weber, Carl J. 1952. *Hardy and the Lady from Madison Square*. Maine, USA: Colby College Press (quotations by kind permission of the publishers)

Wilson, Chris M. & Oswald, Andrew J. May 2005. *How Does Marriage Affect Physical and Psychological Health? A Survey of the Longitudinal Evidence*. Discussion Paper No 1619. Bonn, Germany: IZA

Winchcombe, Anna. 1981. *Hardy's Cottage*. London: The National Trust

Windle, Bertram C.A. 1902. *The Wessex of Thomas Hardy*. London: John Lane, The Bodley Head

Woodhall, Augusta Noreen. 2006. *Norrie's Tale: An Autobiography of the last of the 'Hardy Players'*. Lulworth Cove, Wareham, Dorset: A Lullworde Publication

# Index